The Saffron Walden Branch

by
Peter Paye

THE OAKWOOD PRESS

First Edition published by the Oxford Publishing Company, 1980
This edition published by Oakwood Press an imprint of Stenlake Publishing Ltd, 2017

British Library Cataloguing in Publication Data
A Record for this book is available from the British Library
ISBN 978 0 85361 202 5

Printed by Claro Print, Unit 2, Kirkhill House, 81 Broom Road East, Glasgow, G77 5LL

By the same author and published by Oakwood Press:

The Snape Branch (2005)
The Hadleigh Branch (2006)
The Jersey Eastern Railway (2007)
The Framlingham Branch (2008)
The Wisbech & Upwell Tramway (2009)
The Bishop's Stortford, Dunmow and Braintree Branch (2010)
The Mellis & Eye Railway (2012)
The Aldeburgh Branch (2012)
The Hayling Railway (2013)
The Ely & St Ives Railway (2014)
The Axminster & Lyme Regis Light Railway (2015)

Note
Much of the rolling stock used on the Saffron Walden branch was also used on many other ex-Great Eastern Railway branches. For this reason plans published in the author's earlier titles have not been repeated in this volume.

Front cover: Ex-North Eastern Railway 'G5' class 0-4-4T No. 67322 at Bartlow, having arrived with the branch passenger train from Audley End on 25th August, 1956.
R.C. Riley

Rear cover: The 1946 Ordnance Survey, one inch to one mile, showing the route of the Saffron Walden branch. *Crown Copyright*

Title page: 'G5' class 0-4-4T No. 67279 propels its train through the cutting near Painter's bridge No. 2122 and is making for Saffron Walden and Audley End in the summer of 1956. *Dr I.C. Allen*

Oakwood Press, 54-58 Mill Square, Catrine, KA5 6RD,
Tel: 01290 551122   *Website:* www.stenlake.co.uk

Contents

Saffron Walden station facing Bartlow in July 1956. Behind the signal box is the cattle dock. At the platform 'G5' class 0-4-4T No. 67279 waits to leave with a push-pull unit for Audley End. Note the ornate yard gas-lit lamp on the cast-iron standard. *H.C. Casserley*

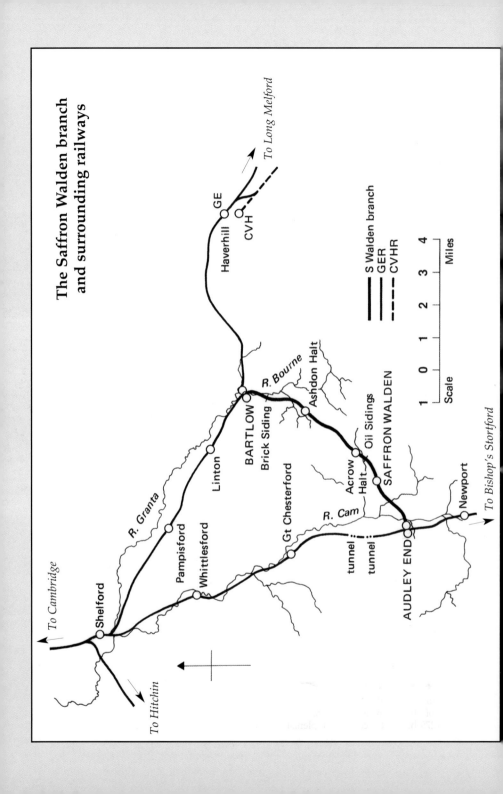

The Saffron Walden branch and surrounding railways

To Long Melford

GE
Haverhill
CVH

S Walden branch
GER
CVHR

1 0 1 2 3 4
Scale   Miles

To Cambridge

Shelford

R. Granta

Pampisford

Linton

Whittlesford

BARTLOW
Brick Siding

R. Bourne

Ashdon Halt

Gt Chesterford

R. Cam

Acrow Halt
Oil Sidings

SAFFRON WALDEN

tunnel
tunnel

AUDLEY END

Newport

To Bishop's Stortford

To Hitchin

Introduction

The Saffron Walden line, some 7½ miles in length, traversed the undulating countryside formed by the East Anglian Heights in the picturesque north-west corner of Essex.

For 99 years the branch served the locality with quiet efficiency. The by-passing of the town some two miles to the west, by the Eastern Counties Railway, forced local businessmen to engender their own railway to avoid economic stagnation.

As the Saffron Walden Railway (SWR), the branch had a perilous infancy and was soon in the hands of the receiver. Even after absorption by the Great Eastern, the desired use of the line as a through route to Suffolk never materialized, and the branch gradually settled as a two section railway - the western end between Audley End and Saffron Walden carrying far greater traffic than the eastern section thence to Bartlow. During the halcyon days before the advent of the motor vehicle, business was good and the branch provided an essential service to this rural area, including at one time a through train to London.

As roads improved, passenger and freight traffic turned to the internal combustion engine for door-to-door service and trade rapidly declined. Despite the influx of commuters in the late 1950s and early 1960s, Dr Beeching advised closure. Now all is silent, many fixed assets are gone, and the track formation in most places has reverted to farmland.

I have attempted to trace the history of the branch and details have been checked with available documents. This revised edition has been prepared as a result of the demand made by those who were unable to obtain the original book, which has been out of print for many years. This new impression contains much additional information and certain revisions which have become apparent since the first volume appeared, but, as before, apologies are offered for any inadvertent errors.

In the final years the coaling of locomotives from the coaling stage was abandoned in favour of direct transfer from a coal wagon stabled in the adjacent siding. 'G5' class 0-4-4T No. 67279 has just received a replenishment of fuel at Saffron Walden on 4th August, 1952. *D. Clayton*

Chapter One

Construction and Opening

Saffron Walden is a small market town nestling on the edge of the East Anglian Heights, 40 miles from London on the north-western border of the county of Essex. The name Walden is derived from the Saxon 'Wold' a forest and 'Dene' a valley - The Forest Valley. The prefix Saffron was said to have been added early in the reign of Edward III and refers to the intense cultivation of the saffron plant in the area, once in great demand for dye colouring and medicinal purposes. Although the trade ceased by 1790 the name remained. The main industry of the town then became malting but with the opening of the River Stort to navigation in 1769 came the decline. Bishop's Stortford at the head of the navigation became the main malting centre with over 100 establishments. Trade declined quite rapidly in Saffron Walden and by 1848 only 24 working malt kilns remained from a total of 53 establishments in 1831.

The decline was caused by the inability of the poor roads in the area to withstand the conveyance of waggon loads of malt away from the town, and the imports of coal and manure. Delays were inevitable and the excessive time taken to get commodities to and from London and the local market towns caused a serious loss of trade. In the late 18th century plans were made to build a canal from the Stort at Bishop's Stortford to the River Cam but after surveys were made the scheme was strongly opposed by Lord Howard of Audley End mansion, who had spent £100,000 on improvements to his estate. Geoffrey de Mandeville founded a priory, which became an abbey in 1190, located on the western perimeter of the town. Henry VIII gave the abbey to Thomas Audley (later Lord Audley) Speaker of Parliament, whose approval of the appropriate Acts led to the dissolution of the monasteries. Having destroyed much of the building, Audley converted the remainder into a house before he died in 1544. His daughter Margaret brought the house to the Howard family by marrying the fourth Duke of Norfolk. He was subsequently beheaded for involvement with Mary, Queen of Scots and the first Audley End house passed to his son Thomas Howard, who became Lord Howard, Earl of Suffolk. Thomas Howard built Audley End mansion between 1603 and 1616. Lord Howard, the first Baron Braybrooke had no children and the title passed to Richard Aldworth Neville, who became the second Baron Braybrooke. Later the Braybrooke family brought considerable influence to bear on the routing and bulding of the Eastern Counties Railway (ECR) through the area.

Despite opposition, meetings were held in the many public houses at Saffron Walden and Great Chesterford to obtain support for the scheme and over £9,000 was raised in 1781.

The main turnpike, which by-passed the town some two miles to the west, thus remained the only access to the metropolis whilst an undulating route across country linking Cambridge with Chelmsford ran by way of Thaxted and Great Dunmow and served as the only other main road in the area.

Some excitement was caused in 1835 when Joseph Gibbs surveyed the route of a railway from London through Dunmow and Saffron Walden to Cambridge and thence to York. Presented to Parliament as the Great Northern Railway, the Bill was defeated at the second reading in 1836 and the scheme fell into oblivion. When the Great Northern Railway was again mooted 10 years later it followed a course to the west through Hitchin and Huntingdon. Gibbs' survey was not the only one carried out, for James Walker had surveyed a route for the proposed Northern and Eastern Railway (N&ER) from London to Cambridge. Walker's route, however, followed the gradual rise of the Lea and Stort valleys to Bishop's Stortford and thence over the watershed at Elsenham to Newport and Great Chesterford, by-passing Saffron Walden two miles to the west. The Bill in support of this scheme successfully passed through both Houses to become law on 4th July, 1836.

The Northern and Eastern line was duly opened to traffic from Stratford to Broxbourne on 15th September, 1840; Harlow was reached on 9th August, 1841; Spelbrook on 19th November, 1841 and Bishop's Stortford on 16th May, 1842. From 1st January, 1844 the activities of the N&ER were taken over by the ECR. The N&ER had obtained powers in 1843 to build the line on to Newport, and the ECR subsequently obtained the Royal Assent on 4th June, 1844 to build a line from Newport to Brandon via Cambridge and Ely to effect an end-on junction with the Norfolk Railway. The section from Bishop's Stortford to Brandon was opened throughout on 29th July, 1845. A guest on one of the special trains, which ran for the event, was Lord Braybrooke of Audley End who had compelled the ECR to construct architecturally pretentious portals to Audley End and Littlebury tunnels where the railway passed through his land. Three tunnels had originally been demanded but settlement was made on two. Public services over this section began the following day, with a station provided at Wenden to serve as a railhead for Audley End House and the town of Saffron Walden. The station was renamed Audley End on and from 1st November, 1848.

The decision of the N&ER and ECR to route the railway via Newport, Wenden and Great Chesterford was a blow to the people of Saffron Walden. After urgent discussions at the Town Hall a letter was sent to the ECR Board suggesting that as the line was by-passing the town, a branch railway should be constructed from the main line with the possibility of an extension eastwards to Halstead. The ECR turned down the proposal and after a meeting chaired by the mayor of Saffron Walden in 1845, the town council decided to back proposals mooted as the Eastern and Northern Counties Railway. The route of this line was to pass through the town whilst connecting existing and projected lines from Bedford in the west to Colchester, Harwich and Maldon in the east. The scheme, heavily dependent on rural backing for support, soon fell into oblivion, leaving the town in continued isolation from the railway. Three years later another proposal was put forward, when the ECR planned to extend the Maldon, Witham and Braintree Railway, opened for goods on 15th August, 1848 and passengers on 2nd October, 1848, to Saffron Walden but this failed to materialize.

The failure of the above schemes brought a lull in the activities of attracting a railway to Saffron Walden but on 8th November, 1858 the Colne Valley and Halstead Railway (CV&HR), which was building a line from Chappel to Halstead, resurrected hopes by seeking powers to build to Haverhill and then extending its line to Audley End. The company advised its intention to make application to Parliament for a railway commencing by a junction with the authorized line at or near Parsons Bridge, in the parish of Halstead, in the County of Essex and passing through or into the following parishes and places or some of them: Halstead, Gosfield, Great Maplestead, Little Maplestead, Sible Hedingham, Castle Hedingham, Toppesfield, Great Yeldham, Little Yeldham, Northey Wood, North Wood otherwise Belchamp North Wood, North End, otherwise Belchamp North End, Belchamp St Paul's, Tilbury otherwise Tilbury-juxta-Clare, Ovington, Ridgewell, Ashen, Stambourne, Birdbrook, Steeple Bumpstead, Helion's Bumpstead, Sturmer, Kedington Hamlet, Haverhill Hamlet and Haverhill in the County of Essex; Wixoe, Haverhill Hamlet, Haverhill, Little Wratting and Withersfield in the County of Suffolk; Shudy Camps, Castle Camps, Helion's Bumpstead and Ashdon in the County of Cambridge; Radwinter, Ashdon, Bartlow, Hempstead, Wimbish otherwise Wimbush, Saffron Walden, Sewards End, Little Walden, Audley End, Wenden, Newport and Little Bury in the County of Essex and terminating in the said parish of Wendon by a junction with the ECR at or near the Audley End station. Despite such grandiose plans the scheme, including a diversion away from Saffron Walden and Audley End to run direct to Cambridge, failed to materialize.

It had become very evident to members of the Saffron Walden town council and local businessmen that isolation from the railway was having an unsettling effect on the community. Action had to be taken to arrest the economic depression which had descended on the town and the population had fallen from 5,911 in 1851 to 5,475 in 1861 as trade and tradespeople were drawn to rail-served centres at Bishop's Stortford and Cambridge. It was at this juncture that the Gibson family, who were Quakers with business interests in malting and brewing together with the local bank of Gibson, Tuke & Gibson, joined forces with other prominent businessmen in the area to promote a scheme to reinvigorate Saffron Walden.

At the beginning of 1860 meetings were held to extol the benefits the railway would bring to the town by opening up new markets. As most advocates of the line were also major landowners in the area no opposition was expected. The ECR Board was duly notified of the proposals and whilst agreeing to a railway linking Saffron Walden with their line, wanted no part in the construction, which had to be carried out by the local company if Parliamentary authority was given.

A detailed survey was then made between the town and proposed junction with the ECR at Audley End station, where the main line company insisted on a separate platform for branch traffic. By mid-August enough support had been promised to persuade the promoters that their proposals might become reality and W.B. Freeland, a solicitor, was appointed secretary to the temporary committee. When the ECR approved the proposed plans and the Board subsequently promised monetary assistance, the way was open for the promoters to seek Parliamentary approval for their short line. On 7th November, 1860 Gibson and Freeland attended the ECR Traffic Committee meeting to suggest that their proposed line be included as part of the Sudbury to Clare railway then being mooted. The Directors, however, required an indication of support for such a project before taking any action.

The proposed Bill and deposited plans for the railway signed by W.B. Freeland & Dyson & Co. were forwarded to the Parliamentary agents on 14th

November, 1860, copies being deposited with the clerk of the peace at Chelmsford and the secretaries of the various parish councils through which the line would pass, on 30th November. The land required for the railway was under the ownership of the Eastern Counties Railway, Audley End Estates (Lord Braybrooke), Wyatt George Gibson, William Charles Smith and the Trustee of King Edward VI Almshouses at Saffron Walden.

The Bill passed both the House of Commons and the Lords, receiving the Royal Assent on 22nd July, 1861 as the Saffron Walden Railway Act 1861 (24 & 25 Vict. cap. clxxviii). The statute authorized the construction of a railway, situated wholly in the county of Essex, from a junction with the Eastern Counties Railway, 200 yards south of Audley End station in the parish of Wenden, otherwise Wendens Ambo parish and passing through and into Wenden, otherwise Wendens Ambo, Audley End and Saffron Walden and terminating in a field belonging to the Trustees of Erswell charity adjoining and on the east side of the road from Saffron Walden to Debden, known locally as Rosse Lane. One and a half years was allowed for the purchase of land and three years for the completion of the works. The Act authorized the Saffron Walden Railway Company to raise a capital of £25,000 in 2,500 £10 shares, with further borrowing powers of £8,000 when £12,500 was subscribed and paid up. Under the powers of the statute the ECR was allowed to subscribe £5,000. The problem of the railway crossing the lands of the Audley End Estates was catered for in the Act, and by agreement made on 12th June, 1861 with the Rt Hon. Charles Cornwallis, Lord Braybrooke, two Directors of the company were to negotiate the mode and route of the intended railway. Clause 19 empowered the ECR to erect signals and appoint staff at the junction to protect its line. The first Directors of the railway were Wyatt George Gibson, Chairman, George Stacey Gibson, Vice-Chairman, John Stephenson Robson, James Starling and Joshua Clarke. The first meeting of the shareholders was held on Monday 21st October, 1861 at Saffron Walden town hall.

With attention focused on the local matters, other railways in the area were forging ahead. The Colne Valley & Halstead Railway having received little co-operation from the ECR, sought powers to extend to Cambridge in an effort to evade the shackles of that company. The CV&HR's ultimate goal was to lease their line to the London & North Western Railway, then approaching Cambridge from Bletchley via Bedford. The ECR, however, was in an almost impregnable position. The Sudbury & Clare Railway had been absorbed in the summer of 1860 and almost immediately powers were sought for a line extending from Sudbury via Melford, Clare and Haverhill to a junction with the London to Cambridge main line at Shelford, in direct opposition to the CV&HR. After a strongly contested struggle the Colne Valley & Halstead Bill was rejected and the ECR obtained its Act on 6th August, 1861 (24 and 25 Vict. cap. ccxxxi), just 15 days after the passing of the Saffron Walden Railway Act. The CV&HR was thus forced to terminate at Haverhill. The proposed new railway was of immediate interest to the Saffron Walden Railway Board as it passed through Bartlow, only five miles away, and could provide a useful outlet for trade if an extension could be built to connect with the new line.

Meanwhile after an initial flurry, sales of shares had almost ceased and a sales campaign in local villages in January and February 1862 met with little success.

ANNO VICESIMO QUARTO & VICESIMO QUINTO

VICTORIÆ REGINÆ.

****

Cap. clxxviii.

An Act to authorize the Construction of a Railway from the *Eastern Counties* Railway to *Saffron Walden* in *Essex.* [22d *July* 1861.]

WHEREAS the making of a Railway from the *Eastern Counties* Railway to *Saffron Walden* in the County of *Essex* would be attended with great local and public Advantage: And whereas the estimated Expense of the said Railway is Twenty-five thousand Pounds, and the Persons herein-after named, with others, are willing, at their own Expense, to construct the Railway: And whereas a Plan and Section of the Railway, showing the Line and Levels thereof, with a Book of Reference to the Plan containing the Names of the Owners and Lessees or reputed Owners and Lessees and of the Occupiers of the Lands through which the said Railway will pass, have been deposited with the Clerk of the Peace for the said County: And whereas it is expedient that the *Eastern Counties* Railway Company should be authorized to enter into the Arrangements herein-after contained with respect to the working and Management of the Railway, and also that they should have Power to subscribe thereto; but the Purposes aforesaid cannot be accomplished without the Authority of Parliament: May it therefore please Your Majesty that it may be enacted; and be it enacted by the Queen's most Excellent Majesty,

[*Local.*]   29 *L*   by

The first page of the Saffron Walden Railway Act of Parliament 22nd July, 1861.

Having obtained their Act the Saffron Walden Directors were anxious to get work started. Land agents concluded the preliminaries of the purchase of land required for the line by April and the Engineer appointed, John Samson Pierce, was preparing final drawings for a contractor, who had still to be appointed. Pierce was also involved with the Hatfield & St Albans Railway in neighbouring Hertfordshire. On the ECR approval was given on 12th March, 1862 for the extension of the platforms at Audley End as the proposed junction would entail more trains stopping at the station.

Despite the difficulties in raising the necessary capital for their modest line, several of the Directors were adamant that the salvation of the railway, and indeed the trade of the town, was for the extension eastward to join with the proposed Shelford to Haverhill line. Others, however, were of the opinion the company had attempted the impossible with the authorized line and wanted no more liabilities. After heated arguments during a meeting in the spring of 1862, the optimists won the day and it was decided to further the scheme to extend to Bartlow as a matter of urgency. Another resolution passed was that because of the inability of the company to purchase rolling stock or provide staff to work the line, the company would ask the ECR for a working agreement. The ECR Board was duly advised at the end of June.

By this time the ECR had leased or taken over the working of all major railways in East Anglia and a scheme was prepared for the amalgamation of the Eastern Counties, Eastern Union, East Anglian, Newmarket and Norfolk Railways into a new undertaking to be known as the Great Eastern Railway (GER). The Act sanctioning the union, the Great Eastern Railway Act 1862 (25 and 26 Vict. cap. ccxxiii), obtained the Royal Assent on 7th August, 1862, but took effect retrospectively from July of that year.

The strain on railway capital was beginning to tell and on 11th September, 1862, Freeland wrote to the newly formed GER Board reminding them of the obligation made by the Eastern Counties Railway in the Act of 1861 into subscribing £5,000 to the local company. He stressed that the paramount object was now to join up with the Sudbury, Haverhill and Cambridge line at Bartlow, to facilitate through running and open up the district to inhabitants of Saffron Walden. To this end the Saffron Walden Railway Company was to approach Parliament with a view to obtaining an Act to enable construction of such a line. Freeland even suggested that the GER construct the Bartlow to Saffron Walden section at the same time as work was being carried out on the Shelford to Sudbury line.

The matter was placed in the hands of Sinclair, the GER Engineer, who after investigation, reported on 30th September that it was desirable for the GER to agree to one of the proposals, that of the completion of the Audley End to Saffron Walden section and the working of the line. It was evident the desire to extend the line to Bartlow was not shared by all Saffron Walden Railway Directors and, despite heated arguments at their meetings in April, Sinclair was of the opinion Freeland was the driving force behind the proposal. The GER Engineer advised his Directors that the ECR had only offered assistance, both financial and technical, to complete the line from Audley End, and if the GER had control of the two miles section being prepared, the extension thence to Barlow could be left to local interests. The estimated cost of the extension to

SAFFRON WALDEN RAILWAY COMPANY.

The Saffron Walden Railway Act, 1861.

To *Deborah Gibson and George Stacey Gibson*

and all other Parties (if any) interested in the Lands and Property hereinafter referred to.

As SECRETARY to and for and on behalf of "THE ~~EASTERN COUNTIES AND~~ SAFFRON WALDEN RAILWAY COMPANY," **I hereby give you Notice,** that the said Company require to purchase and take under and by virtue of an Act of Parliament, made and passed in the session of Parliament held in the 24th and 25th years of the reign of her present Majesty, Queen Victoria, intituled "*An Act to authorize the construction of a Railway from the Eastern Counties Railway to Saffron Walden in Essex,*" and shortly styled "*The Saffron Walden Railway Act,* 1861," and of the "Companies Clauses Consolidation Act, 1845", "The Lands Clauses Consolidation Act, 1845," "The Railway Clauses Consolidation Act, 1845," and "The Lands Clauses Consolidation Acts, Amendment Act, 1860," and other the Acts incorporated therewith, the Lands and Property particularly mentioned and described in the Schedule on the other side hereof, for the purposes of the Railway and works by the said "Saffron Walden Railway Act, 1861," authorized to be constructed. And that the said Company hereby demand from you the particulars of your Estate and interest (if any) in the said Lands and Property, or any part thereof, and of the claim or claims made by you in respect thereof, and that the said Company is willing to treat for the purchase of the said Lands and Property, and every part thereof, and as to the compensation to be made to you for the damage that may be sustained by you, by reason of the execution of the works by the said "Saffron Walden Railway Act, 1861," authorized to be made and constructed.

And I also give you Notice, that by the said last-mentioned Act, or the Act or Acts incorporated therewith, it is provided, that if for twenty-one days after the service of such Notice as above written any party shall fail to state the particulars of his claim in respect of the Lands and Property required by the said Company, or to treat with the said Company in respect of his interest therein, or if such party and the said Company shall differ as to the amount of the compensation to be paid by the said Company to such party for any such interest or for any damage that may be sustained by him, by reason of the execution of the said works, the amount of such compensation shall be settled in manner therein provided for settling cases of disputed compensation.

DATED this *Twenty fourth* day of *December* 1862.

W. B. Freeland
Secretary to the
EASTERN COUNTIES AND SAFFRON WALDEN RAILWAY COMPANY.

N.B.—It is requested by the said Company, that all particulars of your Estate and interest in the Premises above referred to, and of your claim or claims in respect thereof, may be left with, or sent to, MR. WILLIAM BENNETT FREELAND, the Solicitor of the said Company, SAFFRON WALDEN, ESSEX. The said Company likewise request your particular attention to the provisions of the "Land Clauses Consolidation Act, 1845," (8 VIC. c. XVIII.,) under which the present Notice is given. And in returning an answer to this Notice, the said Company will be much obliged by your specifically informing them of the nature of your tenure of the premises referred to by this Notice; and especially, if you claim to be interested as owner therein, whether the same are Freehold or Copyhold, and if Copyhold, who is the Lord of the Manor of which the same is holden; and if you claim to be interested as Occupier, whether you claim title as "Tenant at Will," or as a "Tenant for a Year," or as a "Tenant from Year to Year," or as a Tenant under a Lease, for any and what term of years yet unexpired.

[For Schedule see over.]

Compulsory purchase order served on Deborah Gibson and George Stacey Gibson on 24th December, 1862, prior to the construction of the Saffron Walden Railway.

Bartlow was £50,000, to which Sinclair added a rider that if the local company raised a larger part of the required subscribed capital, then the GER could provide a small amount of capital and offer to work the line.

Following this advice, the GER Board notified the Saffron Walden company that they would provide £5,000 in the event of the smaller company guaranteeing to raise the required capital. Only then if the GER were satisfied, would they construct the line and work the extension railway.

The terms were evidently not acceptable to the Saffron Walden Board, for on 27th September, 1862, a deputation led by G.S. Gibson visited the GER headquarters at Bishopsgate station. After being courteously received, the Saffron Walden men were advised that following further discussion with the GER Directors, the company would be prepared to find one-third of the required capital and work the line for 50 per cent of the gross receipts, if two-thirds of the proposed share capital could be found locally. To these proposals the Saffron Walden deputation readily agreed.

In the meantime a survey had been made of the extension to Bartlow. Estimates and plans were subsequently drawn up and the Parliamentary agents notified of the intention to seek authority for the line. The notice of application for the Bill and the deposited plans were forwarded to the Parliamentary agents and deposited with the clerks of the peace at Chelmsford and Cambridge on 28th November, 1862.

Finances and the working agreement were worrying the SWR Board, for on 16th February, 1863 Freeland again wrote to the GER Board outlining the items mentioned in the 1861 Act and the ECR promise to subscribe £5,000 of the £25,000 capital. The new Bill before Parliament requested an additional capital of £70,000 to complete the five miles to Bartlow and help was again required. He also requested in writing the working agreement made in November 1862. At the same time the application to the GER to construct the new line was dropped as Pierce, the Saffron Walden Engineer, was negotiating with the newly appointed contractor to complete the whole line between Audley End and Bartlow. The GER quickly replied to Freeland, requesting details of the total share subscription received and on 5th March 1863, it was announced that £25,070 had been subscribed and the SWR Board were making every effort to reach a total of £30,000.

The ceremony of the cutting of the first sod was performed in a field occupied by Thomas Smith, halfway between Audley End station and Saffron Walden town on Monday 18th May, 1863. A large crowd gathered for the event and, led by the town band, the leading dignitaries of the town and the railway company Directors were conveyed by horse carriages to the site. Unfortunately the ceremony was so well organized that nobody remembered to bring a spade and the resplendent company had to wait while a man was sent to the nearby farmhouse to bring back the implement. G.S. Gibson, representing by far the largest shareholding in the district, performed the actual deed, turning the spit of earth into a small wheelbarrow, constructed especially for the occasion. After speeches by Gibson, Freeland and Clarke a number of the principal promoters and others dined at the Rose & Crown Hotel.

William Hanson had been awarded the contract to build the line and as soon as construction work commenced over 200 navvies arrived in the district seeking

ANNO VICESIMO SEXTO & VICESIMO SEPTIMO

VICTORIÆ REGINÆ.

****

Cap. lxxxiii.

An Act for authorizing the *Saffron Walden* Railway
Company to make and maintain Railways to the
Great Eastern Railway at *Bartlow;* to raise
further Monies ; and for other Purposes.
[22d *June* 1863.]

WHEREAS by the *Saffron Walden* Railway Act, 1861, the
Saffron *Walden* Railway Company (herein-after called " the
Company") were incorporated, and were authorized to make
and maintain the *Saffron Walden* Railway, and to raise a Capital of
Twenty-five thousand Pounds in Shares and Eight thousand Pounds by
borrowing : And whereas the making of a Railway which would connect
the *Saffron Walden* Railway with the *Great Eastern* Railway at *Bartlow*
would be of local and general Advantage : And whereas the Company
are willing at their own Expense to carry into effect the Undertaking by
this Act authorized : And whereas Plans and Sections showing the Lines
and Levels of the intended Railways, and Books of Reference to the
Plans containing the Names of the Owners in and through which those
Railways are to be made and maintained, have been deposited with the
respective Clerks of the Peace for the County of *Essex* and the Clerk of
the Peace for the County of *Cambridge*, and those Plans, Sections, and

24 & 25 Vict.
c. clxxviii.

[*Local.*]   12 Q   Books

Saffron Walden Railway Extension Act 22nd June, 1863.

lodging and shelter. This large body of men included Irishmen and unemployed men from Norfolk and Suffolk, as well as Saffron Walden and the surrounding villages. To serve the needs of the workforce a large corrugated iron room, financed by the Gibson family, was erected close to the Debden Road, near the site of the railway. The building sold light refreshments and non-intoxicating liquor and doubled up on Sundays as a mission hall for services organized by the Revd Ralph Clarke, vicar of the town church. The use of the hut as a refreshment room was a failure as most men lodged in the vicinity of Castle Street, well away from the area of the railway, and were loathe to walk the distance back to the hut after a hard day's work. As with most railway navvies the public houses of the town were far more attractive and there were often skirmishes between the drunken navvies and the lawmen of Saffron Walden.

On 22nd June, 1863, the Bill before Parliament received the Royal Assent as the Saffron Walden Railway Extension Act 1863 (26 and 27 Vict. cap. lxxxiii) authorizing the company to make and maintain a railway, commencing in the county of Essex, in field No. 31 at the end-on junction with the Audley End to Saffron Walden Railway at Saffron Walden and terminating in the county of Cambridge in the parish of Bartlow by a junction with the authorized GER Clare to Shelford line in field No. 16. A second line commencing from a junction with the first railway in the parish of Ashdon, in the County of Essex, in a field on the west side of Ash Brook Road, was to terminate with the Clare to Shelford line in field No. 56, thus forming a triangular junction. This was later abandoned and only the north-facing junction was laid. Two years were allowed for the compulsory purchase of land and four years for the completion of the railway. The GER was to be afforded through running facilities and could subscribe and hold shares not exceeding £23,000 in addition to the subscription permitted in the 1861 Act. Because of this commitment the latter company was allowed to nominate a representative to sit on the Board of the local company. To finance the complete scheme the Saffron Walden Railway Company was authorized to raise an additional share capital of £70,000 and borrow £23,000 on mortgage.

Freeland wrote again to Bishopsgate in July suggesting that the GER shareholders subscribe to the line immediately now the Act had been passed. The Secretary of the GER replied that his company would subscribe no money until two-thirds of the £95,000, formed by £70,000 and the original £25,000 had been raised. The GER Directors authorized the raising of £23,000 debentures to pay for their portion of the Saffron Walden Railway capital in August.

The Saffron Walden Directors although plagued with financial worries were relieved that the construction of the railway had commenced within the time allowed by the 1861 Act. The contractor was urged to get as much work done before the winter weather delayed progress. A narrow brown swathe soon appeared in the fields as earth was removed from cuttings to form embankments on the undulating two-mile section of line. Additional access tracks were made across the fields from the Audley End road to enable horses and waggons to get to the work site. Construction was affected in September when earthworks were delayed for two weeks by heavy rainfall.

As a result of the clause in the 1863 Act, the GER appointed Messrs Green and Starling to the Saffron Walden Board to look after their interests. The GER Board received a letter from Freeland dated 30th September, 1863 stating that the subscription now prepared, inclusive of the one-third subscription by the GER, had raised only £63,350 and the remaining amount would necessitate the issue of debentures. The contractor agreed to accept £21,000 in debentures and the remaining £10,000 would be purchased locally. The GER had still to provide £5,000 capital against the original Act and £23,000 for the Act authorizing the extension to Bartlow. Freeland concluded by stating that the Saffron Walden company had borrowed money for land purchase, to enable work to commence. The original section was expected to be completed by May 1864 but the extension work required capital, which as yet, was not forthcoming and he earnestly requested the GER to settle 'their apportionment so that construction could commence'.

A month later the solicitor to the GER reported that the local company had received nothing like the two-thirds subscriptions required, and on 7th January, 1864 confirmed that the local railway could only raise approximately £31,666 or about a third of the complete amount needed. The Saffron Walden Board, anxious to raise the two-thirds of the £95,000 required so that they could take advantage of the £31,000 borrowing powers, then asked the GER if they would subscribe a similar £31,666. This suggestion was flatly refused.

Faced with delays to the construction of their line and indeed the abandonment of such a scheme, the Saffron Walden Board met in early February 1864 to discuss the dilemma. The success or failure was now solely in the hands of the GER but when Freeland again wrote to Bishopsgate requesting a reduced GER subscription of £26,000, if the SWR could raise £53,000, he met with a similar rebuff. The situation was now quite desperate and at the end of the month Freeland travelled to Bishopsgate for a meeting with the GER Directors to reiterate the local company's case.

It was almost three months after that meeting on 26th May, 1864 that the GER Secretary wrote to Saffron Walden asking for a 10 per cent discount on the shares taken by his company because of its own precarious financial position. Suitable arrangements were duly made between the two companies and on 2nd June, 1864, a cheque for £7,000 was sent to the SWR.

In September 1864 the SWR Directors voiced concern over the station at Saffron Walden and accommodation for the station master. The Engineer, Pierce, allayed all fears in a letter from his office in London dated 16th October, when he replied that the station would be larger than most provided for a town the size of Saffron Walden. In addition to the building, a canopy some 15 ft wide would cover the platform by the booking office and waiting room, for the convenience of passengers. Pierce was of the opinion that it was a disadvantage to have the station master and his family located in accommodation on the platform when the company had a site in the Debden Road with a whole view of the station. The Directors were adamant, however, that they required the station master on the station and subsequently a two-storey building was erected. The Engineer also referred to a coal siding for nine wagons situated at right angles to the main branch line at Saffron Walden and stressed the inconvenience such a siding would cause to traffic on the main line as well as the increasing cost of installation. Referring to the Bartlow extension, he stated that the new line could be constructed for £60,000 as earthworks required were not heavy and no intermediate station would be required.

By September 1864 construction work was well advanced. The Cam Valley was crossed on an embankment 48 ft high, which required 136,000 cu. yds of earth in its construction. The cutting beyond this involved the excavation of 120,000 cu. yds of earth to reach a depth of 52 ft. The embankment over the Fulfen valley, which attained a maximum height of 45 ft, involved the use of 65,000 cubic yards of earth in its construction. As well as being involved with heavy earthworks west of Saffron Walden, the contractor's men were also advancing with the formation towards Bartlow.

It was anticipated with the opening of the new railway that additional shunting of wagons would be experienced at Audley End, and consideration was given to providing a second horse to assist with the outsorting of vehicles transferring to and from the Saffron Walden line. On 23rd November, 1864 authority was duly given to extend the stable at the junction station to accommodate the additional animal.

Pierce, in his letter of 10th December, 1864, stated that considerable grain and cattle traffic from East Anglia to Saffron Walden would boost the receipts of the company by an estimated £2,800 per annum or 2s. 0d. per mile per week. If the line was worked to its full capacity it could amount to £8 per mile per week. Under the terms, of the working arrangements, with the GER taking 50 per cent of the gross receipts, the SWR would receive £3,900 per annum of the £7,800 total receipts.

On 29th October, 1864 Horatio Love and Col Palmer were elected to represent the GER interests on the SWR Board replacing Messrs Green and Starling. By early December 1864 the SWR was sinking further into financial troubles and on 22nd December they suggested payment for a further £7,000 from the GER. Payment was authorized but deferred until 19th January, 1865.

To assist with the finishing touches to the Audley End to Saffron Walden section of line and construction of the extension to Bartlow, William Hanson ordered a small 0-4-0T locomotive from Manning, Wardle of Leeds and *Little Eastern*, as it was named, was delivered by horse-drawn waggon to the line in January 1865.

The construction of the Saffron Walden Railway had been remarkably free from accident but on the afternoon of Saturday 11th February, 1865, a 27-year-old navvy, Henry Garwood, received fatal injuries. Garwood was working with 30 men in a cutting nine feet deep on the site of Saffron Walden station between Rosse Lane and Mill Lane. Their task was to shovel soil, which had been loosened from the top of the bank, and load it into wagons, which were then pulled by *Little Eastern* to the embankment near the Thaxted Road where the soil was utilized. The method used to dislodge the bank was for the lower soil to be cut away so as to loosen and dislodge the upper crust. Wooden stakes were then driven into the top of the bank to let the earth fall. Evidently Garwood had been warned several times by his foreman for endangering himself. As the locomotive was shunting three loaded wagons away from the site a mass of soil fell from the top of the bank pushing Garwood on to the rails where the three wagons passed over him, killing him instantly.

On 15th June, 1865 a further £7,000 was handed over to the local company and acknowledging receipt, Freeland wrote saying that it was his Directors' desire to open their line for goods traffic at some time during July if the GER could make the necessary arrangements, but nothing further transpired. To accommodate the projected increased traffic and interchange of wagons at

Little Eastern built by Manning, Wardle and ordered by William Hanson, the contractor, being delivered to the site at Saffron Walden in January 1865.   *Saffron Walden Museum*

Audley End, Sinclair the GER Engineer submitted proposals for additional sidings and infrastructure at the junction at an estimated cost of £1,172.

On 16th August, 1865 the GER Board heard from their General Manager and traffic superintendent that the Saffron Walden line was nearing completion and authorized the construction of the junction at Audley End, complete with associated signalling. They also approved the installation of additional sidings to handle the interchange of traffic together with a warehouse, dock and coal storage accommodation and an approach road to the SWR station. The SWR later advised that they had requested the Board of Trade (BoT) to inspect the line and arrangements regarding the proposed working of goods trains were agreed. Initially the SWR Board sought to commence a goods service before the BoT inspection but on advice this was dropped.

Meanwhile Sinclair, investigating the cost of working the line, concluded on 21st August, 1865 that a much higher rate would have to be charged for goods traffic only between Audley End and Saffron Walden than to work the whole line, including the extension to Bartlow, for both goods and passenger traffic. The SWR was duly informed that the GER was ready to fulfill the terms of agreement as soon as the line was fully completed for all traffic. In the meantime if it required any part of the line to be worked the GER was prepared to undertake the operation at cost price.

The Saffron Walden Directors were concerned about future receipts and Freeland wrote again to Bishopsgate on 14th September, 1865, saying that whilst the GER should apply all or as much receipts as necessary to cover working expenses when the line opened, the SWR should not be called to guarantee any payments beyond the gross earnings of the line, if a deficit should accrue.

Capt. H.W. Tyler conducted the Board of Trade inspection of the line on 17th October, 1865 and noted that the railway being offered for examination was 2 miles and 2 chains in length, running from a station and junction with the GER at Audley End to a station at Saffron Walden. The steepest gradient on the line was 1 in 100 and the sharpest curve, near the junction, of 12 chains radius. The earthworks were very heavy involving the removal or installation of 425,000 cu. yds of earth and Tyler recommended the removal of large stones and boulders from the sides of the cuttings. The inspector was satisfied with the permanent way, save that he would have preferred fang bolts to secure the rails at the intermediate sleepers instead of wood screws. Much to the dismay of the Directors, Tyler found that the fencing alongside the railway for its whole length was inadequate. This fencing consisted of oak posts set at nine feet intervals with six wire stretch strands connecting, the upper wire being scarcely 3 ft 6 in. above the ground. The inspector suggested that a height of 4 ft should be the minimum and that a brick post should be erected between each wooden post to strengthen the fencing. On the day of the inspection the site for the engine turntable at Saffron Walden was pointed out, but no work on construction had been carried out.

Capt. Tyler noted there were six underbridges and three overbridges on the line, of which the greatest span was 36 ft 8 in. All appeared to have been substantially constructed and standing well but on inspecting the wrought-iron 'Fighting Cocks' underbridge at 23 chains from the junction at Audley End, Tyler required the side plates of the parapets to be set back to allow adequate clearance for the train to pass, whilst two of the cross girders in which two holes had been punched through the lower flanges, had deteriorated to the extent that the leaves required changing. The arches of two culverts, 36 chains from the junction, had materially altered in shape and the inspector required a longitudinal wall to be inserted in each of them widening out at the soffit for the better support of the arch. At Audley End the SWR had set up check blocks on the main single line to protect the GER line from an overrunning train. The captain stated that this was totally contrary to proper protection and instructed the installation of catch points, interlocked with the main line signals, to protect the GER line. At Saffron Walden much work was outstanding; the local company had omitted to install a pair of points to enable the locomotive to run-round its train, the station platform was incomplete, and connections to the main single line were not connected. Tyler was advised the single line was to be worked by the GER on the Train Staff principle but refused the opening certificate because of the incompleteness of the works.

The Directors were crestfallen that the railway was not to be opened, but it must have been obvious that in the absence of run-round facilities at Saffron Walden and the imperfections at Audley End, the inspector would refuse to issue the necessary certificate. The Engineer and contractor made a detailed survey of the line and programmed the remedial work the following day. All contractor's men working on the Bartlow extension were called back to rectify the deficiencies and within 10 days both the BoT and the GER were notified regarding re-examination.

As the second BoT inspection was imminent, the GER traffic superintendent held a meeting with the local Directors to arrange the train service and on 8th November, 1865 the timetable was sent to the Saffron Walden Board for approval. As expected the branch timings were satisfactory but the GER declined to stop some of the main line expresses at Audley End to provide connections to London or Cambridge. A subsequent visit to Bishopsgate by some of the Directors and Freeland failed to reverse the decision. In the meantime General Manager and Robertson, the traffic superintendent, advised that arrangements for working the line had been agreed with the SWR Board.

For freight charges the SWR received similar terms from the GER as the Ware Hadham & Buntingford, Lynn & Hunstanton and Tendring Hundred railways with a minimum charge of 6 miles. The rates were London terminals on carted traffic 5s. 0d. per ton, London terminals non-carted traffic 1s. 6d. per ton, Saffron Walden carted traffic 3s. 0d. per ton, Saffron Walden non-carted traffic 1s. 6d. per ton.

Capt. H.W. Tyler conducted the second BoT inspection on 17th November and found that all items referred to in the previous report had been attended to except fencing. Freeland, the Secretary, and Pierce, the Engineer of the SWR, were adamant the fencing was adequate. They assured the inspector that the fields in the vicinity of the railway were never used for the grazing of horses or heavy cattle and that sheep mainly grazed on fodder; the occupants of the land were 'perfectly satisfied' with the existing fencing. In these circumstances the inspector and the SWR's representatives came to a mutual agreement whereby the fence would remain at 3 ft 6 in. in height but extra wooden posts would have to be installed; two months being allowed for the completion of the works. On inspecting the 'Fighting Cocks' bridge it was found that the new wrought-iron girder had been cast on site and located but required further setting back by a few inches to enable carriage doors to clear the structure. On looking at the track at the junction at Audley End, the inspector was of the opinion that tongues of points required additional securing at the heel.

The two culverts, 36 chains from the junction received a comment when the captain approved of the long support walls but he noted that two adjacent brick culverts had altered shape and might require changing or at the least careful watching. The junction at Audley End was again referred to in connection with the catch points, which now required an earth drag to stop trains fouling the main line if they ran through and jumped the track. The GER and SWR authorities emphasized that no passenger train would run through the junction at Audley End to destinations beyond, and if they ever contemplated such working or made it a train crossing point, a second platform would be erected at Audley End. Similarly, with the extension of the line to Bartlow, if the company desired to use Saffron Walden as a crossing point for passenger trains a second platform would be installed. The captain finally stressed the method of working freight trains through the junction at Audley End, as agreed with the GER traffic superintendent, whereby down trains used the platform road, whilst up trains used the loop road. This would require the alteration to the interlocking of one pair of points. Tyler was agreeable to the opening of the line to all traffic, subject to the early completion of the remedial work.

The BoT certificate duly arrived on Tuesday 21st November, 1865 and on Wednesday placards signed by W.B. Freeland, the Secretary, were posted at prominent places in Saffron Walden announcing the opening of the line the following day.

The opening of the railway on Thursday 23rd November, 1865 coincided with a day of heavy rain showers. Large crowds gathered at the flower-bedecked station and amassed round the entrance gate, booking hall and even into the goods yard. The Saffron Walden town band, dressed in fine regalia, played a selection of tunes for the benefit of the crowd. The Directors of the company, their friends and important business colleagues of the town together with the mayor stepped down from their respective carriages at the station entrance to join GER officials on the platform for the short run to Audley End. Promptly at 7.20 am guard Charles Newson waved his green flag and driver John Duce opened the regulator of locomotive No. 60 as she pulled slowly away from the platform, whistle blowing to acknowledge the cheers of the townspeople. The train formed of three coaches and luggage van conveyed over 50 passengers. The initial return fares between the two stations were first class 9*d*., second class 6*d*., third class 4*d*. and Parliamentary 2*d*. A total of 144 people travelled on the line on the first day of operation. The provision of the large Sinclair 2-2-2 main line tender locomotive No. 60 by the GER, was apparently for prestige purposes, for on the following day an unknown tank locomotive was substituted.

To effect a better approach to Saffron Walden station, improvements were also made to the High Street by lengthening the lower end and sinking the surface at the upper end. The work was paid for by subscriptions, organized by G.S. Gibson, and Hanson, the contractor of the railway completed the task.

Despite the efforts to get goods traffic on the move prior to the official inspection, freight traffic was not handled until Monday 27th November. The total number of passengers conveyed on the branch and the associated receipts for the first week were encouraging to the Directors:

		No. of passengers				Receipts		
		1st	*2nd*	*3rd*	*Total*	*£*	*s.*	*d.*
Thursday	23rd November, 1865	30	86	28	144	5	12	7
Friday	24th November, 1865	8	24	19	51	4	15	6
Saturday	25th November, 1865	5	26	29	60	3	18	0
Monday	27th November, 1865	16	30	30	76	8	19	0
Tuesday	28th November, 1865	9	32	19	60	7	3	4
Wednesday	29th November, 1865	10	20	20	50	3	10	0
Total		*78*	*218*	*145*	*441*	*33*	*18*	*5*

Receipts for the week ending 24th December, 1865 showed:

	£	*s.*	*d.*
Passengers (1,886)	32	9	0
Parcels	7	8	4
Goods	104	11	2
Total	*144*	*8*	*6*

The successful opening of the railway completely overshadowed the steady progress made by the contractor's men on the extension. Preliminary earthworks had been completed in September and Bartlow was reached in December. Although horses and waggons remained in use for the conveyance of spoil and materials to work sites, the locomotive *Little Eastern* proved a valuable asset once the permanent way was in position and in some cases the time taken for ballasting was halved.

THE EIGHTH HALF-YEARLY ORDINARY GENERAL MEETING OF THE SHAREHOLDERS,

To be held on Friday, the 28th of September, 1866, at the TOWN HALL, *Saffron Walden.*

Report of the Directors.

Your Directors have to congratulate the Shareholders on the near completion of the Line to Bartlow.

The Government Inspector has appointed the 25th instant for the inspection of the Works between Saffron Walden and Bartlow.

Your Directors anticipate a satisfactory Report, and that they may be able at the Meeting, on the 28th instant, to announce the opening of the Line for public Traffic early next month.

The Works, owing to the state of the weather through the whole Summer, and the delays arising from the financial pressure, have been much retarded, but your Directors are pleased to be able notwithstanding, to report that their labours, in so far as regards the completion of the Line for through Traffic, are nearly at an end.

From a Report received from the Great Eastern Railway Company, of the Receipts for the Half-year ending 30th June last, it appears that the sum actually earned by the Company for that period is £1058 15s. 1d., a result shewing that the Line to Walden has produced £20 per week per mile, which your Directors consider upon the whole satisfactory. This amount is to be applied in discharge of the actual working expenses, under a special arrangement with the Great Eastern Company, until the Line is opened in its entirety to Bartlow for general traffic, when the whole Line will be worked by them, upon a payment of £50 per cent. of the gross Receipts.

The account of Expenditure, during the past Half-year is annexed, duly audited, and with the former Accounts shew a present Total of Expenditure of £113,079 10s. 4d., on account of Capital.

Annexed is the Engineer's Report, which the Directors are gratified to find gives a good account of the state of the Works on the Line.

G. S. GIBSON, Chairman.

20th September, 1866.

TO THE DIRECTORS OF THE SAFFRON WALDEN RAILWAY.

GENTLEMEN,

Since I last reported to you, I beg to state that the length between Audley End and Saffron Walden has been continuously worked both for Passenger and Goods traffic, and that all the Works continue in a perfectly sound condition.

SAFFRON WALDEN TO BARTLOW.

These Works are now completed and are ready for the Inspection by the appointed Officer of the Board of Trade. The continued wet weather has retarded their completion considerably and has rendered it necessary to use extreme care, in order to keep the Road, and Cuttings generally, free from the Effects of the surplus water.

I expect that the Inspecting Officer will go over the Line early next week.

I have the honour to be,

Gentlemen,

Your obedient humble Servant,

JOHN SAMPSON PIERCE.

Report of the Directors and of the Engineer at the eighth half-yearly shareholders' meeting.

At the seventh half-yearly meeting of the shareholders held in the town hall at Saffron Walden on 28th March, 1866, it was announced that £105,606 17s. 7d. had been expended on building the line. The Engineer reported that although bridges had been completed, the wet weather encountered during the winter months had caused delay in completing the earthworks at Ashdon and the station site at Bartlow. By June 1866 the railway was completed between Saffron Walden and Bartlow and *Little Eastern* hauling some ballast wagons made the first trial run over the completed section on 10th June. The works between Saffron Walden and Bartlow had not been an easy task for Hanson and his navvies. A cutting east of Painters Lane involved the removal of 46,300 cu. yds of earth and the construction of a three-arch bridge, whilst at Ricketts the embankment required the settling of 54,000 cu. yds of soil and the diversion of a stream.

In the meantime the GER Traffic Committee were reviewing working arrangements on many of their lines with view to cutting operating costs and making the best use of locomotive power. On 20th June, 1866 it was decreed that the Saffron Walden branch engine would make an additional trip from Saffron Walden to Audley End and return with a passenger train to provide a connection with the up main line service due in London at 9.10 am.

On 2nd August, 1866 the GER asked the SWR Board to take their 4½ per cent stock at par in lieu of £7,000 cash. This, the SWR agreed to do, but at 5½ per cent and only if an outstanding £2,100 in cash was paid at the same time. Despite the GER financial difficulties payment was made in October.

With the extension almost completed Freeland advised the Board of Trade and the GER that the line was ready for inspection. After cancellation of a visit on 3rd September, Capt. F.H. Rich duly arrived on 25th September, 1866 to conduct the inspection. He found the extension line ran from Saffron Walden to a junction with the GER at Bartlow. The new section was 5 miles 41 chains in length with formation wide enough and bridges built for double line, but only a single track railway had be laid. Except for minor alterations, the permanent way was suitable for all traffic. The steepest gradient was 1 in 67 and the sharpest curve of 20 chains radius. There were three brick-built overbridges and five brick underbridges, and a further underbridge of 27 ft span with cast-iron girders. There was also a cast-iron girder over a 9 ft wide drain. Bridge deflections were tested and found to his satisfaction. There were two stations on the line at Saffron Walden and Bartlow, the latter close to the GER Bartlow station. Rich noted that if passengers wished to travel beyond Bartlow they had to walk across from one station to the other but he required improvements to the footpath linking the two platforms. The physical junction at Bartlow was not to be used for passenger traffic. There was a locomotive turntable at Saffron Walden but not at Bartlow and the inspector recommended the line be worked at a moderate speed as there were five miles of reverse curves of 40 chains radius without any straight portion between the curves, and most on steep gradients. Rich required an undertaking from both companies that a tank engine would be used on the line until a turntable was provided at Bartlow. Despite the absence of any reference to the mode of working, Rich gave his consent to the line being opened to traffic after confirmation from John Pierce that all relevant matters had been attended to.

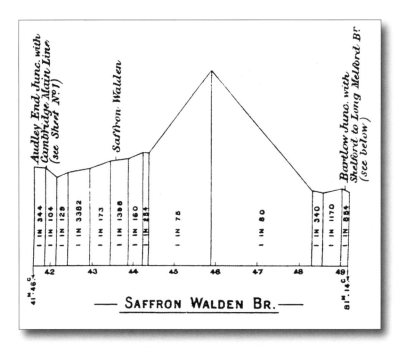

Saffron Walden branch gradient diagram.

The eighth half-yearly meeting of the shareholders was held on 28th September, 1866 when it was announced that the BoT inspection had taken place three days earlier. The poor weather during the summer months and lack of finance had again retarded progress. The ordinary share issue had reached £70,091, whilst debenture issues and temporary loans from Gibson's Bank taken to avoid delay in the progress of the line amounted to £42,988 10s. 4d. The cost of the works to 30th June, 1866 amounted to £84,586 5s. 3d. and the Engineer had received £2,900 in payment during the month. Joshua Clarke and J.S. Robson were re-elected Directors and R.D. Thurgood, auditor. The gathering heard that gross earnings for the six months ending 30th June, 1866 had totalled £1,058, being at the rate of £20 per mile per week. The company had expended £113,000 on the opening of the line and the construction work on the extension to Bartlow.

Freeland forwarded a copy of the BoT certificate to the GER authorities on 10th October, 1866 and plans were formulated to open the extension to traffic on 22nd October, 1866. One proviso was that the line was to be worked by a tank locomotive, whilst another stipulated an engine turntable was to be installed at Bartlow within a period of three months.

The opening of the line to Bartlow was not such a grandiose affair as the opening to Audley End and on Monday 22th October, 1866 only a few people journeyed on the first train to Bartlow. The outward journey was uneventful but on the return trip the train halted abruptly near the top of Ashdon bank when the coupling rod on the leading wheel of the locomotive bent outwards. The footplate staff evidently saved an embarrassing situation by disconnecting the rod completely before continuing the journey to Saffron Walden at a slow speed.

Chapter Two

Independent Days

The completion of the extension to Bartlow and subsequent opening of the line to traffic was a source of satisfaction to the Directors and shareholders. Unfortunately their euphoria was short-lived for within a week of the first train running, drivers were complaining of rough riding and undulating track, not only on the Bartlow section but also between Audley End and Saffron Walden. Some temporary packing was carried out but by 22nd November, 1866 conditions had deteriorated to the extent that the GER sent a ballast train with a permanent way gang from Cambridge to effect repairs. The cost for such work was deducted from the SWR's portion of receipts.

Evidently the remedial measures were not wholly satisfactory for the GER district engineer considered the condition of the trackwork and permanent way deplorable. The contractor, having carried out the maintenance of the Audley End to Saffron Walden section for the first 12 months from the opening of the line, subsequently discharged most of his men at the end of November, much to the chagrin of the Directors. Finding the contract with Hanson for the maintenance of the Bartlow section for the 12 months after opening was not wholly binding, the SWR Board were almost at panic stations. Freeland was sent post-haste to Bishopsgate on 30th November, 1866 and related the complete saga to S.W. Swarbrick, the GER General Manager. The SWR Board subsequently held an emergency meeting the following day and the default in the contract subsequently meant the SWR was responsible for all costs and repairs or maintenance of the line. After heated discussion at the Board meeting it was decided to put the maintenance of the entire railway in the hands of the GER and a letter was forwarded to Bishopsgate requesting that company take over the maintenance as well as the operation of the line.

On 5th December the Secretary of the GER replied, stating that the works of the SWR had not been fully approved by their Engineer as provided for in the working agreement. The GER was only working the line and if the smaller company desired maintenance to be carried out as well, 'a meeting to consider such action would have to be arranged'. After some delay it was resolved that Davis, the GER Civil Engineer, would meet Sampson Pierce, the SWR Engineer,

		SAFFRON WALDEN BRANCH. *Single Line.*																									
Down Trains.					**Week Days.**								**Up Trains.**					**Week Days.**								
Miles	FROM	1	2	3	4	5	6	7	8	9	10	11	12	Miles	FROM	1	2	3	4	5	6	7	8	9	10	11	12
		Pass.	Parl.	Parl.	Pass.	Pass.	Pass.	Pass.								Pass.	Parl.	Parl.	Pass.	Pass.	Pass.	Pass.					
		1 2	1 2 3	1 2 3	1 2	1 2	1 2	1 2 3								1 2	1 2 3	1 2 3	1 2	1 2	1 2 3	1 2 3					
		a.m.	a.m.	a.m.	p.m.	p.m.	p.m.	p.m.								a.m.	a.m.	a.m.	a.m.	p.m.	p.m.	p.m.					
—	Audley End ....dep.	7 45	9 53	10 35	12 38	2 8	5 53	7 43	...	...	...	...	...	—	Saffron Walden ...dep.	7 30	8 50	10 20	11 40	1 45	5 30	7 20	...	...	...	...	...
2	Saffron Walden ...arr.	7 55	9 40	10 45	12 45	2 15	6 0	7 50	...	...	...	...	...	2	Audley End ....arr.	7 37	8 57	10 27	11 47	1 52	5 37	7 27	...	...	...	...	...

The Goods Traffic on this Branch will be worked by the Passenger Trains, and by the Branch Engine making a special trip when necessary.

GER working timetable 1866.

to decide what action was necessary to put the line in a condition acceptable to the GER.

Severe weather conditions precluded any form of site meeting in December 1866 and January 1867 and it was 23rd February before Davis made his inspection and 26th February before he furnished his report, which proved the infrastructure on the SWR was not in the best of condition. Davis found the earthworks, bridges and fencing, 'which should have been the responsibility of the contractor for twelve months after the opening of the line', had received little if any maintenance. 'The banks are in a deplorable condition - it is quite as much as we can do to keep the line open at all'. Before the GER would even contemplate taking over the line, the SWR was to 'provide 8,400 cubic yards of good, sound and clean ballast so that the whole line could be lifted, the chalk and gravel removed and replaced by ballast'. The formation required complete boxing in and the drainage cleared. Davis also found that several cuttings had been cleared of slips and drained whilst the platform at Bartlow was slipping down the embankment and required making good. The GER Engineer also suggested removing the turntable from Saffron Walden to Bartlow. In conclusion Davis advised the GER Directors that the SWR should be made to understand that they were fully responsible for the shortcomings and should pay the GER to make good the works. In the meantime he advised Pierce that a speed limit of 10 mph be imposed on branch traffic or, failing that, all traffic would be stopped and the GER assistance withdrawn until all works were put right. Swarbrick also advised the GER Directors that the SWR was in the process of issuing preference stock, which would be prejudicial to the main line company and on 27th February the law clerk was instructed to stop the SWR from obtaining such powers without the satisfactory protection of the GER subscription to the SWR line.

When Pierce advised the SWR Board of the state of their railway, they were stunned to say the least. Pierce, however, was well aware that he was partially to blame for the deterioration of affairs of the company and offered to forgo six months' consultation fees to arrange the remedial action. It was considered that action should be taken against Hanson but unfortunately there is no evidence that this was pursued.

The SWR Secretary wrote to the GER Board on 12th March stating that all steps were being taken to get the railway in order. The following day Davis advised the Traffic Committee that the defects were principally the fault of the contractor, who had been suitably admonished and the Saffron Walden Company had agreed that all remedial work was to be completed to the satisfaction of the Engineers of both companies. The local company had no objections to the removal of the recently installed turntable from Bartlow provided the GER undertook to work the line as an integral part of their system and fully connect with the district beyond. Gamble was asked to comment on the latter and report at a subsequent meeting.

The GER traffic superintendent still had serious misgivings over the viability of the Saffron Walden to Bartlow section of line and reported on 28th March, 1867 that the 5½ miles section, involving three trains each way for six days per week and aggregating 198 train miles, was earning a mere 8s. 0d. per day. The Traffic Committee requested the law clerk and chief officer to report on the GER's legal liability for working the line. Then on 24th April the Saffron Walden

Company Secretary submitted a claim for payment of £541 15s. 1d. owing for GER internal traffic. After due investigation the application was refused as the SWR owed the GER £700 for remedial and maintenance work.

The 10 mph speed limit ordered by Davis was rigidly enforced immediately and during the next three months as work was carried out on track repairs. The SW Board managed to obtain the ballast from a local pit, although the actual source is not recorded. Payment for the 8,400 cubic yards of material was made with the help of a loan from Gibson's Bank. GER gangers and navvies carried out most of the remedial work on the embankments and cuttings during weekdays, whilst the lifting and working on the track between Saffron Walden and Audley End took place between the running of normal service trains. Minor remedial work on the track between Saffron Walden and Bartlow was also executed between trains on weekdays, with major lifting and re-ballasting being carried out on Sundays when no trains ran.

To help pay for the extensive work carried out by the GER, the SWR sought Parliamentary and Board of Trade authority and was subsequently granted an additional capital certificate to raise a further £25,000 in shares, with borrowing powers of £8,000. How exactly the Directors hoped to get this money and who would buy such shares is not known, for many of the existing shares remained unsold with no likelihood of prospective purchasers. Unsatisfactory negotiations with the GER Traffic Committee in June, concerning the retiming of passenger services on the line and connections with main line services at Audley End and cross-country services at Bartlow, added to the moribund situation. Matters finally reached a head in early July 1867, when two claims against the SWR for £2,718 1s. 3d. and £1,869 4s. 10d. were received in respect of outstanding payments for land purchase.

With liabilities of £67,503 8s. 4d. against assets of only £48,284 19s. 9d. the company had reached the end of the road. All attempts to fight off the impending insolvency had been exhausted and the only way out was to admit bankruptcy and appoint a receiver. Thus on 3rd August, 1867 the SWR took the unprecedented step of appointing Freeland, the Secretary, as official receiver. Then at the beginning of September 1867 the General Post Office wrote to the SWR and GER offering an annual payment of £5 for the conveyance of a few mailbags between Audley End and Saffron Walden.

At the tenth half-yearly meeting of the shareholders held in Saffron Walden town hall on 26th September, 1867, the Directors had little cheering news to tell. The unsatisfactory monetary position of the GER had reacted on the Saffron Walden line. The hoped-for alterations in the passenger timetable and the increase in goods facilities at Bartlow had fallen on deaf ears at Bishopsgate. The gross income received for the six months ending 30th June, 1867 amounted to £1,193 2s. 7d. After deducting 50 per cent for working the line, the GER had, with the Directors' approval, retained the remainder as part payment for an outstanding bill of £1,442 14s. 0d. in respect of payment for the completion of the railway and the junctions at Audley End and Bartlow. The shareholders were also informed of the precarious state of the company; creditors were pressing for payment of outstanding debts.

The completion of the upgrading of the trackwork by the GER engineers enabled the speed limit to be restored to 20 miles per hour. All attempts by the local company to persuade the GER to divert through traffic onto their line, however, met with refusal and relations between the two companies reached straining point, so that plans for additional sidings at Bartlow were temporarily put in abeyance.

In an effort to save money Pierce was requested to consult with the land agent to determine pockets of land surplus to the railway's requirements with a view to possible sales to adjoining landowners. The railway came in for criticism early in February 1868 after an old man narrowly missed being run down by an Audley End to Bartlow train on an occupational crossing near Church End, Ashdon. It was stated by a witness working in a nearby field, that the engine whistle only sounded when the driver saw the man on the crossing. As a result a whistle board was erected on the approaches to the crossing to give earlier warning and an offending tree was cut down to give the driver of an approaching train a clearer view of the crossing.

The eleventh half-yearly meeting on 30th March, 1868 heard that debentures remained unpaid; the GER had received £1,332 18s. 8d. for operating the line during the six months ending 31st December, 1867 but again had retained the full amount to cover outstanding debts. Because of the monetary involvement in the SWR, two GER Directors, Lord Cranborne and Mr Currie, were elected to the local Board in April 1868.

In spite of the worries, frustrations and problems associated with the SWR, the Directors were delighted to learn in June that the extension of the railway to Bartlow and the general usefulness of the line had finally brought about an increase in passenger and freight receipts, and Freeland reported an income of £4,413 14s. 9d. against working expenses of £3,685 17s. 1d., leaving a healthy credit balance of £727 17s. 8d. Unfortunately the whole of this amount had again been paid over to the GER for outstanding debts. Later in August, Mr Houblon made an offer of £60 for a small tract of railway land at Bartlow. The Engineer considered it inadvisable to sell because of the insecure state of the ground, the low price offered and the position of the turntable in relation to the property. On 19th August, 1867 the GER Engineer reported to the Traffic Committee that he had met with Pierce, the SWR Engineer, on the question of the future of the line and would prepare a joint report by 15th September. The General Manager, however, stipulated that the GER could not take over the line until the permanent way and infrastructure was 'put into proper repair and the two engineers had agreed as to what was to be done'. At a GER Board meeting held on 7th August, 1868 the Marquis of Salisbury and Mr G.W. Currie were delegated to represent the GER on the SWR Board.

At the twelfth half-yearly meeting of the shareholders held on 30th September, 1868 the Directors were highly critical of the GER. Despite receipts of £1,253 13s. 6d. for the six months ending 30th June, 1868, an increase of £60 10s. 11d. over the corresponding half year for 1867, reference was made to the 'objectionable arrangement existing for working the line, which is rendered almost useless', a statement alluding to the continued stalemate between the two companies over the working of GER through traffic between Audley End and Bartlow.

At the GER Directors meeting on 4th February, 1869 it was announced that the credit for traffic at 30th June, 1868 on the Saffron Walden line was £4,413 14s. 9d.

against a debit of £3,685 17s. 1d. for ballasting, stores and general works and it was agreed the balance of £727 17s. 8d. was to be paid over to the smaller company.

The question of charging merchants a rental for use of the coal ground in Saffron Walden goods yard was raised early in March 1869. After consultation with the goods manager at Cambridge, who was of the opinion that by raising a rental such action might deter customers and drive away trade, it was resolved no charges would be raised.

In April 1869 Freeland wrote to the GER Board regarding a proposed goods yard at Bartlow for the Saffron Walden line and a siding for Mr Slater's farm and brickfield near Ashdon. The cost for the yard was estimated at £452 and the siding at £170. After deliberations and investigations the GER goods manager turned down the application for the yard stating that adequate facilities existed at the GER station. Approval was, however, given for the farm siding and a single siding at Bartlow for the local company. New plans were submitted on 19th May, 1869 and the siding at Bartlow was installed in October at a cost of £180 to the SWR. On 8th July, 1869 C.H. Turner and George Wodehouse Currie were elected to represent the GER interests on the SWR Board. At that time other members of the Board were George Stacey Gibson, Chairman, John Stephenson Robson, Vice-Chairman, the Marquis of Salisbury and Thomas Shirley. Three weeks later it was agreed to issue free passes to the Saffron Walden Directors to enable them to travel to London for meetings.

Meanwhile on 28th July an application to purchase excess land alongside Saffron Walden goods yard was received from Mr Wilkins of Waltham Abbey. It was his intention to erect limekilns and the only suitable chalk lay in the area of the yard. His application was turned down as the land was required for the possible extension of the yard and it was thought that the smoke would prove an inconvenience and annoyance to people living in the locality.

The assurances given by the Secretary and the Engineer of the SWR to Colonel Rich regarding the fencing of the line rebounded as early as September 1869 when it was found that the wooden posts were rotting at various points along the line, with the result that animals were straying on the railway by crossing or breaking the support wires.

At the 14th half-yearly meeting on 29th September, 1869, the Engineer referred to the imminent installation of a siding adjacent to Mr Slater's brickfields at Ashdon. The shareholders were informed that the company was pressing the GER for the increased siding accommodation at Bartlow and Saffron Walden to attract further trade. Although surplus land had been sold for £1,683 10s. 8d., £14,240 of ordinary shares and £25,000 debentures issues remained unsold. The Secretary also advised gross receipts for the half-year to 30th June, 1869 totalled £1,337 14s. 3d., an increase of £84 0s. 9d. over the previous six months.

In late January 1870 the Electric Telegraph Co. wrote to the GER offering to erect a telegraph route between Audley End and Saffron Walden. The application after endorsement was passed to the SWR Board for action. Freeland duly replied stating that the SWR had no funds at its disposal to pay for the installation and 'had little encouragement to induce them to make any outlay while the line is practically unworked between Saffron Walden and Bartlow'. Final approval of the installation of telegraph on the branch was given

GREAT EASTERN RAILWAY

A DAY AT THE SEA-SIDE.

On Wednesday, August 2nd, 1876,

A SPECIAL CHEAP

EXCURSION TRAIN

TO

WALTON-ON-THE-NAZE

AND BACK,

Will run as under :—

From	Train at	Fares to Walton & back.	
		First Class.	Covered Cars.
	a.m.		
Cambridge........	6 20		
Shelford..........	6 26		
Linton	6 40	6s.	3s.
Saffron Walden....	6 25		
Bartlow	6 45		
Haverhill	7 0		
Clare	7 20	5s.	2s. 6d.
Melford	7 40		
Walton, arr. about	9 45		

Returning from Walton at 7.0 p.m. the same day.

No Luggage allowed.

London, July 1876.   **S. SWARBRICK, General Manager.**

PRINTED AT THE COMPANY'S WORKS, STRATFORD.

Seaside excursion train notice, issued by the GER in 1876.

on 19th February, 1870 when it was installed between Audley End and Saffron Walden stations at the end of the following month, the SWR paying £28 to the telegraph company.

Following further representation by Messrs Gibson and Freeland early in 1870, the GER adopted a more lenient attitude towards the affairs of the SWR. After a tour of inspection of lines in the Cambridge area in March 1870, S.W. Swarbrick advised the local Board that subject to their approval, arrangements would be made for joint detailed site meetings at Saffron Walden and Bartlow to discuss operating problems. Six months elapsed, however, before the site meetings were held when the GER was represented by the Way & Works and Traffic Committees. Very little was achieved by the meeting other than a promise to increase the passenger train services with improved connections at Audley End and Bartlow. The GER representatives were adamant that no further sidings would be added at Bartlow as the GER goods yard could handle any interchange of traffic. The subject of through traffic using the line was avoided, except that it was stated that better facilities for marshalling and exchanging traffic from south of Audley End bound for the Haverhill line existed at Cambridge.

The Essex Agricultural Show held at Saffron Walden in June 1870 attracted much needed trade to the line. Passenger traffic increased and the demand for loading, unloading, feeding and watering livestock necessitated the import of staff from other GER stations in the Cambridge area. Revenue for the half-year ending 30th June, 1870 amounted to £1,545 4s. 7d., an increase over the previous six months of £173 8s. 2d. and the corresponding half-year of 1869 of £207 9s. 5d.; the increase being wholly due to the show.

At the beginning of September 1870 several gentry, merchants and farmers, and other residents of Haverhill and surrounding area, sent a memorial to the GER suggesting the Saffron Walden line between Bartlow and Audley End be made available as a direct connecting link between Haverhill and its neighbourhood and the metropolis. The petition also asked for an increased train service on the Saffron Walden line. The matter was discussed at the meeting of the Traffic Committee on 14th September when it was agreed that the Directors would include a visit to the line on Thursday 22nd September during a tour of inspection of the area. In the meantime Freeland was asked to advise the petitioners that the Directors would meet with a deputation on that date. The meeting was duly held and the General Manager reported on 12th October that a better class of carriage was to be used on the branch, whilst a small improvement could be made to the train service by better utilization of the engine allocated to work the line. On 15th September, 1870 it was announced that the Marquis of Salisbury as a past Director of the SWR held bonds to the value of £100 in the company. On 12th October authority was given for additional sidings on the branch at a cost of £349 15s. 0d. As the SWR was insolvent the GER agreed to pay full costs.

However, the new proposals for an enhanced train service were not to the liking of the inhabitants of Saffron Walden for on 25th October J.G. Billingham wrote to the General Manager offering alternative alterations to the timetable. The correspondence was passed to the traffic superintendent, and the Traffic Committee considered his comments at their meeting on 26th October:

We can agree to the following extension of the 7.58 am train ex-Audley End to Bartlow and return from Bartlow at 9.00 am to Saffron Walden. This will cut off the connection with the down main line 6.45 am Parliamentary train from London, and the Saffron Walden Company ask that we should book Parliamentary passengers from Saffron Walden to Cambridge and stations between, by our 8.00 am train instead of the existing Parliamentary train. This we concede but there will not be any other Parliamentary passengers other than from the Saffron Walden line by our 8.00 am train. The 9.00 am train ex-Bartlow will afford passengers who connect at the station at 8.41 am by our 7.35 am train ex-Sudbury, a means of getting to London by our 9.00 am train ex-Cambridge, due at Bishopsgate at 10.55 am, instead of by the 9.37 am up express and the 9.45 am Parliamentary train due in London at 11.08 am and 12.30 pm respectively. This will no doubt divert the position of traffic from stations on our branch and the Colne Valley Railway, which now finds its way either via Cambridge or Marks Tey. The Manager is also of the opinion that we agree to the extension of the 9.30 am and 10.28 am trains from Audley End to Saffron Walden on to Bartlow, also the return trains from Bartlow at 9.58 am and 12.20 pm, also to run a train on Thursdays only for Bishop's Stortford market. Passengers would return from Audley End to Bartlow at 4.48 pm, in connection with the 2.45 pm train from London necessitating a return journey from Bartlow to Audley End. This will involve 154 additional train miles per week. We cannot agree to the GER Company running any train between Bartlow and Haverhill with Saffron Walden Company passengers, unless that Company pay especially for the service, as our own train loading is very light.

At the end of 1870 the GER authorities were contemplating altering the terms for working the line to 60 per cent of gross receipts but because of the continuing serious financial state of the local company the idea was shelved. At the same time both Freeland and the GER goods manager wrote to GER headquarters requesting the provision of a goods shed at Bartlow. They also asked for the diversion of Haverhill goods traffic from stations south of Audley End over the Saffron Walden line instead of going via Cambridge and Shelford. The Traffic Committee considered the matter on 4th January, 1871 when the General Manager was instructed to advise Freeland that the company had no objection to the provision of the shed provided plans were submitted and agreed between the two companies and that the GER was allowed use of the building. The second request was bluntly refused; 'We cannot, however, bind ourselves to sending by the Saffron Walden line, traffic from places beyond it or to run a train on our line to Haverhill in accordance to the submitted timetable'. Receipts on the line were encouraging for the 7½ mile branch earned £2,556 or £341 per mile in 1867 but by 1870 the receipts had increased to £3,077 or £410 per mile.

In early March 1871 the SWR Board complained of the poor mechanical condition of the locomotives working the line and requested heavier and stronger machines. The GER Board advised that the locomotives used were adequate for the existing service and if more powerful locomotives were required, traffic would have to increase considerably, the track be relaid and the formation strengthened. Then on 11th of the month Freeland wrote to the GER management regarding the shortcomings of the branch train service and the traffic superintendent was asked to investigate. The subject was raised at the Traffic Committee meeting on 26th April which must have reconsidered the discussions heard the previous October. It was announced that a draft reply had been sent to the SWR Secretary stating that it had been agreed to extend to Bartlow the 7.58 am train from Audley End, returning from Bartlow to Audley End at approximately 8.55. As a result of these alterations the 8.45 am Saffron Walden to Audley End train and the 9.04 am return workings were to be discontinued. The 9.35 and 10.28 am trains from Audley End were to be extended to Bartlow returning at approximately 9.58 am and 12.20 pm respectively. On Thursdays, Bishops Stortford market day, a train to Bartlow would connect at Audley End with the 2.45 pm train from London to convey branch passengers and this would return from Bartlow to Audley End at 5.15. The 5.50 pm train from Audley End was to be extended to Bartlow returning from Bartlow to Audley End at 6.45. It was also agreed that the through booking of passengers from Bartlow via Saffron Walden to London and principal intermediate stations and vice versa would be permitted and a mileage proportion allowed to the SWR on passengers carried by the SWR route.

The new arrangements were subject to certain regulations. As there was only a narrow margin of time between the arrival of the 9.35 and 10.28 am trains from Audley End at Bartlow, and the required departure time to allow the return trains to connect with the GER main line services at Audley End, it was stipulated that the arrangements were experimental and depended on the branch train being able to work to the junction without causing delays to the main line trains. With regard to the goods traffic, the SWR was to be allowed their mileage proportion on any traffic from Bartlow to London and principal intermediate stations and vice versa, if conveyed by the Saffron Walden line, also the mileage proportion on all goods traffic consigned by their route from GER stations between Bartlow and Long Melford, including to Saffron Walden and Audley End, and from stations east of Long Melford to Ipswich inclusive.

On 14th September, 1871 Messrs Lightly Simpson and G.W. Currie were nominated to represent the interests of the GER on the SWR Board. The shareholders at the 18th half-yearly meeting held at Saffron Walden town hall on 27th September, 1871 were informed by the local Directors that tentative arrangements had been made with the GER for an improvement in the working of the line. However, any improvement would be useless unless through traffic to Haverhill, Clare and Sudbury was diverted across the line and the GER used the route as part of their system. The receipts for the half-year ending 31st December, 1871 amounted to £1,634 4s. 8d., an increase over the half-year ending December 1870 of £102 7s. 11d., due to more traffic accruing following improved working arrangements at Bartlow. The improvements appear to have been short-lived for the Directors were soon complaining that the Haverhill and Clare traffic was still being worked via Shelford and not Saffron Walden, a view which was voiced at the half-yearly meeting of shareholders on 20th September, 1872. In June 1872 the £100 shareholdings of the Marquis of Salisbury and R. Young were transferred to the GER.

The steep gradient of Ashdon bank, which faced trains leaving Saffron Walden and Bartlow meant that locomotives were working hard to get their loads to the summit. The elderly motive power supplied to work the services often belched sparks from the chimney as they struggled to get their trains over the summit. This was of no consequence during winter but in summer months the dry

TIME TABLE.

SAFFRON WALDEN RAILWAY.

SEPTEMBER, 1872.

DOWN TRAINS.

FROM	Week Days						Sundays		
	morn. (Parl.)	morn.	morn.	even.	even.	even.	morn.	even.	even. (Parl.)
	1 2 3	1 2 3	1 2 3	1 2 3	1 2 3	1 2 3	1 2 3	1 2 3	1 2 3
LONDON ....dep.	6 45	8 0 11 0		2 45	4 6	6 0	6 30	2 15	9 0
STRATFORD	6 58						6 41		9 47
BROXBOURNE	7 50	8 39 11 30		2 39	4 42	6 33 9 51	7 27	2 53	9 51
BPS. STORTFORD..	8 29	9 7 12 12		4 15	5 18	7 9 10 23	8 8	3 33 10 19
STANSTEAD	8 37	9 12 19		4 22	5 25	7 16	8 16	3 41
ELSENHAM	8 44	12 29		4 29	5 *		8 23	3 51
NEWPORT	8 53	12 38		4 38			8 33	4
Bartlow ....departure	8 55 11 10		5 12	6 45				
S. Walden ....ditto	9 15 12 25 4 20		5 25	7 15				
Audley End ... arrival	9 22 12 32 4 37		5 32	7 22				
AUDLEY END junc.	8 59 9 26 12 37		4 44	5 44	7 36 10 43		8 39	4 11 10 41
Audley End..departure	9 35 12 42 4 48		5 50	7 38				
S Walden .... arrival	9 42 12 49 4 55		5 57	7 45				
Bartlow ....ditto	9 64 1 4 5 7		6 10					
CHESTERFORD	9 8 12 46 4 53		5 53	7 45 10 54			8 48	4 22 10 50
WHITTLESFORD	9 16 12 54 5		5 *				8 56	4 33
SHELFORD	9 23 5 9		6 30	8 10 11 16			9 4	4 45 11 12
CAMBRIDGE	9 40 9 57 1 30 5 20		6 15 7 1	8 10 12 0			9 15	4 55 12 0
ELY	10 22 10 29 1 50 6 15		7 1	12 45				5 55 12 43
PETERBORO'	12 20 2 0 30 30 7 40		9 10	2 35				7 35 1 43
NORWICH	1 0 3 55		9 10	2 35				8 20 2 35
YARMOUTH	2 23 4 55		9 55	3 30				9 30 3 30

UP TRAINS.

FROM	Week Days						Sundays		
	morn.	morn. (Parl.)	morn.	even.	even.	even.	morn.	even.	even. (Parl.)
	1 2 3	1 2 3	1 2 3	1 2 3	1 2 3	1 2 3	1 2 3	1 2 3	1 2 3
YARMOUTH			9 25		1 50	8 40			8 40
NORWICH		7 15 10 44		3 0	4 10 0			4 10 0
PTERBOROUGH		11 28		4 23	4 40 10 58			4 40 10 58
ELY	7 10	9 3 12 46		5 10	6 12 5		9 50	2 45 6 12 5
CAMBRIDGE	7 18	9 43 1 45		5 17	6 5 1 20		9 58	4 20 5 20 1 20
SHELFORD	7 25	9 54 1 37		5 24	*		10 6	5 28
WHITTLESFORD	7 33	10 11 1 52		5 33	7 16		10 15	5 35
CHESTERFORD		10 11 1 52		5 33	7 16			5 47
Bartlow ....departure	8 55	9 58		3 12	6 45			
S. Walden ...... ditto	7 30	9 15 10 10		1 48	5 23	7 15		
Audley End ... arrival	7 37	9 22 10 17		1 53	5 32	7 22		
AUDLEY END junc.	7 42	9 31 10 23		2 1	3 43	7 26 1 56		10 26	5 58 1 56
Audley End..departure	7 58	9 35 10 28		2 5	5 50	7 38		
S. Walden .... arrival	8 5	9 42 10 35		2 12	5 57	7 45		
Bartlow ....ditto	8 25	9 54 10 50		6 10				
NEWPORT	7 47	10 29	2 6	5 48			10 32	6 4
ELSENHAM	7 57	10 41	2 19		7 40		10 43	6 16
STANSTEAD	8 3	9 46 10 48	2 27	6 2			10 36	6 23
BPS. STORTFORD ..	8 11	9 53 11 0	2 57	6 11	7 54 2 30		11 0	6 33 2 30
BROXBOURNE	8 47	10 21 11 42	2 56	6 46	8 23 3 9		11 37	7 15 3 9
STRATFORD		12 20	3 36		9 14 4 0		12 31	4 0
LONDON	9 30	10 59 12 30	3 36 7 30		9 10 4 15		12 45 7 53	4 15

PRINTED BY J. M. YOUNGMAN.

* will stop when required, notice being given at the preceding Station.

§ These Trains run To and From Bartlow on Thursdays only.

Saffron Walden Railway public timetable for September 1872. At this period the majority of trains ran through to Bartlow.

conditions and the open fields alongside the line meant a danger to crops. Drivers were advised to take preventative action. Despite this instruction, sparks set fire to a field of wheat in August 1872, although fortunately the blaze was brought under control before much damage was done.

The advent of the railway in this area of north-west Essex was not welcomed by all and several attempts were made to derail the branch train. As late as 14th September, 1872 a down train formed of a locomotive and three coaches hit a wooden post placed across the line near Bartlow. Fortunately the offending post was brushed aside and except for jolting the locomotive and rolling stock suffered no damage. At the end of the month Messrs C.H. Parkes and G.W. Currie were elected to serve as GER representatives on the SWR Board.

Despite the GER Board's statement of faith made in March 1871, the choice of motive power supplied to the Saffron Walden branch left much to be desired and failures were commonplace. On Saturday 4th January, 1873 the 8.15 am ex-Bartlow train failed near Ashdon when the steam chest on the locomotive fractured. Such was the shortage of motive power that a four-hour delay was incurred whilst a fresh locomotive was brought from Cambridge to rescue the failed train. In the same month continuous heavy rain caused several landslips on the branch. The damage was more severe than originally thought and repairs near Saffron Walden and Bartlow were still in hand in March 1873.

Five months later on 17th May 1873, the 5.25 pm Saffron Walden to Audley End train was passing through the deep cutting near Beechy Ride when the train ground to a halt. The connecting rod on the locomotive had fractured and ploughed into the ballast causing the sudden stoppage. With the locomotive a total failure, passengers had to alight and walk the rest of the way to Audley End. The branch service was again disrupted for three hours awaiting a replacement locomotive from Cambridge and the removal of the failure. Later in early October of the same year Mr Armstrong, the station master at Bartlow, reported that residents who lived near the station were complaining of nuisance caused by the unloading of rotting fish, which was used as manure by the local farmers. From enquiries it appeared that the fish merchants at Lowestoft and Yarmouth were all too eager to dispatch the highly aromatic manure, but the farmers in question were slow to remove the rotting flesh and bones from the goods yard.

On 24th March, 1874 the GER Directors noted that the junction between the two lines at Bartlow was still not interlocked. With the liquidation of the company's debts finalized in June 1874 and the outstanding unissued shares and debentures on hand, the SWR Board requested the GER to take over the SWR 'on favourable terms'. On receipt of the proposal, the GER Executive Committee studied details of the traffic receipts and outstanding liabilities before replying that they were unable to make a decision until further investigations had been made. These revealed that shares to the value of £82,490 had been created but £12,510 remained unissued; £25,000 preference shares were not issued, whilst debentures to the value of £30,985 had been issued leaving £8,015 debentures unsold. The GER authorities, however, were evidently happy with receipts of the line, which had risen almost 50 per cent in three years, for when the traffic superintendent notified the GER Board of the scope for further increase, imminent takeover appeared possible. On 28th September a tour of inspection by the Traffic Committee found the station masters re-affirming this view. On 6th August, 1874, Messrs C.H. Parkes and G.W. Currie had been re-elected as GER representatives on the SWR Board.

Gas prices for supplies to Saffron Walden station were 6s. 8d. per thousand cubic feet, a price that was considered above average for GER country stations during a survey conducted in February 1875. On 19th May, 1875 it was announced that Messrs T. Cave MP and A. Young had been appointed by the SWR to serve on the GER and SWR Joint Committee, whilst the General Manager was to investigate the full extent of the repairs required to bring the railway up to standard. By 16th June the Engineer's report had been forwarded to Saffron Walden.

The increase in goods traffic on the branch necessitated the installation of a loading gauge in the siding at Bartlow in June 1876. In March of the same year the GER was involved with a rating appeal after new assessments were made on the buildings at Audley End station. The original figures for main line platforms and the branch platform were £5,356 and £341 but the revised rates was advised as £11,819 and £986 respectively. To this both the GER and SWR Companies took exception and contested the totals with the local rating authority. Their efforts were not in vain for after investigation the rates charged were reduced to £8,034 and £447.

On 8th April, 1876 a fire broke out at Saffron Walden station when a pig and its sty were engulfed and destroyed in flames. The flames spread to the station roof at one time but no damage was sustained and the fire was quickly brought under control. The unfortunate pig and its accommodation belonged to station foreman/porter Smith, who was severely admonished by the railway authorities for letting such an occurrence happen. On 11th July, 1876 the provision of locking bars to points at Audley End was approved at a cost of £40. Then on 24th August it was revealed a Mr Taylor had approached the railway company for provision of a footpath to Saffron Walden station running alongside the goods yard but the scheme was rejected by the Way & Works Committee as being too dangerous as it crossed several railway tracks in its proposed path.

In the autumn of 1876 the GER solicitor and Freeland were finalizing details of purchase agreements as the larger company was preparing to apply to Parliament for a General Bill, which would include the takeover of the SWR. The few shareholders that bothered to attend an extraordinary meeting in September were informed officially of the imminent purchase and voiced no strong objections. Indeed some were happy to expect some cash return in the future. At the GER Traffic Committee meeting on 28th November, 1876 the General Manager reported the capital of the SWR totalled £151,000, formed of £31,000 five per cent debentures due for settlement in 1881, £25,000 three per cent preference stock and £95,000 ordinary shares of which the GER had subscribed £28,000. It was announced that the Board had agreed to offer £31,000 four per cent debentures, £12,500 five per cent preference shares, whilst ordinary shareholders were to receive not exceeding £40 of GER ordinary shares for every £100 SWR shares. Davis, Morgan & Co. agreed to accept the terms on behalf of the SWR and on 29th November, 1876 it was announced that Parliamentary powers would be sought in the GER 1877 Bill.

From May 1877 a new innovation was a through 'slip coach' detached at Audley End for Saffron Walden off the 2.40pm Liverpool Street to Norwich train via Cambridge. This was a long-lasting service, for it was retained until 1914.

The last joint act of the two Boards was made on 12th June, 1877 when advice was received from the goods manager at Cambridge that a college was about to be built at Saffron Walden by Messrs Bell. The total cost of the project was £8,000 and the contractor had advised a greater proportion of the building material would be received by rail. Unfortunately there was no fixed crane at Saffron Walden goods yard to offload the bricks and cement. Authority was quickly given for a 5 ton capacity crane, later reduced to 1 ton 10 cwt to be installed at an estimated cost of £150.

Under the provisions of the GER Act of 12th July, 1877 (40 and 41 Vict. cap. lxxxiii) the GER purchased the total assets of the SWR for £70,750. The capital authorized to be raised by the local company was £120,000 formed of £82,470 ordinary shares, £12,530 ordinary stock and £25,000 preference shares, although many remained unsold. In addition a total of £31,000 had been borrowed. The GER purchase price of £70,750 was paid over as £12,500 GER five per cent preference stock, £26,800 ordinary shares, £31,000 GER four per cent debentures and £450 cash. The Saffron Walden preference holders received £50 of GER stock for each £100 holding, whilst the debenture stock was divided between the local debenture holders. Ordinary Saffron Walden shareholders shared the ordinary stock and £450 cash. The GER financed this exchange of shares by itself creating £11,130 five per cent preference stock, £1,370 preference stock being created with effect from 30th January, 1878, £26,800 ordinary stock was issued out of a balance of £34,100 existing preference stock and £31,000 four per cent debenture stock, £1,370 preference stock being created with effect from 30th January, but the takeover was officially backdated to take effect from 1st January, 1877.

On enquiring into the financial state of the SWR after the passing of the Act, the GER Board was shown the following statement on 19th December, 1877:

Cash from traffic receipts – 1877	£	s.	d.
January	126	17	7
February	129	1	1
March	144	12	3
April	114	11	4
May	127	9	1
June	124	5	4
July	132	5	1
August	140	4	6

From these receipts the SWR paid £23 6s. 3d. income tax and after expenses were left with a balance of £494 1s. 1d., the GER retaining the remainder.

At the time of takeover by the GER, the SWR Board was formed of G.S. Gibson, Chairman, J.S. Robson, Vice-Chairman, both of Saffron Walden, Thomas Shirley of Newport, Thomas Cave of Richmond and Alexander Young of London EC, the last two gentlemen being representatives of the GER. The Secretary during the independent years was W.B. Freeland, who also acted as solicitor and the Engineer J.S. Pierce. The banking for the railway was in the hands of the Saffron Walden partnership of Gibson, Tuke & Gibson.

SAFFRON WALDEN RAILWAY.

Saffron Walden,

8th August 1878.

Sir,

I beg to acknowledge the receipt of Certificates, No. *100*

3621 to 3720 both numbers inclusive

for £10 each, in the Saffron Walden Railway Company, and I hereby undertake to hold them on your behalf until I have handed you in exchange a Certificate for Great Eastern Ordinary Stock, which will be issued to you with a Cheque for any Dividend that may have been declared thereon.

I am, Sir,

Your obedient Servant,

W. B. FREELAND,

Secretary.

G. S. Gibson Esqr.

for Mr Wm Hanson.

Letter of receipt of Saffron Walden Railway share certificates from the Company Secretary to a company shareholder after the Great Eastern Railway takeover.

Chapter Three

Great Eastern Ownership

At the GER Directors' meeting held on 21st January, 1878 it was announced that the SWR purchase had been completed and the line was now part of the GER. The takeover brought little change to the Saffron Walden line and the new acquisition continued to operate purely as a branch, feeding at one end the Cambridge main line and at the other a cross-country branch. Nevertheless gradual improvements were made as traffic increased. The following day approval was given to the planting of gorse on the railway embankment near Saffron Walden station to consolidate the escarpment.

The station master at Saffron Walden complained in May 1878 of the lack of facilities and privacy for him and his family in off duty hours. After investigation by the Way & Works Committee, a new washhouse was erected in August alongside the station house, together with higher and stronger fencing at a cost of £30. Along the line at Bartlow there had been complaints regarding station master Armstrong's inappropriate dealings with customers. After submission of a letter from Mr Clayden of Barham Hall and a memorial from the farmers of Linton and district and an internal inquiry, the Traffic Committee dismissed Armstrong from the company's employ in September 1878.

The GER received little praise for their attempts at improvements in the station area at Saffrom Walden. New fencing was erected around the goods yard in 1879 and caused an immediate complaint from a prominent townsman who stated he could not see when a horse-drawn vehicle was leaving the yard, and that accidents were likely. The railway authorities suitably ignored this but retaliated against the local council when they complained of the state of the station road entrance to the goods yard. The railway company was adamant that their entrance was fully made up and that it was the local authority's roadway, which was 'full of ruts and uneven for vehicular traffic'.

On 6th April, 1880 it was announced that gas prices to Audley End station were fixed at 5s. 6d. per thousand cubic feet. Then on 21st April, 1880 signalling and permanent way alterations totalling £1,710 were authorized at Audley End. The work, including the provision of a new signal box and involving the main line and branch facilities, was completed in August 1880 at a cost of £760 for permanent way and £950 for signalling. As freight increased at Saffron Walden the cramped track layout caused congestion during shunting operations, often to the point where wagons were left at Audley End or passenger trains delayed. To ease the problem a new goods siding was installed in October 1880 at a cost of £80. In the meantime W.B. Freeland, now clerk to Saffron Walden town council and former Secretary of the SWR, requested the GER to provide railway telegraphic communication along the branch from Audley End to Bartlow. The telegraph superintendent reported on 17th August, 1880 that the work could be completed for the relatively small outlay of between £30 and £40, as the posts were already erected alongside the line for the postal telegraph route. The Traffic Committee approved the outlay and work was completed in November.

The year 1881 was best remembered for the snowstorm, which obliterated the landscape from about 5 pm on Tuesday 18th January. The storm continued unabated until 9 am the following morning. Train services were severely disrupted and the last down train from Audley End in the evening made three attempts to reach Saffron Walden before arriving safely.

To handle the increase in cattle traffic passing through the railhead at Bartlow to markets at Saffron Walden, Haverhill and Cambridge, a new cattle pen was installed at the junction station in August 1881 at a cost of £35. The facility helped to increase cattle traffic on the branch and reduced the numbers of drovers walking their animals to market along the Ashdon Road. In April of the following year a plot of land for future expansion was purchased at Audley End at a cost of £37.

On 6th February, 1883 authority was given for signalling improvements at Bartlow and Linton at a combined cost of £154. At both stations the signals were to be resited to provide better braking distance between distant and home signals. The work was completed at Bartlow later in the year at a cost of £130. The former Chairman of the SWR, George Stacey Gibson, died in 1883 at the age of 65 and over 5,000 people attended his funeral service held at the Saffron Walden Quaker Meeting House. A special train ran from Liverpool Street conveying Quaker businessmen and other professional men, all wearing top hats and morning dress. Once on the branch the train was the responsibility of Saffron Walden guard 'Captain' Scarlett, who was at the time the Railway Mission leader, town Co-operative Society pioneer and, before that, the Salvation Army captain.

The decision to again hold the Essex Agricultural Show at Saffron Walden in 1884 brought an unexpected boost to the GER when the organizers requested the railway company to convey all livestock to the event by rail from many points in East Anglia. As early as 5th February the goods agent was seeking authority to finance additional siding accommodation for horseboxes and cattle trucks. The estimated £690 was authorized in March and construction appears to have been completed well in advance of the show's opening date. Facilities included the extension to the cattle dock. On 1st April authority was given for the provision of water supply for cattle at Audley End at a cost of £22, in case any animals were detained at the junction station. By 1885 a second slip coach was detached at Audley End for Saffron Walden.

In January 1886 pedestrians using South Road bridge complained of the narrow structure and the danger from passing carts, and petitioned for the bridge to be widened. Their action had arisen because of an increase in pedestrian and vehicular traffic using the road and bridge, which crossed the railway to the east of Saffron Walden station. The surface of the road had deteriorated and the Saffron Walden council decided to widen the road on either side of the structure. They duly notified the GER authorities of their intentions and requested the bridge to be widened from 14 to 24 ft to avoid a bottleneck. After making enquiries, the GER solicitor notified the Board that the railway company was legally liable for maintenance and alterations to the particular structure and authority was duly given on 20th July, 1886 at an estimated cost of £300, the work being completed the following year. In the meantime W.H. Hall, E.P. Frost and other local residents approached the GER with a proposal for a railway from Bartlow to Six Mile Bottom on the Cambridge to Newmarket line. The matter was discussed at the Directors' meeting on 4th May, 1886 when the Secretary was asked to reply that the GER was unable to say, what, if anything, they might recommend to the shareholders.

The cramped office conditions at Saffron Walden station meant that the station master often handled important meetings with traders, staff and even railway officers in the booking office or the waiting room. To obviate such shortcomings authority was given on 15th January, 1887 for a small office to be built for the station master, at the west end of the platform near the signal box at a cost of £70. The work, however, was not considered top priority and was completed in April 1888.

In anticipation of the forthcoming Regulation of Railways Act and to ease train working, authority was given on 18th October, 1887 for the introduction of block working between Audley End and Saffron Walden; the cost of £2,845 included work on four other branches and was charged to the interlocking account. Work was not completed until September 1888.

On Friday 2nd August, 1889 one wagon of a train of five being shunted from the main line into the goods yard became derailed at Saffron Walden. The 11.50 am and 12.15 pm trains from Saffron Walden were subsequently cancelled. Fortunately the Cambridge breakdown train was soon on the scene and the offending wagon was re-railed within two hours. Just over a month later on 9th September the engine for the 9.05 am Audley End to Saffron Walden train became derailed whilst shunting wagons at Audley End. After some connivance between the footplate crew, the shunter and the signalman, the locomotive was re-railed using old sleepers, thereby restricting the delay to 45 minutes.

As a result of the legislative Regulation of Railways Act 1889, the GER Signal & Telegraph Department erected new and improved signal posts on the branch in March 1890. At the same time preliminary work was carried out in connection with the introduction of block signalling between Saffron Walden and Bartlow Junction signal boxes as authorized by the GER Board on 3rd December, 1889.

The undulating countryside around Saffron Walden became a favourite area for the army to conduct troop exercises and manoeuvres. On one occasion, 11th April, 1890, the 3rd Cambridgeshire Volunteer Battalion (Suffolk Regiment) arrived by special train at the station before marching through the town to their temporary field headquarters. This training ground was subsequently used by thousands of troops until after World War I.

At a town council meeting in June 1890 Councillor Gilling introduced a motion that the GER should be approached regarding improvements in the passenger and freight services on the Saffron Walden branch. After consultation his fellow members agreed to form a sub-committee to monitor the service provided to the town.

As a result of the Regulation of Railways Act, interlocking of points and signals on both the Shelford to Marks Tey and Saffron Walden lines at Bartlow was completed by Saxby & Farmer Ltd in August 1891. Major General C.S.

Hutchinson conducted the Board of Trade inspection of the new works at Bartlow on 6th October, 1891. He found the alterations comprised the lengthening of the station loop line on the Shelford to Sudbury route and the provision of a new double line junction for the Saffron Walden branch at the Shelford end of the station, together with new and altered siding connections and a rearrangement of the signalling 'on the modern principle'. The signals and points were controlled from two new signal boxes, Bartlow Junction containing a 39-lever frame with 31 working and eight spare levers and Bartlow East [later 'Station'] signal box containing a 20-lever frame with 12 working and eight spare levers, the latter at the Haverhill end of the station and not affecting Saffron Walden branch services. Hutchinson found many discrepancies when checking the interlocking. In the Junction signal box, Nos. 3 and 34 levers required interlocking; levers Nos. 22 and 37 should not be preceded by No. 8 but only by No. 17; lever No. 37 was to be interlocked with lever No. 2; lever Nos. 14 and 34 should not have been interlocked; lever Nos. 13 and 34 required interlocking; lever No. 19 should have locked lever No. 18 in either position; lever Nos. 19 and 28 and 34 and 36 required interlocking; lever No. 32 should have released lever No. 35 and lever No. 38 should lock lever No. 18. In the East signal box, lever No. 18 should release No. 20 and levers Nos. 8 and 19 should not have been interlocked. The down distant signal also required electrically repeating. The Major General sanctioned the use of the new works subject to the correct coupling of the levers with the points and signals and early re-inspection. He also noted that Bartlow main line station had no footbridge or subway connecting the platforms and asked the GER to consider the provision of one or the other for the provision of public safety. Major General Hutchinson duly re-inspected the works at Bartlow on 19th November, 1891 and found all remedial work had been satisfactorily completed.

On 19th July, 1892 the contract for the interlocking of signals at Saffron Walden was awarded to McKenzie & Holland. The firm was unable to carry out the work and the contract was transferred to Saxby & Farmer who provided a new signal box containing a 32-lever frame.

On 1st January, 1893, second class passenger accommodation was abolished on all GER lines except in the London suburban area and on boat trains. The following month on 14th February, 1893, a lad named F.A. Parker committed suicide when he jumped in front of a train near Saffron Walden.

The following year the ironwork on Ashdon Road bridge, No. 2120 at 44 miles 44 chains from Liverpool Street between Saffron Walden and Bartlow, showed signs of fracture and necessitated urgent repairs. Authority was given for the remedial work on 3rd April, 1894 and the contract was awarded to J. Westwood of Napier Yard, Millwall at a cost of £176 10s. 0d. Work included the replacement of some corrugated cross troughing and plate parapets and was completed within four months.

The GER carried out improvements at Audley End main line station when an improved brick-built waiting room and other accommodation was built on the down platform. Authorized on 5th September, 1893 at a cost of £600, the works were completed by Collins & Barker in September 1894 at a cost of £360. Three years later the position of the waiting room and booking office in the up side platform buildings were reversed to provide improved accommodation for waiting passengers, the cost of conversion being £270. On 18th December, 1894 authority was given for the replacement of Train Staff & Ticket working between Shelford and Bartlow with the Electric Tablet system of single line working at a cost of £540.

Essex Foxhounds often held their meets in the Saffron Walden area around the turn of the century. The railway line was crossed on many occasions during the hunt and drivers of trains were warned to keep a sharp lookout for hounds and riders. Nevertheless on two occasions hounds narrowly missed being run down by trains near Ashdon in 1890 and again in 1895.

On 13th September, 1895 a fire broke out at T. & H. King's flour mill, which adjoined the railway at Saffron Walden. The outbreak was discovered at 3.00 am by local railwaymen, who feared the spreading flames would engulf coaching stock standing in the adjacent sidings. Fortunately the branch engine, standing in the shed with a head of steam, was quickly utilized to haul the coaches clear before the building collapsed across the line. In the event this did not happen but the building was gutted.

The companionship amongst railway staff on the Saffron Walden branch was made evident by social activities held around the turn of the century. In January 1896 the goods staff from Saffron Walden held their annual dinner at the Railway Hotel whilst the Railway Mission, which reopened in 1892, had over 80 people attending their dinner on 30th January, 1896. On 3rd March, 1896 a heavy thunderstorm and resultant hailstorm caused flooding of the line near Ashdon and trains were delayed over an hour until the water receded.

In preparation for the replacement of oil-lit carriages to gas-lit stock on the branch services, the General Manager in February 1896 reported that a gas storage holder was to be provided at Saffron Walden to enable coaching stock to be replenished with gas for lighting. The tank was to be refilled from a travelling gas tank wagon as and when required. The cost of £1,200, which included nine other stations was approved on 4th February. Further costs were approved on 28th July when authority was given for the provision of five additional gas tank wagons at a cost of £1,200 and £200 for the cost of the necessary piping and one filling point at each location. On 8th July, 1896 goods porter Charles Rider received fatal injuries as a result of an accident during shunting operations at Saffron Walden goods yard.

The 7.40 am Saffron Walden to Liverpool Street train was involved in a collision at Tottenham North Junction on 19th November, 1896 when it ran into a shunting locomotive standing on the main line. Both locomotives were severely damaged but fortunately the enginemen and several passengers received only slight injuries. At the subsequent inquiry the cause of the accident was established as signalman's error. On 1st December, 1896 further alterations were authorized at Audley End including the repositioning of a home signal at a cost of £30, alterations to a crossover and associated signalling at £240 and alterations to offices estimated at £30.

On 15th and 16th January, 1897 services were affected when drifting snow blocked the shallow cuttings near Ashdon and Bartlow. Traffic was delayed for some hours on both days. By the end of 1896 the timekeeping and quality of through train services between Saffron Walden and Liverpool Street had deteriorated. The local council wrote on a number of occasions to Liverpool Street but no action was taken to obviate the shortcomings. Incensed by the GER's lethargic attitude, a deputation of dignitaries from Saffron Walden formed by the mayor J. Gilling, deputy mayor E. Taylor, the town clerk, and two others met the GER Directors on Wednesday 1st January, 1897. As well as airing their views on the through services, opportunity was taken to discuss the local branch timetable. After much deliberation the GER authorities responded to the Saffron Walden council's request by introducing, in the July 1897 timetable, a new train with a 5.25 pm departure from Liverpool Street running direct to Saffron Walden arriving at 6.40 pm. This obviated passengers changing trains at Bishop's Stortford and Audley End and saved 17 minutes in the overall journey time. A slight adjustment was also made to the 8.35 am up departure from Saffron Walden, which was altered to 8.38 am.

On 5th April, 1898 authority was given to replace the Train Staff & Ticket working of the single line between Bartlow and Haverhill with Electric Tablet working at a cost of £368.

Before the advent of steam heating on passenger trains, travellers not wishing to endure the rigours of sitting in a cold compartment for a winter journey, with ice forming on the inside of the windows, could take advantage of foot warmers. For many years Saffron Walden station was a storage and refilling point for foot warmers and in June 1898 a small foot warmer house was erected at a cost of £80 to improve the servicing of the metal canisters.

In the following month authority was given to provide an up advanced starting signal at Saffron Walden to facilitate the movement of trains in the station area. When the Board of Trade inspector inspected the line he stipulated that if trains were to pass at Saffron Walden a second platform was to be provided. The dictates of the inspector had been allowed to lapse but very often a second train required usage of the platform on the main single line as soon as the first up train had departed. With only an up starting signal this movement was not possible. The provision of the advanced starter was also deemed necessary by the length of goods trains, which with a single starting signal had to be backed out on to the main line thus occupying the platform until the section to Audley End was clear. With the advanced starter it was possible to start the train direct from the goods yard. The signal was duly installed and interlocked in November 1898.

Goods traffic handled at Saffron Walden goods yard was increasing steadily each year, from 12,100 tons in 1889 to 19,700 tons in 1897. Originally staff had been kept to a minimum but by September 1898 tonnage had reached such a level that it was considered necessary to employ two additional clerks in the goods office. Unfortunately the existing structure was rather small and, with the additional staff, the office accommodation became rather cramped. To ease the situation the office was enlarged during the following spring at a cost of £60.

In September 1898 William Adams, the town clerk of Saffron Walden, forwarded a petition to the GER Board requesting consideration for the extension of the Saffron Walden branch from Bartlow to Six Mile Bottom on the Cambridge to Newmarket line. The document endorsed by Saffron Walden town council, Haverhill Urban District Council and the parish councils of Bartlow, Balsham, West Wickham and West Wratting was raised at a meeting of the Traffic Committee on 20th September and declined, as it was considered insufficient traffic would be forthcoming.

During a tour of inspection of the system on 27th, 28th and 29th October, 1898, the GER Directors visited the Saffron Walden branch. At Audley End approval was given for the provision of a footbridge to connect the up and down main line platforms and for an additional siding on the branch to accommodate 36 wagons. At Saffron Walden it was agreed to earmark a portion of land on the down side of the line at the Bartlow end of the station, east of South Road overbridge, for the Engineer to prepare plans for a possible goods yard. The existing booking office was also to be enlarged as a temporary measure, for it was also thought the existing passenger facilities could be transferred to a new station to be built on the newly acquired property, thus releasing the land occupied by the existing station for extension of the goods yard. At Bartlow the station was inspected. The Directors then continued to Linton, Pampisford and on to the Lynn to Hunstanton branch.

On 4th July, 1899 a slip connection from the up loop line to a dead end and a new starting signal was authorized at Audley End at a cost of £250, the BoT inspection being made on 25th November, 1899. At the same meeting the Directors sanctioned the erection of a footbridge to connect the up and down main line platforms at a cost of £450. The contract was subsequently awarded to A. Handyside on 6th June, 1900 after tendering at £445 9s. 4d.

A severe blizzard on 14th February, 1900 blocked the line between Saffron Walden and Ashdon for over 24 hours before permanent way staff managed to clear the drift. Roads were also impassable and once cleared the branch railway provided the only communication with the surrounding area for some days.

The GER received a number of letters in February and March 1901 complaining of the poor state of the roads over the railway bridges at Saffron Walden. The frost and snow of the winter had destroyed the surface, leaving the highway fragmented. The maintenance of the bridges and road surfaces was at that time a matter of consultation between the railway company and the town council and a letter regarding the future repair of roads over the bridges was sent to Saffron Walden council in April.

About the turn of the century Saffron Walden became a popular destination for railway staff outings. On one such occasion on 7th July, 1901, 50 members of the blacksmith's department at Stratford Works visited the town for their annual outing. Arriving at 10.00 am they made the King's Arms in Market Hill their headquarters before visiting places of interest in the town. Needless to say a rather merry party left the station at 7.00 pm on their return journey.

At 6.30pm on the evening of Saturday 8th February, 1902 during shunting operations at Saffron Walden, two wagons detained on the main line ran out of control and collided with a passenger train. Three wagons of a goods train had been left standing on the main line as the train was being divided, when two of the wagons started to roll slowly away down the gradient in the darkness. The shunter, realising the situation, ran and applied the hand brake to the rear wagon but was unable to secure the brake on the leading wagon as both gained

Audley End main line station facing north *circa* 1902 and showing the up platform to the right and covered footbridge connecting to the staggered down side platform. Oblivious to the dangers of any approaching traffic, station and goods yard staff pose for the cameraman on platform and track.   *Author's Collection*

The junction at Audley End facing south in 1910. The Saffron Walden branch is in the foreground and the main line to Cambridge on the right. the station platforms are behind the photographer.   *GERS/Windwood Collection*

speed. A telegraph message was sent to Audley End to stop the down passenger train leaving that station but unfortunately it had already departed, and when entering the deep cutting near Beechy Ride the tender of the locomotive collided with the runaway wagons. Both wagons were derailed and extensively damaged whilst the tender of the locomotive was badly dented, although it remained on the rails. With the impact, the coaches of the passenger train became uncoupled from the locomotive but the automatic application of the Westinghouse brake prevented the vehicles running away. As a result of the crash driver Beaumont suffered shock, a cut head and damaged abdomen, whilst fireman Braybrooke received only slight injuries. Fortunately no passengers were hurt but guard Mumford received cuts and bruises. The passengers were detrained and walked to Saffron Walden where station master Brown organized a train to convey passengers to Bartlow. An emergency train service was introduced between Saffron Walden and Audley End via Bartlow and Shelford until the line was cleared. The breakdown train arrived from Cambridge at 9.00 pm and the line was available for traffic by 3.00 am on Sunday morning.

The provision of the additional office for the station master at Saffron Walden in 1888 had eased the problem of congestion for a short while but by 1900, with passenger and parcels traffic on the increase, the booking office and booking hall became totally inadequate to handle traffic. After a visit by the local engineer, the Way and Works Committee on 2nd October, 1900 authorized the building of a new waiting room and the conversion of the old room into a larger booking office. After competitive tender, the contract was awarded to J. Glasscock of Bishop's Stortford for £160 in March 1902. On 4th February, 1902 authority had been given for the extension of the refuge sidings on the main line at Audley End at an estimated cost of £625. The new footbridge connecting the up and down main line platforms at Audley End was completed by the end of May 1902 but at an increased cost of £686 against an estimate of £450. The new refuge sidings were completed in December 1902 but at the reduced cost of £402 against an estimate of £625.

In May 1902 the locomotive superintendent was asking for routes to be upgraded and bridges to be strengthened to take engines with heavier axle loading. After discussion, the GER Board recommended on 4th June that certain lines including Audley End to Bartlow could be removed from the scheme to save costs as it was unlikely any locomotives with the heavier weight would be used on the branch.

On 22nd May, 1903 acting fireman George Daniel Bush aged 22 years, received injuries from an accident at Saffron Walden, which necessitated him being sick from work for a month. On the day in question Bush was working with driver G. Whiffen on tank locomotive No. 93 which had worked a train from Bartlow to Saffron Walden. The next part of the diagram involved a light engine movement to Stansted. As the locomotive, working boiler first, departed from Saffron Walden, Bush left the footplate with a tail lamp and walked round the bunker to place it in position. Whilst so engaged and in a stooping position, his head came into contact with a wagon standing in Dix's siding, near the main line on which the engine was travelling. The acting fireman was thrown to the ground sustaining injuries to his left shoulder, left side and left ear. At the subsequent inquiry it was revealed that horse shunter William Munden had left the wagon too near the main line; he admitted in evidence that he had disregarded Rule 184(c) [wagons to be left clear of the fouling points of adjacent lines]. At the same time signalman A.W. Sutton, who knew the wagon was very close to the main line, was remiss in not informing Whiffen and Bush of the position of the vehicle before permitting the engine to leave the loop line, as it had stood close to the signal box whilst Bush was engaged on engine duties. Driver Whiffen was absolved from blame as he was looking ahead for signals when Bush left the footplate. The acting fireman was also blameless because there were no instructions definitely forbidding him to leave the footplate of the engine when in motion. He had also only 12 to 13 minutes allowed at Saffron Walden between the arrival of the train from Bartlow and the departure to Stansted to perform many duties. It was therefore of no surprise that he failed to notice the position of the offending wagon. From evidence the inspecting officer found that Rule 184(c) had previously been disregarded at Saffron Walden and he required the GER to take steps to strictly enforce the rule in future. It was also considered desirable to issue instructions forbidding enginemen from leaving the footplate when the locomotive was in motion.

On 16th June, 1903 the contract for repairs and painting of Saffron Walden station was awarded to Messrs Proctor after the firm quoted a price of £135. Then in April 1904 new up main and up main to branch signals worked from Bartlow Junction signal box were erected 30 yards nearer to Shelford than the signals they replaced. The up main post also carried the Bartlow Station signal box distant signal arm.

The goods office at Saffron Walden was again extended when it was realized additional clerical staff would have to be employed to handle the increased paperwork. Authority for such an extension was given on 6th December, 1904 at an estimated cost of £140 but prices escalated and when the structure was completed by November 1905 it had cost £205. In March 1905 gas prices were reduced at Saffron Walden by 5d. per thousand cubic feet.

In January 1906 the railway suffered a set back when the London mails were dispatched by motor vehicle from Saffron Walden via Bishop's Stortford to Epping. The initial service was not a complete success as on two or three occasions the vehicle caught fire or broke down on the road, necessitating the conveyance of the mails by rail.

A violent electrical storm raging in the area on 8th February, 1906 caused the block bells to ring in the signal boxes and for a while rendered the instruments inoperative. Trains were signalled by telephone until linemen had repaired the block instruments. During a particularly heavy thunderstorm on 27th July, 1906, lightning struck a telegraph pole and wires near Saffron Walden. So severe was the flash that it put the block instruments out of action for the rest of the day. In the same storm, engine cleaner Eider, working on an engine by the adjacent engine shed, was thrown off the footplate to the ground and rendered unconscious, while another youth passing over South Road bridge and under the wires was severely dazed.

Audley End branch and main line stations were repainted during the late summer of 1906, the contract being awarded to A. Coe who tendered at £169. At 5.40 pm on Saturday 13th April, 1907 whilst shunting coaching stock into Audley End branch platform, the branch engine became derailed at the run-round points. The branch line remained blocked for two hours before an engine of a main line goods train pulled the locomotive back on the track with the aid of sleepers packed under the derailed wheels. Within 12 days a derailment occurred at the same spot when the locomotive working the 6.50 pm goods train from Audley End ran off the line with three wagons. Branch services were diverted via Shelford and the Cambridge breakdown gang subsequently cleared the line by 10.00 pm. An immediate investigation into the derailments at the same spot found the tongues of the points of the run-round loop were worn and these were quickly replaced.

Wednesday 14th August, 1907 proved an eventful day when the Excelsior Band had their annual outing to Clacton by train. Over 320 passengers joined the special train at Saffron Walden and this proved too much for the locomotive, which succeeded in losing time to Bartlow. Here the Saffron Walden portion was to be coupled up with another special from Cambridge for the remainder of the journey but because of the length and weight of the train, it was decided to run it forward in two portions from Bartlow to Clacton, a decision which added further delay. For the intrepid band and its followers their troubles were not over, for on the return journey the locomotive failed on Ashdon bank between Bartlow and Saffron Walden. After a delay of over an hour the train was divided and taken forward in two portions, the last of which arrived with its disgruntled passengers at Saffron Walden a few minutes before midnight.

As a result of correspondence started in 1901 Saffron Walden council commenced the widening of Borough Lane, Saffron Walden early in 1908 and on 17th March requested the railway company to widen the bridge from 15 to 25 ft to comply with the works. As the GER was under statutory obligation to widen the bridge, estimates were drawn up and tenders sent to contractors, the cheapest of which was £500. On reflection the GER Civil Engineering Department advised the rejection of such tenders and subsequently undertook the task. Work was completed on 16th December, 1909 at a cost of £355. In the meantime the dilapidated building on the Saffron Walden branch platform at Bartlow received its first repairs since the opening of the line and was repainted during October and November 1909 at a cost of £120 5s. 0d.

The Railway Brigade of St John Ambulance was formed by railway staff at Saffron Walden in 1911 and lasted until the outbreak of World War II.

For some years the residents of Ashdon, led by Col Proby and other influential gentlemen of the neighbourhood had been petitioning for the provision of a halt to serve the village. The matter was finally raised at a meeting of the Traffic Committee on 2nd March, 1911 when the General Manager reported that the village of some 800 residents was located two miles from Bartlow and $4^1/_2$ miles from Saffron Walden. The inhabitants of the village had to walk the two miles to Bartlow to travel by rail to Saffron Walden and the Engineer considered a halt could be provided at Fallowden Lane for an estimated £146. The committee agreed to the provision of the new halt provided costs were kept to a minimum. The traffic superintendent reported that no staff would be employed and fares would be based on the halt mileage, as if charges were the same as Bartlow or Saffron Walden very little traffic would be secured. The halt, completed at a cost of £73, was opened on Monday 14th August, 1911 and from that date all branch passenger services were booked to stop. The platform was formed of raised earth and clinker with sleeper frontage to the track and sleeper edging. As the halt was unstaffed the

Bartlow Stour Valley line station viewed from Bartlow Junction signal box facing east towards Haverhill in 1910. A 'Y14' class 0-6-0 tender locomotive is standing in the dock road which served cattle pens. Note the Bartlow tumuli on the skyline surmounted by trees and the timber buffer stops on the spur at the end of the up reception siding.   *GERS/Windwood Collection*

Looking east from Bartlow Stour Valley line station with the small goods yard at the east end of the platform in 1910. The Bartlow to Ashdon road is spanned by bridge No. 2147 in the foreground whilst the noted Bartlow Hills tumuli are on the horizon. Bartlow Station signal box can be seen in the background partially obscured behind the brick-built lamp room.

GERS/Windwood Collection

following instructions were issued to staff regarding the issue and collection of tickets in the GER *Appendix to the Working Timetables*:

HALT FOR PASSENGERS
BETWEEN SAFFRON WALDEN AND BARTLOW STATIONS

A halt called 'Ashdon Halt' is provided on the Saffron Walden branch, about 3½ miles on the Bartlow side of Saffron Walden station. No signals are provided.

All trains - both Up and Down - are to call at Ashdon Halt to set down or take up passengers.

Tickets are issued from Audley End, Saffron Walden and Bartlow to Ashdon Halt.

The guard of the train is to collect the tickets from all passengers alighting at the Halt and hand such tickets to the Station Master or other person in charge upon arrival at Saffron Walden or Bartlow, as the case may be.

Tickets will not be issued at the Halt but in the case of passengers joining a train there, the guard of the train must take a record and inform the Station Master or other person in charge at the station - Saffron Walden, Audley End or Bartlow as the case may be - at which the passengers alight, with a view to the fares being collected from those passengers who are not in possession of return halves of tickets.

In the event of passengers arriving at Bartlow or Audley End for a more distant destination, such as Bishop's Stortford, Chelmsford or London, without a ticket, the fare from the Halt or the return half of the Halt ticket is to be collected and the passengers requested to re-book to their destinations.

Saffron Walden station and signal box received a welcome coat of paint in April 1912 when Clarke & Sons were awarded the contract at £132 10s. 0d. In the same year on 3rd October the land agent recommended the purchase of an additional six acres of land at Saffron Walden to improve railway facilities. The General Manager reported that some years previously a scheme had been prepared to improve passenger and goods facilities at the station but the estimated costs of £22,908 had been considered excessive. Goods traffic was increasing rapidly from 38,984 tons handled in 1907 to 54,911 tons in 1911. The accommodation in the existing goods yard was restricted, as public roads surrounded it on three sides and it was not possible to extend the present site. The goods manager would not propose plans for an immediate increase in accommodation but because of future developments it was imperative the company purchase the land. The land agent reported he had not approached the owners of the required property but estimated the cost at £1,000. The proposal was endorsed by the Traffic Committee, who at the same meeting authorized an 85 ft extension and raising of the down main line platform to a height of 3 ft at Audley End, at a cost of £144. The existing platform was too short to accommodate certain main line trains, which were delayed drawing up twice to enable passengers to alight.

Important army exercises were held near Cambridge in 1912. To ease congestion on the main line, at least two trains from Aldershot traversed the branch. Because of the severe gradient north-east of Saffron Walden the trains were double-headed between Audley End and Bartlow.

On 27th May, 1913 a severe hailstorm hit Bartlow, Ashdon and nearby Hadstock causing severe damage to crops and property. The branch railway was affected by the torrential downpour as nearly all the glass in the station platform lamps at Bartlow station and Ashdon Halt was shattered.

Looking south from Bartlow Junction signal box towards the Saffron Walden branch platform in 1910. The main single line serves the platform and the run-round loop runs parallel with the headshunt to the right. The down starting signal stands sentinel at the end of the platform protecting the junction, whilst Hills Farm is in the distance. Permanent way staff are making minor alterations. The building on the platform was later replaced by a less ornate structure.

GERS/Windwood Collection

The Saffron Walden branch platform at Bartlow looking south towards Audley End in 1910. The open shelter is flanked by waiting rooms for the comfort of intending passengers at this exposed location and oil lamps are provided on the platform for night-time illumination. The down home and up starting signal, sharing the same post are in the background.

GERS/Windwood Collection

At about 2.45 pm on 16th January, 1914, 38-year-old foreman Samuel Brown sustained fatal injuries during shunting operations at Saffron Walden. At the subsequent inquiry the inspecting officer Amos Ford established Brown was walking alongside a wagon, which was being taken along the slip road by a shunt horse, when he ran forward apparently to check the numbers of two of the four wagons in front. As the single wagon was closing up to the other four vehicles Brown, for unknown reasons, attempted to pass between the buffers of the second and third wagons, standing some 18 inches apart. As he passed between the wagons they closed up and he was crushed and died from his injuries the same day. Ford attributed the cause of the mishap to 'want of care by Brown'.

At the end of May 1914 the first inroads into the monopoly enjoyed by the branch came when proposals were mooted for a motorbus service from Saffron Walden to Cambridge via Great Chesterford and Sawston.

Lieutenant P.G. Von Donop belatedly carried out the Board of Trade inspection of Ashdon Halt on 23rd July, 1914. He found the 150 ft-long platform was located on the up side of the single line and was 7 ft wide and 3 ft in height. It was provided with a nameboard, oil lamp and a means of approach from the adjacent level crossing. The inspector found the arrangements satisfactory and recommended the use of the halt 'by trains of a suitable length'.

The outbreak of World War I on 4th August, 1914 found the GER with other British railway companies under Government control. Train services continued to run to pre-war timetables as passengers travelled to business or on pleasure. Goods traffic quietly flourished as increased produce was dispatched from farmlands to towns and cities to make up for the loss of imported food. Local railwaymen soon answered the call to arms, four staff from Saffron Walden, two from Audley End and one from Bartlow joined the colours within a month.

From 4th October 1914 a 'Radical Alterations' timetable resulted in the Audley End 'slip coach' being withdrawn and the Saffron Walden coach or coaches being 'slipped' at Newport. The branch locomotive then ran light to Newport to work the stock forward to Audley End and Saffron Walden. By October 1916 Saffron Walden coaches were being detached at Newport, but one service had been reinstated to Audley End. At the end of 1916 all 'slip coaches' were withdrawn.

During World War I the training of troops in the countryside around Saffron Walden was accelerated and many troop trains were dealt with, as well as horse traffic and goods and other provisions required for the men. In some cases soldiers were sent to the front direct from the training ground and in this instance through trains were run to the Channel ports. In 1914 soon after the beginning of hostilities the GER set up a War Relief Fund with collections being made at the company's stations. The first call resulted in a total of 4s. 4d. being collected at Saffron Walden, whilst the fourth call in January 1915 showed an increase to 15s. 3d., with Bartlow collecting 4s. 3d. and Audley End 6s. 10d. For the three month period ending 31st December, 1917 travellers at Saffron Walden contributed 16s. 0d. with £1 0s. 3d. in the following quarter. Despite the hostilities, Audley End station came in for repainting in May and June 1915 when Clarke & Sons were awarded the contract after tendering at £133.

From 1916 an old GER carriage body was provided as passenger waiting accommodation at Ashdon Halt. The vehicle had the internal fittings removed

Saffron Walden station viewed from South Road overbridge on 9th December, 1910 with Massey Bromley 0-4-4T No. 097 approaching on the main single line with the branch goods train from Audley End. Next to the main single line is the run-round loop and beside that sidings serving the unloading bank. The 202 ft-long platform was host to the ornate station buildings fronted by a canopy and beyond can just be seen the Station signal box. The down starting signal stands guardian at the Bartlow end of the platform.   *GERS/Windwood Collection*

A view from Debden Road overbridge looking towards Saffron Walden station in 1910 with the goods yard to the left, and goods shed to the centre. The main single line threads the layout whilst Dix's siding to the right is occupied with mainly empty merchandise wagons. Alongside Dix's siding is Saffron Walden up starting signal. Beyond the various yard offices to the left can be seen the Railway Arms public house, built in similar style to Saffron Walden station building. South Road overbridge spans the line beyond the station.   *GERS/Windwood Collection*

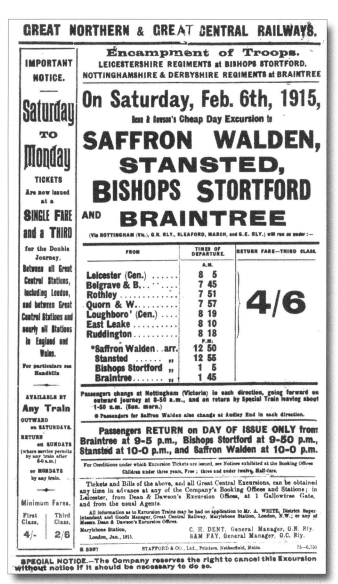

A notice of an excursion to Saffron Walden on 6th February, 1915 in connection with troop encampments at Bishop's Stortford and Braintree.

and wooden benches placed around the sides. In the same year on 6th July, Clarke & Sons were awarded the contract for repairing and painting Bartlow station after tendering at £89 17s. 0d.

The GER serving a mainly rural community was always keen to promote ideas which could add to revenue. An exhibition train on egg and poultry production was one of their publicity outlets in World War I. It made many visits to locations in 1916 when the train was stabled at Saffron Walden for a few days to enable the local farmers and landowners to view the latest techniques in farming as well as promoting traffic.

Saffron Walden goods yard from the up side loading dock in 1910, with Saffron Walden Station signal box to the right. The brick-built goods shed, with storage capacity for 250 quarters of grain and the attendant goods office are prominent, whilst a GER cattle wagon and GER covered van stand in the cattle dock road. Dix's road is to the left, with the run-round loop and then main line next the signal box. A GER covered lime wagon stands at the head of a rake of wagons by the goods shed. *GERS/Windwood Collection*

The approach path from the branch platform at Bartlow looking towards the main station building on the Haverhill line. This attractive scene taken in the 1920s with shrubs bordering the path was a far cry from the unkempt access of the latter years. Note the well-tended vegetable plots on each side. *Author's Collection*

The strain of the war was taxing the resources of the railways and in December 1916, the Railway Executive Committee issued an ultimatum to the effect that they would only carry on if drastic reductions were made to ordinary services. Locomotive power was short, through lack of coal supplies. The Lloyd George Coalition thus agreed to the reduction of passenger train services from 1st January, 1917. Despite this edict the Saffron Walden branch services remained virtually unchanged because of the flow of militia to the local training ground.

After the cessation of hostilities on Armistice Day flags were displayed at Saffron Walden and Bartlow stations. The festivities were short-lived for from 26th September to 5th October, 1919 a general railway strike brought the suspension of services on the Saffron Walden branch. Two years later the miners' strike affected coal supplies; although services were not curtailed, some short-term cancellations were unavoidable.

After the war the GER decided to revive 'slip' coach services although on a much reduced scale. On 20th March, 1920 a slip coach was detached at Audley End for Saffron Walden off the 8.35 am Liverpool Street to Yarmouth service. However, the prolonged miners strike in 1921 resulted in the permanent withdrawal of the Audley End slip coach from 15th April.

At 12.45 am on 19th January, 1922, engine cleaner D.J. Newman was engaged coaling a locomotive standing on one of the shed roads at Saffron Walden engine shed when a large lump of coal fell from the top of an adjacent wagon crashing on to his hand and severely crushing a finger. The subsequent inquiry was conducted by J.P.S. Main who established that there were no fixed lights in the yard or at the shed, where two locomotives were stabled. The work of cleaning and coaling was principally performed during the night and on the night in question Newman was using two oil lamps as well as having the advantage of full moonlight. Main was of the opinion the accident could not have been attributed to the want of fixed lights. He noted that an application had been made some seven months before the accident for both the shed and yard to be provided with lighting. It was now desirable for the GER to provide the lighting at an early date.

The industrial dispute of 1919 began the decline in railway freight. Farmers and growers realized for the first time that with improving roads, goods could be sent by motor lorry using in some cases vehicles purchased second-hand from the army, thus motivating short haul journeys cheaper than the rates charged by the GER. The door-to-door service was more convenient than the double handling caused by loading and unloading into and out of railway wagons. The primitive commercial road vehicles of the day, however, were not capable of continuous long hauls and the middle and long distance freight traffic remained safely in the hands of the railway company. Fortunately the same problem was not as acute with passenger traffic, few local people owned cars and were in the main reliant on the branch for all journeys. The GER did not have the complete monopoly, however, for infrequent bus services had commenced between Saffron Walden and Cambridge and Saffron Walden and Haverhill. Thus was the position of the branch when, as a result of the 1921 Railways Act, the GER was grouped with the Great Northern, Great Central, North Eastern, North British and other minor railways to form the London & North Eastern Railway (LNER) from 1st January, 1923.

'G4' class 0-4-4T No. 8114 waiting to depart from the branch platform at Bartlow with a train for Saffron Walden and Audley End in 1929. The train is formed of a six-wheel brake third and a bogie clerestory composite. No. 8114 was the first of the quartet of 'G4s' used on the branch to be withdrawn, going for scrap in September 1931.   *Dr I.C. Allen*

'G4' class 0-4-4T No. 8122 departing Audley End for Saffron Walden with a two-coach branch train on 17th May, 1930. The bogie coach dating from 1901 survived in traffic until 1955 whilst the six-wheeler, dating from 1899, was withdrawn from service in 1935. The building in the background is the Neville Arms Hotel.   *E.R. Wethersett*

Chapter Four

Grouping

From 1st January, 1923 the Saffron Walden line changed ownership for the third time to that of the London & North Eastern Railway. The new ownership brought few changes to the branch working but a seven-day railway strike from 20th January, 1924, brought a further decline in the use of the branch. Would-be passengers turned to road transport and some of those travelling short distances were never to return to the railway.

The increasing competition for passenger and local goods traffic brought an increased in-depth investigation into possible economies in working. In the autumn of 1924 the Deputy General Manager (Southern Area) announced that savings could be achieved by concentrating the working of all signals and points at Bartlow station on Bartlow Junction signal box, thus allowing the abolition of Bartlow Station signal box and the saving of two signalmen's posts. Future renewal and maintenance costs would also be obviated. Major G.L. Hall subsequently conducted the Board of Trade inspection at Bartlow on 28th July, 1925. He found that Bartlow Station signal box had been abolished and alterations had been made to the control of the east end single line loop points and to the siding points at that end of the station. The loop points were now controlled from Bartlow Junction signal box via a battery point machine and the detection was mechanical and not electrical. The siding points were situated quite close to the loop points and were worked by a single-lever ground frame controlled by Annett's key in conjunction with lever No. 8 in the Junction signal box. Hall noted that track circuits were provided for a distance of 100 yards on the approach side of the down home signal and through the facing points for a short distance both sides of the loop. The track circuit when occupied locked lever No. 7, which controlled the electric point machine in both positions. The railway officers attending the inspection advised the Major that instructions had been issued to the Junction signalmen that a train was not to be accepted from Haverhill when the release lever for the ground frame was pulled over. Hall observed that Bartlow Junction signal box contained a 39-lever frame, with 37 working and two spare levers and was satisfied with the new works.

For many years Saffron Walden branch passengers had only the comfort of footwarmers in winter months. These were gradually withdrawn and the need for warmth for travellers was uppermost in the minds of the management. Most of the bogie coaching stock was fitted with steam heating pipes but many of the six-wheel and four-wheel vehicles used on East Anglian branch lines were sadly lacking this asset. In October 1925 the LNER took remedial action and arranged for 184 vehicles to be equipped with steam heating pipes. The Saffron Walden branch gained from this innovation, and in January 1926 the five vehicles normally allocated for branch services were fitted with this equipment.

The branch was again affected by an industrial dispute during the General Strike of May 1926 when union members withdrew their labour in support of the miners. Train services could not be guaranteed and the Saffron Walden branch service was suspended for several days. Fortunately within a week or so regular railwaymen returned to work but the impact of the continuing miners strike meant coal stocks were low. The LNER authorities decided on the only course of action available and reduced train services for a short period to conserve coal supplies. From 31st May, when the revised timetables were introduced, two trains in each direction were withdrawn.

In 1926 Bartlow station was awarded a first class certificate in the Best Kept Station awards. This success for station master Beales and his staff followed a third class prize in 1923 and second class prizes in 1924 and 1925, the latter earning a £5 monetary award.

Snow again blocked the line in December 1927, falling on Christmas Day. Because all services had finished for the day, the swirling snow quickly filled some of the cuttings. Several abortive attempts were made to open the line by running a light engine to Audley End and Bartlow the same evening but each time its progress was baulked by a drift. After permanent way men worked through the night the line was eventually cleared by mid-morning on Boxing Day.

As part of the ongoing programme of repairs and painting of stations, N.S. Long received the contract for work at Saffron Walden station on 26th April, 1928. The work was completed by September at the much reduced cost of £152 9s. 0d. against an estimated £229.

Despite various reductions in operating costs, the loss of traffic caused by the strikes and the attractions of an almost door-to-door service by the competitive bus services, the decline suffered by the Saffron Walden branch was minimal compared with many other East Anglian branches as the receipts for the period 1923 to 1928 show:

	No. of passengers	Passenger receipts £	Parcels receipts £	Season ticket receipts £	Total receipts £
1923					
Audley End	30,507	2,334	436	227	2,997
Saffron Walden	66,611	6,577	1,514	2,420	10,511
Ashdon Halt*	187	10			10
Bartlow	13,193	1,166	431	25	1,622
Total for branch	*66,798*	*6,587*	*1,514*	*2,420*	*10,521*
1924					
Audley End	30,181	2,487	350	339	3,176
Saffron Walden	64,509	6,449	1,471	2,276	10,196
Bartlow	12,542	1,061	281	32	1,374
Total for branch	*64,509*	*6,449*	*1,471*	*2,276*	*10,196*
1925					
Audley End	32,645	2,783	406	426	3,615
Saffron Walden	66,177	6,627	1,599	1,594	9,820
Bartlow	12,758	989	322	71	1,382
Total for branch	*66,177*	*6,627*	*1,599*	*1,594*	*9,820*

---

*   Receipts for 1924 to 1928 from Ashdon Halt included in Saffron Walden total.

	No. of passengers	Passenger receipts £	Parcels receipts £	Season ticket receipts £	Total receipts £
1926					
Audley End	29,424	2,412	453	431	3,296
Saffron Walden	60,681	6,145	1,578	1,446	9,169
Bartlow	10,440	859	384	94	1,337
Total for branch	*60,681*	*6,145*	*1,578*	*1,446*	*9,169*
1927					
Audley End	29,869	2,340	391	422	3,153
Saffron Walden	63,695	6,307	1,532	1,341	9,180
Bartlow	11,383	837	208	96	1,141
Total for branch	*63,695*	*6,307*	*1,532*	*1,341*	*9,180*
1928					
Audley End	30,845	2,229	375	430	3,034
Saffron Walden	61,397	5,837	1,561	1,115	8,513
Bartlow	11,657	837	313	76	1,226
Total for branch	*61,397*	*5,837*	*1,561*	*1,115*	*8,513*

Very few travelled from Audley End or Bartlow to Saffron Walden.

The average number of passengers travelling daily from Saffron Walden in 1923 was 184 but this had reduced to 169 by 1928, whilst daily passenger receipts reduced accordingly from £18 1s. 10d. to £16 1s. 4d. In comparison Bartlow with 42 passengers daily in 1923 had reduced to 37 in 1928 and daily takings at the booking office window had fallen by £1. Audley End with 84 passengers booking daily in 1923 showed an increase to 85 in 1928 but receipts had reduced from £6 8s. 2d. to £6 2s. 5d.

Passenger traffic receipts picked up in the mid-1930s when holidays and rambles in the country became popular. Branch trains at weekends and bank holidays carried large numbers of passengers eager to take advantage of their free time in the countryside. The LNER issued a useful little booklet at this time featuring 'Rambles in Essex'. Local bus services, however, also increased in frequency and motor coaches were handling most day and weekly trips to the sea.

In September 1931 the LNER management was seeking to effect operating economies on the branch especially on lightly-used services by replacing the normal locomotive and two- or three-coach formation with a Sentinel steam railcar. Accordingly No. 2203 *Old Blue*, which had previously worked from Guisborough in the North Eastern section and St Margarets, Edinburgh, was transferred initially to Norwich for trials on branches between 14th and 19th September. The car then went to Ipswich for two days before taking up trial duties at Cambridge from 21st to 25th of the month, where she was sent to work the Mildenhall branch before running test trips between Audley End, Saffron Walden and Bartlow. Its usefulness was questioned as mixed trains ran on both the Mildenhall and Saffron Walden branches and *Old Blue* was duly sent back to Guisborough and no further attempt was made to introduce steam railcars.

Late in 1931, with the increase in traffic between Whitemoor to Temple MIlls, additional loop lines were provided on the up and down sides of the main line

Saffron Walden engine shed on 27th June, 1936. 'G4' class 0-4-4T No. 8139 is standing in the shed, whilst 'F4' class 2-4-2T No. 7174 stands on the main single line.   *H.C. Casserley*

'G4' class 0-4-4T No. 8139 pulls out of the goods yard and on to the main line at Saffron Walden during shunting operations on 2nd June, 1936. The signal box is to the right.   *V. Webster*

Branch motive power at Saffron Walden on 2nd August, 1936. *From left to right*: 'G4' class 0-4-4T No. 8139, 'F4' class 2-4-2T No. 7174 and 'G4' class 0-4-4T No. 8105. The Saffron Walden up home signal is in the background. *V. Webster*

'G4' class 0-4-4T No. 8105 standing by the water column at Saffron Walden engine shed on 27th June, 1936. The 'G4' class were allocated to Saffron Walden shed and operated the branch services in the 1930s. *H.C. Casserley*

Saffron Walden shed in the late 1930s with two 'C12' class 4-4-2Ts, led by No. 4534 standing by the water column. An 'E4' class 2-4-0 is standing in the single-road engine shed.

Author's Collection

The branch train in wartime. 'C12' class 4-4-2T No. 4520 approaching Bartlow with the 3.20 pm ex-Saffron Walden on 9th September, 1943.   *E.R. Wethersett*

north of Audley End station - the up later becoming a track-circuited passenger loop, the signal box frame being enlarged to 60 levers to control the new facilities.

The LNER management in their quest for reduction in permanent way maintenance costs in the 1930s gradually introduced motor trolleys and trailers on sections of line to assist staff in their duties. On 28th September, 1933 the Way & Works Committee agreed to the provision of one motor trolley and trailer at a cost of £617, to cover the section of line from Shelford to Bartlow and across the branch to Audley End. Together with a similar scheme for the Bishop's Stortford to Felsted section of the Dunmow branch, the 54 men maintaining the 44½ route miles involved could be reduced to 41 men, with the estimated saving on the Shelford to Bartlow and Saffron Walden branch of £255 per annum.

On 27th July, 1939 authority was given for alterations to the station buildings at Audley End at an estimated cost of £488. With the imminent outbreak of World War II the LNER and other major railway companies came under the control of the Railway Executive Committee from 1st September, 1939. Within weeks the Saffron Walden branch was carrying evacuees from the London area and the south coast and the last of the children did not arrive in the area until 1940.

Most of the cheap day facilities were withdrawn and excursion traffic curtailed during hostilities. Local bus services were reduced or removed from the road by petrol rationing and the branch again came into its own as most trains ran with a full complement of passengers. In May 1941 first class facilities were withdrawn from the branch, a feature which remained in force for a decade.

To safeguard against air raids, especially at night, station lamps remained dimmed and staff utilized shielded hand lamps to attend to train and shunting duties. As a precaution against evening attacks station nameboards were also removed and stored in lamp rooms and other out of the way places. The agricultural nature of the freight handled by the branch was of the utmost importance as the vital provisions of home grown food, grain, vegetables and fruit traffics were dispatched to the markets. In addition to the outward flow of produce, the war years brought an influx of tinned food by rail to Saffron Walden for distribution to Ministry of Food storage depots in the area.

Despite the close proximity of airfields at Debden, Duxford, Castle Camps, Hadstock and Wethersfield, a branch train running between Ashdon and Saffron Walden narrowly escaped being 'shot up' by a Luftwaffe fighter-bomber early one morning in May 1941. The crew of the aircraft flying south after a raid further inland spotted the steam from the locomotive and altered course to attack. Fortunately the train succeeded in reaching the cutting near Painter's bridge where the driver halted the train. Nothing further developed and the aircraft after swooping low over the train headed south-east to escape possible attack by RAF fighters from the nearby airfields.

Two further separate incidents involving branch trains occurred during the early years of the war. On 16th December, 1940 'C12' class locomotive No. 4520 was hit by shrapnel from a bomb, which exploded narrowly missing the stream bridge on the main line at Audley End. The fireman sustained minor injuries from the shattered cab windows as he was attending to the locomotive standing with the train in the branch platform. The other incident involved a train running between Audley End and Saffron Walden which was machine-gunned

'C12' class 4-4-2T No. 4509 approaching Audley End with a three-coach branch train in 1946.
E.R. Wethersett

'C12' class 4-4-2T No. 7385 leaving Saffron Walden goods yard with a goods train for Bartlow and Cambridge in 1947. The signalman is handing over the single line staff.   *W.A. Camwell*

Saffron Walden goods yard and station viewed facing east from the Debden Road overbridge in the bitter winter of 1947. The yard and Dix's siding to the right are almost full to capacity with wagons showing evidence of the importance of railway for the conveyance of commodities to the community in the last year of LNER ownership. *D. Campbell*

Saffron Walden engine shed and yard in the winter of 1947 with a 'J15' class 0-6-0 tender locomotive beside the shed building and a 'C12' class 4-4-2 tank locomotive taking water. During these severe periods of cold a lighted brazier was kept near the water column to prevent supplies freezing up. The main single line is to the left. *D. Campbell*

Saffron Walden station facing Audley End in the bitter winter of 1947. Note the GER down starting signal with lower quadrant arm, which was later replaced by an upper quadrant arm.

D. Campbell

'C12' class 4-4-2T No. 7375 near Fighting Cocks underbridge No. 2107 on the approach to Audley End with a two-coach branch train in 1947.

as it crossed the embankment near Beechy Ride by a low flying German aircraft. The locomotive and coaching stock sustained minor damage whilst the fireman was hit in the arm by a bullet.

The five airfields mentioned received considerable quantities of supplies via Saffron Walden and Bartlow stations during hostilities, including armaments, which were mostly off-loaded at night and transhipped by road. The ammunition was usually conveyed in open wagons, sheeted over to conceal their deadly cargo, although the prominent red flashed labels advised 'Shunt With Great Care' and 'Place As Far As Possible From The Engine, Brake Van and Wagons Labelled Inflammable'.

Although the branch had no strategic importance for troop movements as in World War I, it resumed considerable importance with the transit of essential fuel supplies when petrol sidings were installed half a mile east of Saffron Walden on the up or south side of the line in 1939. As airfields in East Anglia became operational demand for petrol had rapidly increased and the Petroleum Board had put down installations for loading tank cars at Sandy on the London Midland & Scottish Railway (LMS) cross-country line from Bedford to Cambridge. Supplies were drawn by pipeline from Stanlow and Avonmouth and trains were then loaded and dispatched to six destinations including Saffron Walden. As demand for further supplies increased the Petroleum Board installed a further pipe line from Thames Haven to Sandy and augmented the rail supplies to Saffron Walden, Thetford and Hethersett. The sidings at Saffron Walden consisted of two reception roads, which could each accommodate six tank wagons. These served fuel storage bays with capacity for 7,000 tons of aviation fuel in buried and semi-buried underground tanks. In all 498 trains served the sidings between August 1939 and March 1944 by which time the depot was served by pipeline direct from Sandy. By the end of 1943 a direct pipeline was also installed from Thames Haven to Saffron Walden which led to a reduction in supplies received by rail. Individual yearly totals were 1939 - 6 trains, 1940 - 29 trains, 1941 - 67 trains, 1942 - 118 trains, 1943 - 260 trains and 1944 - 18 trains. Many of the trains were worked via Shelford and Bartlow to prevent some of the high-octane fuel passing through Saffron Walden. Danger was greatest when a train on the branch was being shunted during an air raid but fortunately the coincidence of these two operations was rare. The sidings remained in use for supplies sporadically until 1949.

After the war the railways resumed peacetime services with run-down rolling stock and equipment and stations in need of maintenance. Questions were raised in Parliament regarding the poor condition of the rolling stock and deteriorating services offered by the railways and the Saffron Walden branch was no exception, with engine failures during the latter part of 1945 and early 1946 becoming commonplace.

The severe weather in 1947 with heavy snowfall brought many delays to services and at one stage in February the line was blocked twice near Ashdon, necessitating the use of the Cambridge snowplough to clear the line after the locomotive booked to run all night between Audley End and Bartlow failed to keep the line clear. With the impending nationalization of the railways the LNER continued to operate a frequent service and there were optimistic hopes that the new regime would bring improvements to the Saffron Walden line.

In the event of the normal branch locomotive being unavailable, Cambridge shed often sent an 'E4' class 2-4-0 to deputise. No. 2783 is here leaving Audley End with a two-coach train on 27th March, 1948.
E.R. Wethersett

Saffron Walden station in 1949 with 'C12' class 4-4-2T No. 67375 waiting to depart with a train to Audley End. The locomotive still bears the name of Louth shed on the buffer beam.
W.A. Camwell

Chapter Five

Nationalization and Closure

The nationalization of the railways from 1st January, 1948 brought little change to the branch, which retained its GER/LNER atmosphere for some time. Gradually new posters, paperwork and uniforms appeared. Although stocks of LNER tickets remained in use until the branch closed, those in constant demand were replaced with tickets bearing the legend 'Railway Executive' and later 'British Transport Commission'. Locomotives working the branch soon lost their 'NE' or 'LNER' identity in favour of the more austere 'BRITISH RAILWAYS'. Varnished teak or brown paint remained on the coaching stock until the early 1950s, when crimson red was introduced.

Freight traffic showed a further a decline in the late 1940s and early 1950s as fuel rationing ended and farmers and traders preferred to dispatch or receive their produce and goods by motor lorry. Livestock traffic also fell far short of pre-war figures and sheep and cattle for markets in surrounding areas was sent by road, a method which obviated the double handling of animals at both the sending and receiving stations.

On 2nd November, 1949, Col D. McMullen rather belatedly carried out the Board of Trade inspection of the oil sidings at Saffron Walden, which were installed in 1939. He found the new works consisted of siding accommodation for the Air Ministry on the Bartlow side of the station. A single-lever ground frame, released by the Annett's key on the Train Staff controlled the single connection from the branch line, and the track was formed of 85 lb. per yard new rail. McMullen noted the siding was used extensively during the war years as they served a petrol depot but at the time of inspection the sidings were not being used.

On the same day McMullen also inspected alterations at Bartlow. He found that the works had been carried out to enable the Saffron Walden branch line engine to run-round its train without obstructing the down main line, and also with a view to track rationalization. The short shunting neck into which the branch line engine ran before commencing the run-round movement was not provided with trap points. The inspector observed that passenger trains did not, as a regular course, run through from the Shelford to Haverhill line towards Saffron Walden, but it was known for excursion trains to use the connection. As a result of on-site discussions with railway officers it was agreed an instruction would be issued to the effect that the shunting neck was to be kept clear of vehicles during the passage of a train from the Shelford to Haverhill line to the Saffron Walden branch. The new track was laid with 85 lb. per yard rails and the portion of the relevant locking was checked in Bartlow Junction signal box and found satisfactory.

In 1945 Premier Travel Services Ltd of Cambridge had acquired the business of Weedens Motor Services Ltd, which operated motorbus services in the Saffron Walden area for some years. This service was further consolidated in 1949 when Premier Travel also took over the Pullman Services of G.F. Burgoin

Members of the 'C12' class provided the regular branch motive power in the 1940s. Here the former GNR 4-4-2T No. 67375 is running into Audley End branch platform with a train from Saffron Walden. The goods shed is in the left background and to the centre is the Neville Arms Hotel.   *W.A. Camwell*

'C12' class 4-4-2T No. 67375 waiting to depart from the branch platform at Bartlow with a train for Audley End in 1949. Bartlow Junction signal box can be seen in the background.
                                                                                                                              W.A. Camwell

(Haverhill) Ltd who operated a through service to London. Premier Travel at once augmented the bus routes in the Saffron Walden area and the direct services from Stradishall and Haverhill via Saffron Walden and Bishop's Stortford to London (route 38), operated in competition against the railway, outlived the closure of the branch line.

The usual arrangement for changing locomotives on the branch was for Cambridge men to bring the fresh engine light from Cambridge to Audley End and on to Saffron Walden. The exchange was then made and the relieved locomotive, manned again by the Cambridge men, hauled the 2.20 pm goods train from Saffron Walden to Cambridge via Bartlow. On one such occasion, in March 1951, the 'C12' class locomotives were exchanged at Saffron Walden in the usual way before No. 67367 set off for Cambridge with a heavier than usual goods train. The locomotive was priming badly but managed with some effort to top Ashdon bank. On the descent, however, the driver was unable to hold the load with the vacuum or steam brake and the train gathered speed on the falling gradient towards Bartlow. Fortunately the driver sounded the whistle continuously as the train lurched towards the junction and with great presence of mind the Bartlow Junction signalman, having no other traffic, set the road from the branch for the train to continue towards Cambridge. With squealing flanges and sparks from the brakes on the locomotive and brake van, the train sped round the curve through Bartlow and to safety on the Haverhill to Cambridge line, with no more than a bruised driver, fireman and guard.

After some years of deliberation the railway authorities introduced push-and-pull working on the branch from July 1951, utilizing three ex-North Eastern Railway 'O' class, LNER 'G5' class, 0-4-4 tank locomotives and two 2-coach push-and-pull coaching sets formed of ex-GER main line bogie coaching stock, which had previously seen use on the Seven Sisters to Palace Gates shuttle service. The introduction of these trains eliminated the time consumed in coupling, uncoupling and running round at each end of the journey.

The fireman in control of 'G5' class locomotive No. 67269 misread a shunting signal whilst propelling wagons into Dix's siding in 1952. In consequence a number of wagons were derailed and one of the push-pull coaching sets damaged. The line was blocked for seven hours whilst the Cambridge breakdown train was called to attend to the incident and the crane re-rail the stock. No. 67269 was not damaged but because of the shortage of the push-pull set, one of the coaching stock diagrams had to be covered by ex-GER corridor coaches with the locomotive running round the train after each trip.

The increase in car ownership and decrease in passengers using railway services brought about the closure of two neighbouring lines, the Bishop's Stortford to Braintree branch to passenger traffic on and from 3rd March, 1952 and the Elsenham to Thaxted branch, opened as a light railway as late as 1st April, 1913; the latter closed to passenger traffic on and from 15th September, 1952, and completely on 1st June, 1953.

Two of the 'G5' class locomotives were in collision in Saffron Walden shed yard in March 1954. One was slightly damaged and was unable to take up its booked working. The other took over all passenger train duties but some delays were inevitable until a replacement locomotive was sent from Cambridge.

'G5' class 0-4-4T No. 67269, carrying an unofficial 'Lucy Belle' chalked headboard standing at Audley End branch platform with the branch train on 30th May, 1953. Audley End signal box, which controlled all points and signals at the station stands alongside the main line to the left of the picture.   *R.E. Vincent*

Saffron Walden station facing Audley End. 'G5' class 0-4-4T No. 67322 on a two-coach push-pull set takes water at the platform, whilst sister locomotive No. 67269 shunts a brake van into Foundry siding.   *D. Campbell*

In 1955 a traffic census on the branch revealed some alarming statistics; for week ending 27th March a total of 932 train miles were run with a load factor of eight per cent, the movement cost to revenue ratio being 858 per cent. Later in the year for week ending 3rd September, the average number of passengers totalled 10 per train, giving a load factor of eight per cent and movement cost to revenue ratio of 860 per cent!

Acrow Engineering Ltd established its works adjacent to the branch, north-east of Saffron Walden, in 1953 and subsequently requested British Railways (BR) to provide a siding to serve the establishment to cater for the receipt and dispatch of large equipment. Authority was duly given subject to the usual annual charges and rebates. Col W.P. Reed carried out the official inspection of the connection leading to new sidings serving Acrow (Engineering) Ltd on 27th August, 1956. A 2-lever ground frame controlled by Annett's key attached to the single line Train Staff controlled the new connection facing trains in the up direction. Reed found the works in good order and the sidings on level ground. As the gradient on the main single line fell at 1 in 75 in the up direction operating instructions were issued that no vehicles were to be left on the main line during shunting operations. It was mooted at the inspection that the firm required a lineside halt to enable workers and visitors to use the rail service to reach the works, with Acrow constructing the platform and shelter at its own expense. Eager to encourage passenger traffic BR officials fully agreed to the provision of the halt.

By the late summer of 1956 the Eastern Region management were concerned by the deteriorating condition of the three ageing 'G5 'class 0-4-4Ts and their antique push-and-pull coaching sets. On 27th August 'N7' class 0-6-2T No. 69720 ran trials across the branch hauling an inspection saloon and another coach to evaluate possible use on the line. The test could not have come at a more opportune moment for in October 1956 the three ageing 'G5' class 0-4-4Ts were all failures at once and Cambridge depot had to resort to the use of equally antique 'E4' class 2-4-0s Nos. 62787, 62788 and 62789 to cover the Saffron Walden branch workings. Thus in the same month three push-and-pull-fitted 'N7' class 0-6-2Ts Nos. 69651, 69690 and 69692 were transferred from Annesley and Lowestoft sheds to Cambridge and together with two Gresley push-and-pull coaching sets commenced operations on the line. Soon after the introduction of the push-pull trains through workings were reintroduced from Audley End to Haverhill, with a reversal at Bartlow, in 1958.

The new halt between Saffron Walden and Ashdon adjacent to the Ashdon Road overbridge, and known as Acrow Halt was opened to traffic on 25th March, 1957. Built to serve the works of Acrow Engineering Ltd, Coronation Works, the opening ceremony was attended by the mayor of Saffron Walden. The driver and fireman of the locomotive of the first train to serve the halt, 'N7' class No. 69651, were each presented with a bottle of champagne!

The renewal of a bridge on the Cambridge main line at Great Chesterford between the hours of 2.00 am and 11.00 pm on Sunday 16th June, 1957 brought extra traffic to the branch when main line services between Liverpool Street and Cambridge were diverted via Saffron Walden, Bartlow and Linton. The arrangements for crossing trains on the single line was complicated because the

'J15' class 0-6-0 No. 65445 waits for Saffron Walden down starting signal to clear before setting off for Bartlow and Cambridge in August 1953. Beyond South Road overbridge a 'G5' class 0-4-4T is engaged in shunting wagons on the shed road and long siding. *D. Campbell*

'E4' class 2-4-0 No. 62787 deputizing for a failed 'G5' class 0-4-4T arrives at Saffron Walden with the branch train on 25th August, 1956. *R.C. Riley*

crossing loops at Saffron Walden and Bartlow were too short for the long trains and only Linton (between Bartlow and Shelford) could be used. The Train Staff & Ticket system was used to the full, with most trains carrying Tickets. Because the workings were unbalanced, 'B1' class 4-6-0 No. 61371 from Cambridge depot spent the day on the branch returning the Train Staff to where it was required and assisting the heavy main line trains over the 1 in 75/80 gradients of Ashdon bank, piloting down trains and banking up services. Most of the Cambridge men were conversant with the route but pilotmen were required for Stratford and Norwich crews. Special authority was given for the 'B1' and 'B17' class 4-6-0s, 'J20' class 0-6-0s, BR '4MT' 2-6-0 s and the BR Standard class '7MT' 4-6-2s to work across the branch, and trains were restricted to a speed of 20 mph throughout and 5 mph over two weak bridges. Locomotives working main line services included BR '7MT' Nos. 70003 *John Bunyan*, 70009 *Alfred the Great* and 70042 *Lord Roberts* as well as '4MT' No. 76034.

On 25th February, 1958 heavy snow caused more disruption to traffic on the branch but in the evening, when the push-and-pull train was returning from Haverhill to Bartlow en route to Audley End it ran into a snowdrift near Wethersfield siding. The Cambridge snowplough managed to free the train some five hours later when the 'N7' class locomotive and its two coaches set off to complete the much delayed journey. Fortunately the Saffron Walden line remained clear and when it became known the train had stuck in a snowdrift the other 'N7' locomotive and push-and-pull set at Saffron Walden took up the internal branch working.

The Saffron Walden branch received the benefit of the British Railways modernization programme from 7th July, 1958 when diesel railbuses built by the German firm of Waggon und Maschinenbau replaced steam traction on passenger services. On the final Saturday of steam traction 5th July, two 'N7' class tank locomotives and two push-pull coaching sets were in operation and over 100 passengers crowded into the last steam train during the evening. The railbuses were initially unpopular and unreliable; they later proved to be suited to the relatively light passenger loadings of the branch, although parcels traffic was transferred to road conveyance because of the limited space available. The commencement of the railbus services led many to believe the line had a secure future but the infamous Beeching Report was to prove otherwise.

In 1961 a total of 54,162 tickets were issued at Saffron Walden earning revenue of £20,370, whilst 86,659 tickets were collected. A total of 16,544 parcels were dispatched and 54,875 received, earning revenue of £3,485. The following year goods traffic received totalled 7,451 tons, whilst 4,945 tons were dispatched.

On Wednesday 27th March, 1963 the Beeching Report was duly published and the worst fears proved correct with the recommendation that the branch passenger services be withdrawn and Saffron Walden station, Acrow Halt and Ashdon Halt closed. The report also recommended the closure of the Shelford to Sudbury line including Bartlow station and the neighbouring St Margarets to Buntingford branch. In evidence the report quoted the following broad statistics for the Saffron Walden branch:

A busy time at Saffron Walden on 25th August, 1956; 'G5' 0-4-4T No. 67322 approaching with the 4.52 pm ex-Audley End train passing 'E4' 2-4-0 No. 62787 and two-coach set in No. 1 shed road. On departure of the 'G5' and train to Bartlow, No. 62787 ran into the platform and round its train before departing tender first to Audley End.   *R.C. Riley*

'N7/3' class 0-6-2T No. 69692 leaving Audley End with a Bartlow train on 25th June, 1958. Audley End main station building is to the right of the photograph.   *R.C. Riley*

'N7/3' class 0-6-2T No. 69692 heads towards Ashdon with an Audley End to Bartlow train on the last day of regular steam push-pull working on the branch. The engine is decorated with flags whilst the smokebox door bears the legends 'Old Faithful' and 'The Last Roundup'.
Author's Collection

Diesel railbus No. E79960 waiting at the branch platform at Audley End ready to return to Saffron Walden in 1960. *N. Williams*

Railbus displaying the earlier 'cats whisker' below the front window standing at Ashdon Halt on a up working in 1958. Only one passenger has alighted at this remote halt.   *N. Williams*

Railbus standing at Acrow Halt in July 1958. This halt was built entirely by Acrow Engineering Ltd using metal shuttering and concrete. The driver of the railbus is Reg Thake.

Author's Collection

Density of passenger traffic	0 to 5,000 passengers per week
Density of freight traffic	0 to 5,000 tons per week

Passenger station receipts	
Audley End (including main line)	over £25,000 per annum
Saffron Walden	£5,000 to £25,000 per annum
Ashdon Halt	£0 to £5,000 per annum
Bartlow (including Haverhill line)	£0 to £5,000 per annum

Freight traffic station tonnages	
Audley End (including main line)	0 to 5,000 tons per annum
Saffron Walden	5,000 to 25,000 tons per annum
Bartlow (including Haverhill line)	0 to 5,000 tons per annum

Later in the month D. Fenton, the traffic manager at Cambridge, officially announcing British Railways' decision admitted that some local railwaymen would become redundant as a result of the closure but that numbers 'could be counted on one hand'.

The closure of the branch immediately became the most important subject on the agenda of the town council and local parish council meetings. The National Union of Railwaymen and the Associated Society of Locomotive Engineers' and Firemen's branches at Cambridge recorded their objections to the closure of the branch lines in the Cambridge area with the Transport Users' Consultative Committee (TUCC) for East Anglia. In the town the Saffron Walden Railway Group was formed to represent the interests and views of individual travellers.

At a meeting of the town council at the end of March 1963 the mayor, D.J. Hawkins pronounced the feeling of all members at the meeting when stating that the closure of the branch railway would cause hardship. Increased use of heavy traffic on the roads of the town would cause a heavier burden on the ratepayers. The mayor stressed that all possible support should be given for the retention of the line. Further meetings were held and on 18th October, 1963 the council made a plea to the local townsfolk to help fight against the closure by writing to the TUCC for East Anglia with whom formal objections had to be lodged by 8th November. Saffron Walden Rural Council and Haverhill Urban District Council added their weight to the proposals.

On 30th May, 1963 a special train formed of Royal coaching stock had worked across the branch via Bartlow hauled by 'B1' class 4-6-0 No. 61119, long after steam traction had officially ceased south of March in September 1962. The special conveyed Prince Philip on a private visit to the area.

The official TUCC hearing was held at the Town Hall, Saffron Walden on Tuesday 13th December, 1963 when over 200 people packed into the meeting. M.J. Mustill presented the Saffron Walden Railway Group's case and claimed that many of the figures quoted as costs by the railway were misleading. Existing bus connections were poor, especially on the Eastern National 301 route. The closure of the line would cause hardship with disastrous effects on the local community. Representatives of the Saffron Walden Borough Council, Saffron Walden Rural District Council, West Suffolk County Council, Haverhill Urban District Council, Essex County Council, R.A. Butler MP and a number of individuals also gave evidence. The Chairman of the TUCC, L.A. Carey was

Saffron Walden station from the east in September 1963. Railbus No. E79960 is at the platform whilst class '03' 0-6-0 diesel-mechanical shunting locomotive No. D2003 is stabled in the Railway Foundry siding.   *Author*

On the penultimate day of passenger working 5th September, 1964, railbus No. E79962 departs Ashdon Halt for Bartlow.   *Author*

adamant that he and his fellow committee would hear no more that evening and caused uproar amongst those present when he stated, 'Many of us have long *car* journeys ahead of us'.

At the resumed TUCC inquiry held at the Masonic Hall, Saffron Walden on 31st December, 1963 at which G.M. Lewis represented the Saffron Walden Railway Group, less than half of the objectors were present although over 170 commuters were represented. After hearing the various proposals of the outstanding objectors and the railway group, Geoffrey Parslew, acting traffic manager at Cambridge stated there was hardly any case for the retention of the line, especially the Saffron Walden to Bartlow section, as on average only nine ticket holders used this section daily. E.W. Lowson, representing Premier Travel told the gathering that his company and Viceroy Coaches had agreed to operate the replacement bus services although no timings had been arranged.

The meeting established that the bulk of the passengers using the line travelled to and from Saffron Walden and it was known 78 held season tickets to London, 20 to Cambridge, including eight scholars, and 20 to Bishop's Stortford, including 15 scholars. A census taken during week ending 27th April, 1963 showed that a daily average of 266 passengers alighted at Audley End from the branch and of these 234 joined at Saffron Walden. In the reverse direction 279 passengers joined the branch trains at Audley End and of this number 250 alighted at Saffron Walden. A further census taken during week ending 20th July, 1963 revealed an increase of 20 per cent. Nearly all passengers arriving from the branch line at Audley End transferred to main line services to Liverpool Street and Cambridge.

In all 224 written submissions and 20 oral representations were considered by the committee. Within the 224 written submissions the main theme was hardship, the complainants feeling that the proposed replacement bus services would not cope with the additional number of passengers. Additional time taken to pick up and set down passengers would cause delay to bus schedules, adding time to the working and school day and missed train connections with main line services at Audley End. It was also thought that inconvenience would be caused to residents of villages along the route, notably Ashdon and Bartlow, who would be unable to convey prams, pushchairs, bicycles and livestock by train. In addition many people put forward the view that bus fares were higher than rail fares. British Railways gave the tentative date for closure as 2nd March, 1964, but as the Minister of Transport had not considered the TUCC report at that time, closure was postponed.

After considering the objections made, the committee recommended withdrawal of passenger services and submitted their report to the Minister on 28th February, 1964. The Minister accepted the recommendation and his decision was made known on 21st May authorizing the closure of the line, subject to licences for additional bus services being granted by the Traffic Commissioner. In a letter announcing the decision the Minister accepted the TUCC view that with their proposal, and due regard to the bus services already provided, most hardship cases would be alleviated.

Additional licences were duly granted to Premier Travel for the operation of a new bus route 59 from Audley End railway station to Saffron Walden and Haverhill via Ashdon and Castle Camps to run at similar times to the former

Railbus No. E79963 forms the 3.02 pm train to Saffron Walden standing at the branch platform at Audley End on 6th September, 1964.   *Ken Paye*

Railbus No. E79961 running into Saffron Walden with a down working on a damp Whit Monday 1963. The short Saffron Walden up starting signal is at the end of the platform.
                                                                                                                          Author

As railway enthusiasts and local people gather in the fading twilight railbus E79963 stands at the branch platform at Audley End prior to working the final train the 7.56 pm departure to Saffron Walden on 6th September, 1964. The train is already almost filled to full and standing. *Ken Paye*

Railbus E79963 standing at Saffron Walden after arriving with the last train, the 7.56 pm ex-Audley End on 6th September, 1964, watched by many local people and enthusiasts gathered on the platform. *Ken Paye*

Right: Cover of the pamphlet announcing the introduction of the replacement bus service in 1964.

Below: Timetable of the new Audley End to Haverhill bus service, effective from 7th September, 1964, after the closure of the railway to passenger traffic.

PREMIER TRAVEL
LTD

Area Office:	Head Office:	Area Office:
CAMPS ROAD	15 MARKET HILL	14 HILL STREET
HAVERHILL	CAMBRIDGE	SAFFRON WALDEN
2138	53327	3374

NEW SERVICE 59

HAVERHILL—SAFFRON WALDEN—
AUDLEY END STATION
via CASTLE CAMPS and ASHDON
(Replacement Service for
Bartlow—Audley End Railway Line)

Commencing
MONDAY, 7th SEPTEMBER, 1964
and until further notice

Showing journeys operated by Messrs. F. C. Moore Ltd. (Viceroy Coaches) and Eastern National Omnibus Co. Ltd., Service 301, and principal rail connections with London (Liverpool Street) and Cambridge

---

MONDAYS TO FRIDAYS

BUS

Haverhill (Market Hill)	dep.	—	—	—	07 06	—	—	08 25	—	12 05	—	16 05	18 12
Castle Camps (School)	,,	—	—	—	07 19	—	—	08 38	—	12 18	—	16 18	18 25
Ashdon (Rose and Crown)	,,	—	—	—	07 27	—	—	08 46	—	12 26	—	16 26	18 33
Saffron Walden (Common)	,,	07 10	07 28	07 39	07 39	07 50	08 10	08 58	10 38	12 38	14 38	16 38	18 45
Audley End (Railway Stn.)	arr.	07 20†	07 38†	07 49†	07 49	08 00†	08 20†	09 08	10 48†	12 48	14 48†	16 48	18 53

RAIL

Audley End (Railway Stn.)	dep.	07 30	07 48	07 59	07 59	08 10	08 30	09 18	10 58	12 58	14 58	16 58	18 58
London (Liverpool Street)	arr.	08 38	08 52	08 58	08 58	09 18	09 38	10 18	11 58	13 58	15 58	17 58	19 58
Audley End (Railway Stn.)	dep.	—	—	07 56	07 56	—	08 56	09 30	11 30	13 30	15 30	17 27	19 05
Cambridge (Station)	arr.	—	—	08 21	08 21	—	09 20	09 46	11 46	13 46	15 46	17 43	19 26

MONDAYS TO FRIDAYS

RAIL

Cambridge (Station)	dep.	07 40	08 00	09 00	10 40	12 40	14 50	16 40	17 50	—	18 40	—	21 20
Audley End (Railway Stn.)	arr.	07 59	08 30	09 18	10 58	12 58	15 16	16 58	18 16	—	18 58	—	21 50
London (Liverpool Street)	dep.	06 32	07 32	08 36	10 36	12 36	14 36	16 36	16 56	17 36	17 56	18 36	19 36	20 42
Audley End (Railway Stn.)	arr.	07 56	08 56	09 30	11 30	13 30	15 30	17 27	17 53	18 36	19 05	19 36	20 30	22 11

BUS

Audley End (Railway Stn.)	dep.	08 00†	09 00†	09 35	11 35†	13 35	15 35†	17 30	18 20†	18 40†	19 10†	19 40	20 39*	2220†
Saffron Walden (Common)	,,	08 10	09 10	09 45	11 45	13 45	15 45	17 38	18 30	18 50	19 20	19 50	20 47	22 30
Ashdon (Rose and Crown)	,,	—	—	09 57	—	13 57	—	17 50	—	—	—	20 02	—	—
Castle Camps (School)	,,	—	—	10 05	—	14 05	—	17 58	—	—	—	20 10	—	—
Haverhill (Market Hill)	arr.	—	—	10 18	—	14 18	—	18 11	—	—	—	20 23	—	—

ROUTE IN SAFFRON WALDEN
Via Ashdon Road, Common Hill, Hill Street, George Street, High Street and London Road

SATURDAYS

BUS

Haverhill (Market Hill)	dep.	—	—	—	07 06	—	08 25	—	12 05	—	16 05	18 12
Castle Camps (School)	,,	—	—	—	07 19	—	08 38	—	12 18	—	16 18	18 25
Ashdon (Rose and Crown)	,,	—	—	—	07 27	—	08 46	—	12 26	—	16 26	18 33
Saffron Walden (Common)	,,	07 00	07 39	07 39	08 00	08 58	10 38	12 38	14 38	16 38	18 45
Audley End (Railway Stn.)	arr.	07 10†	07 49†	07 49	08 10†	09 08	10 48†	12 48	14 48†	16 48	18 53

RAIL

Audley End (Railway Stn.)	dep.	07 20	07 59	07 59	09 08	10 58	12 58	14 58	16 58	18 58
London (Liverpool Street)	arr.	08 27	08 58	08 58	09 28	10 18	11 58	13 58	15 58	17 58	19 58
Audley End (Railway Stn.)	dep.	—	08 06	08 06	—	09 30	11 30	13 19	15 30	17 27	19 30
Cambridge (Station)	arr.	—	08 30	08 30	—	09 46	11 46	13 35	15 46	17 43	19 48

SATURDAYS

RAIL

Cambridge (Station)	dep.	07 40	—	09 00	10 40	12 40	14 40	16 40	—	—	18 40	—	21 20
Audley End (Railway Stn.)	arr.	07 59	—	09 18	10 58	12 58	14 58	16 58	—	—	18 58	—	21 50
London (Liverpool Street)	dep.	06 42	07 42	08 36	10 36	12 36	14 36	16 36	—	17 36	—	18 36	19 36	20 42
Audley End (Railway Stn.)	arr.	08 06	09 06	09 30	11 30	13 30	15 30	17 27	—	18 30	—	19 30	20 30	22 16

BUS

Audley End (Railway Stn.)	dep.	08 10†	09 10†	09 35	11 35†	13 35	15 35†	17 30	18 20†	18 40†	19 10†	19 40	20 39*	22 20†
Saffron Walden (Common)	,,	08 20	09 20	09 45	11 45	13 45	15 45	17 38	18 30	18 50	19 20	19 50	20 47	22 30
Ashdon (Rose and Crown)	,,	—	—	09 57	—	13 57	—	17 50	—	—	—	20 02	—	—
Castle Camps (School)	,,	—	—	10 05	—	14 05	—	17 58	—	—	—	20 10	—	—
Haverhill (Market Hill)	arr.	—	—	10 18	—	14 18	—	18 11	—	—	—	20 23	—	—

NOTES
† These journeys operated by Messrs. F. C. Moore Ltd. (Viceroy Coaches)
* This journey operated by Eastern National Omnibus Co. Ltd., Service 301, terminating at Saffron Walden (Railway Station)
CHRISTMAS DAY—No service

railway timetable on weekdays only. The existing Eastern National route 301, Bishop's Stortford to Saffron Walden and F.C. Moore Ltd Viceroy Coaches provided the other services.

British Railways subsequently announced the closure of the Saffron Walden branch to passenger traffic on and from 7th September, 1964, with the last trains running on Sunday 6th September. Attempts were made to seek an eleventh hour reprieve but to no avail and on Saturday 5th and Sunday 6th September railway enthusiasts and local people crowded on the railbus for their last rides on the branch. On both afternoons the fine weather attracted many people to the line and the railbus was crowded to the doors with passengers sitting in every seat and occupying every available space.

On Sunday 6th September, the final down working, the 7.56 pm from Audley End, departed three minutes late to blasts on the two-tone horn and the explosion of detonators. A large crowd massed on the platform waved to the 130 passengers crowded into the railbus built to accommodate 56 persons. Among the passengers was Nigel Weaver of the Saffron Walden Railway Group, Michael Cornish, prospective Labour party candidate and Saffron Walden town councillor Dennis Weaver. The railbus, in charge of driver Ken Brand and guard Ron Cornell, quickly made the run through the gathering darkness to arrive at the equally crowded platform at Saffron Walden. The passengers alighted and amid the singing of *Auld Lang Syne*, the vehicle was handed over to a Cambridge crew, who after reversal, took the railbus 'light' to Audley End and then over the junction and the down main line to Cambridge.

On the day following the withdrawal of the passenger service, civil engineering staff commenced removing station nameboards and small items of redundant assets from the lineside. Later, office furniture, collectors' items and other assets were removed. The branch remained under the overall charge of the station master at Audley End who was involved with the closing down process. Saffron Walden signal box remained open for the freight traffic, but within a month of the withdrawal of the passenger traffic British Railways announced its intention to withdraw freight facilities from the branch on and from 28th December, 1964.

Freight traffic dwindled rapidly during the remaining months and usually the shunting locomotive made only two trips a week to Bartlow and this sometimes to keep the rust off the rails. As the Christmas holiday intervened, the last day of freight working was Thursday 24th December, 1964, when all wagons were cleared from Saffron Walden yard and the shunting locomotive returned to Cambridge. On the same day Saffron Walden signal box was abolished. Within weeks the once shiny rails were bearing a film of rust whilst weeds and small trees later grew through the trackbed. Railway buildings were vandalized and until a purchaser was found the doors and windows of Saffron Walden station were boarded up. All connections to the Saffron Walden branch at Audley End were removed on 7th February, 1965.

A few months after closure, enquiries were made regarding the reopening of the section between Audley End and Saffron Walden by a private company but by then most people who had regularly used the line were happy with their alternative mode of transport and with the high purchase price unreachable, the scheme fell into oblivion.

Right: Cambridge breakdown crane removing the water column from the end of the platform at Saffron Walden in April 1964.

D. Campbell

Below: The track is removed from Saffron Walden station and yard, to be loaded on to the demolition train in June 1968.

Author's Collection

By June 1965 the track through the branch platform at Audley End had been lifted and the associated run-round loop and sidings were removed, to make way for an extension of the car park. At the other end of the branch the Stour Valley line from Shelford Junction to Haverhill and Sudbury was subsequently closed to goods on 31st October, 1966 and passengers from 6th March, 1967. Prior to these closures the Saffron Walden branch signalling had been abolished at Bartlow on 10th July, 1965 and Bartlow Junction signal box closed on 17th April, 1966.

The remainder of the Saffron Walden branch except for a short section near Bartlow was removed during the spring and summer of 1968. As with the building of the line, work commenced at Audley End in March and continued over a five-month period. To facilitate the loading of scrap by contractors, a daily supply of wagons was propelled from Saffron Walden and after the removal of the run-round facilities there, from Bartlow. The sidings at Saffron Walden were used for sorting empty and loaded wagons from the Audley End section. On the recovery trains the Brush type '2' class '31' diesel-electric locomotives were restricted to loads not exceeding 600 tons. As the gradients on the branch were severe a locomotive was in continuous attendance during loading operations. During the course of removal scrap rail was normally cut into lengths of 24 to 30 ft whilst serviceable rail was dispatched in 45 and 60 ft lengths, with points and crossings, to Chesterton Junction permanent way depot, two miles north of Cambridge.

The Saffron Walden branch gained fame at the last when the track was being removed. By the end of August 1968 only a short section of line near Bartlow remained, and this site was chosen by Colombia (Bristol) Productions Ltd as suitable for the re-enactment of a guerrilla attack on a Malayan train carrying British troops for the film *The Virgin Soldiers*. On 10th September one of the last London Midland Region class '5MT' 4-6-0s to remain in service, No. 44781, which had been purchased by the film company for £3,500, was hauled 'dead' from Carnforth shed to the site at Bartlow with some condemned BR Mark I main line corridor coaches. After arrival the following day the rolling stock was suitably disguised as Malayan Railway stock and No. 44781 received false side tanks and cowcatcher and the tender, false side plates, before being renumbered 531.03. The locomotive and coaches were derailed by a breakdown crane and left at various angles to the track. Explosive charges were then placed under the permanent way to suitably twist the track. The whole train lay within the small wood skirting both sides of the branch and the trees and vegetation received false creepers and other embellishments to simulate the Malayan jungle. Actual filming took place in October during late afternoon and the darkness and simulated steam added the final touches to the occasion. After the staged crash the locomotive was offered to a Saffron Walden enthusiast for £1,700 but the £3,500 cost of salvaging was too prohibitive and No. 44781 and the stock were subsequently cut up on site by A. King & Sons of Norwich.

In November 1969 the contract for the removal of the permanent way from the Stour Valley line was awarded to A. King & Sons of Norwich, whilst Bartlow station and site were sold to the Trustees of the Bartlow Estates. A. King & Sons also lifted the remaining short section of track used for the filming, at the same time as the Stour Valley line.

Most of the former trackbed and railway land has been sold and much of the branch obliterated. At Audley End the former branch platform and station building survive in the centre of the car park. A bungalow now occupies the former trackbed just before the former A11 road whist the Fighting Cocks underbridge was removed soon after the track was lifted on 10th June, 1968, to facilitate the widening of the main road. The entire section of the line across the Cam Valley and Fulfen Slade was subsequently resold to the Audley End Estates. The new owners have, by removing the high embankments and filling in the cuttings, reverted the contours of the countryside to the state it was before the railway was built. Similarly London Road and Borough Lane bridges were removed and the land filled in, in 1969. Saffron Walden station is now a private residence and Cleales Ltd, the local Ford main dealer used the yard and former trackbed. Extensive showrooms were built on the site but the firm ceased trading in 1998.

Between Saffron Walden and Bartlow most of the earthworks are clear and easy to follow although some of the trackbed now forms extensions to fields. Thaxted Road bridge was removed in 1975, whilst Radwinter Road bridge No. 2119 was demolished in 1970 although one abutment was left standing. Ashdon Road bridge was also demolished in 1970. The adjacent halt still stands alongside former site of the Acrow factory whilst Keeper's bridge was included in the sale of land to Audley End Estates in July 1967. Ashdon Halt, now much overgrown, is privately-owned, as is the River Bourn underbridge, No. 2127, which was included in the land sold to Bartlow estates with Bartlow station.

Since the closure of the railway over five decades ago, the population of Saffron Walden has increased with many commuting to London. Except for the reference to Station Street and Station Road, many would be unaware that a railway once served the town. Such is the reliance on the private car that bus services have been cut back to a shadow of former years and the town and surrounding villages function quite efficiently without the branch railway.

Brush type '2' diesel-electric locomotives, later BR class '31', were used on recovery trains when the branch track was removed. No. D5634 stands with flat wagons at Saffron Walden in 1968.   *Author's Collection*

Chapter Six

The Route Described

Audley End station, 41 miles 57 chains from Liverpool Street, via Clapton, on the former GER main line to Cambridge was the junction for the Saffron Walden branch. The main platforms at this station, called Wenden (after the adjacent village of Wendens Ambo) from the opening of the main line on 30th July, 1845 until 1st November, 1848, were staggered, but under the modernization programme were extended. The platforms were and still are connected by a footbridge the original having a corrugated iron roof. The main buildings on the up platform, designed by architect Francis Thompson, with its impressive entrance, included a booking and parcels office, waiting room, gentlemen's toilet, ladies' toilet, waiting room, porters' room and station master's house. The down side platform had a waiting room wedged between two former cottages, which were demolished many years ago. To the north of the up side platform was a loop road with access from the up main line by a trailing connection. This also led to a short loop siding from which wagon turntables gave access to the two-bay goods shed, which could accommodate 300 quarters of grain. The situation of the goods yard was rather cramped by the Neville Arms Hotel and its adjacent garden. In addition to the crane in the goods shed, there was a one ton capacity crane situated on the cattle dock. At the back of the London end of the up platform was a short siding which served the shed of Barnard Brothers, also entered by a trailing connection from the up main line. Opposite the up platform was a reception siding entered by trailing points from the down main line, immediately to the south of the down platform, whilst to the north of the station immediately beyond Station Road overbridge No. 1518 were up and down goods loops. Audley End signal box, latterly equipped with a 60-lever Saxby & Farmer Duplex frame controlled the points on the main line and Saffron Walden branch and was situated on the down side of the main line at the back of the reception siding, to the south of the down platform.

As the mileposts erected on the down or north side of the Saffron Walden branch gave the distance from Liverpool Street via Hackney Downs and Clapton Junction, the following description of the route quotes these distances. From the junction points at 41 m. 44 ch. the main single branch line and passing loop line swung away to the north-east on a 12 chains radius right-hand curve; 332 ft from the junction the main branch road entered the independent branch platform located on the down side of the line, which was 205 ft in length. Passengers from the main line train changing to the branch had to leave the up main platform via the booking hall and pass under the ornate frontage, and across the station forecourt to the small but homely branch platform. The building on the platform included the station master's office, storeroom and open-fronted, covered waiting shelter. Four gas lamps provided illumination of the platform during the hours of darkness. Run-round facilities were afforded by a 255 ft-long loop siding, from which trailing points led to the 1,017 ft-long storage siding on the up side of the line. To the south of the branch platform,

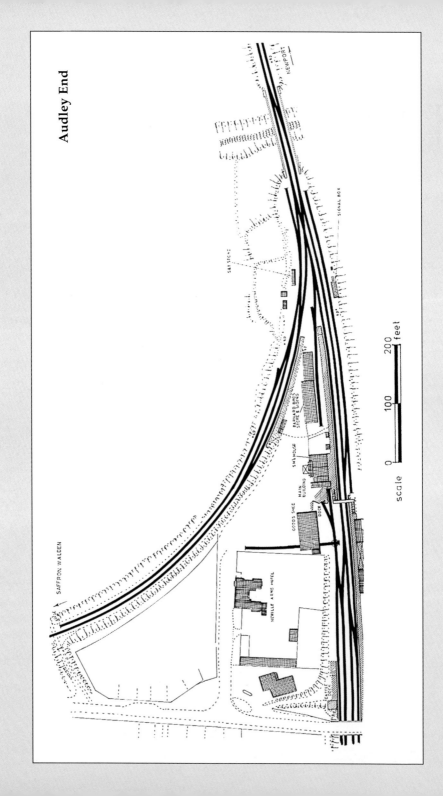

Audley End

Audley End up main line platform facing towards Liverpool Street. The ornate *porte-cochère* station building dating from 1845 contained the booking offices and station master's house.
Author's Collection

Audley End branch platform with small station building and Great Eastern Railway starting signal, view facing Saffron Walden. *Author*

Audley End station from the north with down platform to the right and up platform to the left. By the time this view was taken in April 1968 the platforms had been extended.　　*R. Powell*

Fighting Cocks underbridge No. 2107 at 41 miles 68 chains near Audley End. The structure named after a local hostelry spanned the then A11 main road, which in this view is devoid of traffic.　　*Author's Collection*

points off the up line led to an 80 ft-long shunting spur which also acted as a trap siding to obviate a runaway on the branch blocking the main line.

From the junction the branch climbed initially at 1 in 139/247 and then fell at 1 in 344 past the platform and over an accommodation crossing No. 1, leading to the Mutton Hall Estate on the up side of the line. Five chains beyond, the railway crossed the main A11 London to Norwich road by Fighting Cocks underbridge, No. 2107, named after the nearby public house. Here the line straightened out as the gradient fell for a quarter of a mile at 1 in 104 passing Wenden Mill to the south. The branch passed through a copse after the bridge, then crossed the valley of the River Cam on an embankment 38 ft high, from where good views were obtained of the surrounding low-lying land, including the trees of the Audley End Estate and the quaintly named St Joshua's bridge on the nearby road. The bridge over the River Cam and its adjacent occupational bridge, Nos. 2109 and 2110, were at the base of the embankment on which stood Audley End's up fixed distant signal. From the embankment the branch entered a deep cutting on a rising gradient of 1 in 129 to pass under an occupational three-arch overbridge No. 2111. After the bridge the gradient eased to 1 in 3382 rising, as the line negotiated a short 41 chains radius left-hand curve. Emerging from the cutting on to another embankment the line crossed the Fulfen Slade, a tributary of the Cam, by underbridge No. 2112, where the distance between the rail level and the water was 43 ft.

This small valley, also known as Beechy Ride on account of the number of beech trees in the area, was the site where Irish navvies held their outdoor mass when the line was built. After quick glimpses of Conduit Plantation and the rooftops of Audley End Mansion to the north-west, the branch quickly re-entered a cutting to pass under occupational overbridge No. 2113, again with three arches. Just beyond the bridge near milepost 43, the gradient stiffened to 1 in 173 for half a mile as the line eased round a short 65 chains right-hand curve on the approach to the outskirts of Saffron Walden. All the cuttings along the branch to this point showed the unmistakable whiteness of chalk as evidence of the East Anglian Ridge through which the line passed. When the town was reached, the railway stayed in a cutting, to follow a straight course to negotiate three public road overbridges. The first, London Road, No. 2114, which carried the B1052 from the junction with the A11 near Newport to the town, was followed by Borough Lane overbridge No. 2115, and Debden Road overbridge No. 2116, before the branch passed the goods yard on the down side of the line to enter Saffron Walden station, 43 m. 41 ch. from Liverpool Street and 1 mile 67 chains from Audley End, on a rising gradient of 1 in 1398.

Saffron Walden, built as a through station with one 202 ft-long platform, situated on the down side of the line, had the largest track layout on the branch. The white brick buildings of the station and station master's house, the latter located on the first floor, dated from 1865 and included booking office, waiting room, porters' room, ladies' waiting room and toilets and the station master's office in a detached building by the signal box. For many years the station platforms and buildings were lit by gas but the LNER later installed electric lighting in the buildings.

Opposite the platform was a run-round loop, 270 ft in length, from which the 912 ft-long siding ran under South Road bridge down to the Gas House siding

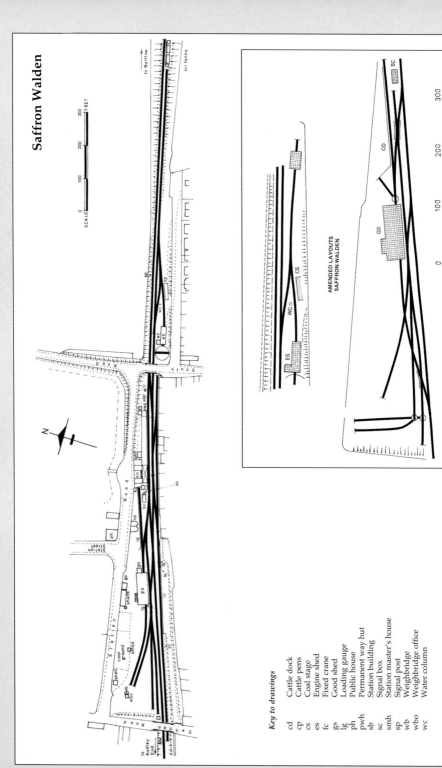

Saffron Walden

SCALE 100 200 300 FEET

to Bartlow

oil tanks

to Audley End

Station Road

Debden Road

Station Street

AMENDED LAYOUTS
SAFFRON WALDEN

scale 0 100 200 300 feet

Key to drawings

cd	Cattle dock
cp	Cattle pens
cs	Coal stage
es	Engine shed
fc	Fixed crane
gs	Good shed
lg	Loading gauge
ph	Public house
pwh	Permanent way hut
sb	Station building
sc	Signal box
smh.	Station master's house
sp	Signal post
wb	Weighbridge
wbo	Weighbridge office
wc	Water column

The ornate frontage of Saffron Walden station, dating from 1865 and designed by J.S. Pierce, with offices at ground level and station master's accommodation above. *J. Watling*

The imposing station at Saffron Walden and the signal box containing a 32-lever frame. This view was taken in October 1954 facing towards Bartlow. *Author's Collection*

Saffron Walden station, view facing west towards Audley End.   *Author's Collection*

Saffron Walden station and station master's house, view facing towards Audley End. To the left are Bell's siding and the run-round loop, whilst in the background are the goods yard and goods shed.   *Author*

and Anglo American Oil Company's tanks. From this siding facing and trailing points led to the engine shed and turntable. Also leading from the run-round loop, facing and trailing points led to a 395 ft-long siding serving the Railway Foundry at the eastern end, opposite the station platform, and the 637 ft-long Dix's siding serving a loading dock and taking its name from the adjacent cement works of Dix, Green & Co. The road entrance to this loading dock, with its 1 ton 10 cwt capacity fixed crane, was via gates by the Debden Road overbridge. The down side yard between the Debden Road bridge and the station had a large 112 ft by 34 ft covered goods shed, containing its own 1 ton 10 cwt capacity crane, loading platform, cattle pens, coal wharves and offices. Entrance to the yard was effected by trailing connections from the main single line. Road access was from gates in Station Road. Saffron Walden yard had capacity for 112 wagons. Points and signals at Saffron Walden were controlled from the signal box, situated by the down side of the main branch line at the western end of the station platform and equipped with a Saxby & Farmer 32-lever Duplex frame.

Continuing on the rising 1 in 1398 gradient, the single branch line ran under South Road bridge No. 2117, past the engine shed on the up side, and continued on a straight course through the outskirts of the town. Soon after passing the end of Gas House siding near the 43¾ milepost, the gradient stiffened to 1 in 160 for the initial quarter of a mile of Ashdon bank. A short embankment led the line to the Thaxted Road underbridge No. 2118. The buildings of the town gave way to open country on the down side of the line as the railway skirted the cemetery on the north side. A short descent at 1 in 264 followed as the line swung on a 60 chains radius right-hand curve over Sewards End Road, underbridge No. 2119, also known as the Radwinter Road. Two chains beyond the bridge were the points leading to the Air Ministry oil sidings installed in 1939, located on the up side of the line and used extensively during World War II to feed the underground fuel tanks. The siding closed in 1949. Beyond the points operated by a single-lever ground frame released by Annett's key on the Saffron Walden to Bartlow Train Staff, the single line began the 1½ miles gruelling climb at 1 in 75 to the summit of Ashdon bank. On the up side across the fields lay the quaintly named Turnip Hall and Pounce Wood, whilst on the down side was St James Hospital and the land of Copt Hall Farm. The branch straightened out for a short distance as it crossed Ashdon Road underbridge No. 2120 to enter Acrow Halt 230 ft in length at 44 m. 47ch., which served Acrow Engineering Company's Coronation Works, from where an elevated path led to the factory. The points leading to the siding serving the factory left the single line on the down side via a trailing connection to the east of the platform; they were controlled from a 2-lever ground frame released by Annett's key on the Train Staff and also by a key attached to the metal tickets.

From Acrow Halt, 2 m. 73 ch. from Audley End, the line continued climbing at 1 in 75 on a 65 chains left-hand curve followed by a 40 chains right-hand curve through open country. At the 45 mile post, Keeper's bridge, underbridge No. 2121, which carried the railway over an occupational track leading to Painter's Cottage and Ten Acre Wood, was crossed. This marked the half-way point on the climb to the summit. The branch then negotiated a 40 chains radius

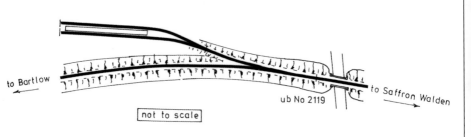

Air Ministry sidings, Saffron Walden

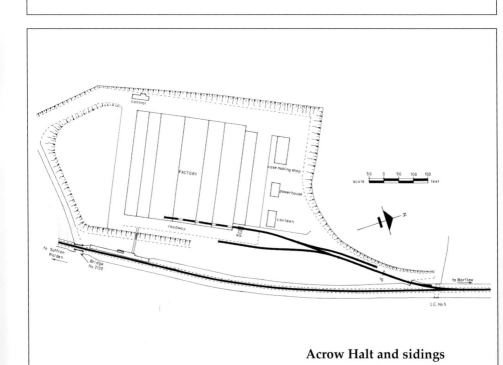

Acrow Halt and sidings

Acrow Halt, 44 miles 47 chains from Liverpool Street, was a late addition to the branch stations and opened on 25th March, 1957 to serve Acrow Engineering, Coronation Works, view facing towards Bartlow.   *Ken Paye*

Close up of Acrow Halt serving the adjacent Acrow factory on 6th September, 1964.   *Ken Paye*

Ashton Halt with oil lamps and old GER coach body serving as waiting accommodation, view facing towards Bartlow.   *Author*

The earth bank timber-faced platform at Ashdon Halt, view facing towards Audley End.
                                                                    Author

left-hand curve entering a shallow cutting before passing under Painter's
bridge, a three-arch structure near the 45½ mile post. Here a public road from
the nearby Saffron Walden to Ashdon road led to the hamlet of Ravenstock
Green and Hadstock Airfield. The branch then emerged from the cutting to
enter a straight level stretch of track to the summit of the line, 374 ft above sea
level. From the summit the line fell at 1 in 80 for 2½ miles, most of the way to
Bartlow. The descent began as the railway fell through a cutting before
negotiating a short 65 chains right-hand curve. The line followed a straight
course on an embankment where Nutts bridge, underbridge No. 2123 was
crossed, before the branch passed through woodland to enter Ashdon Halt, 46
m. 64 ch. Here the platform, 210 ft-long, on the up side of the railway was built
of raised earth and clinker with timber edging. An old GER coach body
converted to a waiting room provided covered passenger accommodation,
whilst three oil lamps on posts illuminated the platform at night, but later
'Tilley' lamps were substituted. In both instances the guards of trains were
responsible for lighting and extinguishing the lamps during the hours of
darkness. Ashdon Halt was actually located in the hamlet of Church End and a
trek of ³/₄ mile was necessary before the intending visitor reached the main road
and the south end of the village. Ashdon Halt was unstaffed for its 53 years of
existence.

Away from Ashdon the branch continued on a 65 chains radius left-hand
curve to cross Ricketts bridge, No. 2124, at 47 m. 20 ch. before entering a shallow
cutting and passing Newnham Hall on the up side of the railway. Open pasture
land was located on both sides of the track before the branch passed under
Ashdon Road bridge No. 2126, at 48 m. 03 ch. Beyond this bridge at 48 m. 17 ch.
a short siding, known as Slater's siding, served by points forming a trailing
connection from the main single line, was situated on the down side. The points
were initially locked and unlocked by keys kept in the possession of the Bartlow
station master, but later they were operated from a single-lever ground frame
released by Annett's key on the Train Staff. Initially installed to serve a brick
works, but when this trade became exhausted around the turn of the century it
was used as an agricultural siding by local farmers and was finally removed
about 1931. The branch continued on an almost straight course alongside the
infant River Bourne. At the 48¼ mile post the gradient eased to 1 in 340 falling
before the line crossed the river. There then followed a short rise at 1 in 1170
through woodland and over Brocklebank's crossing No. 24 before negotiating a
20 chains radius left-hand curve past the branch platform at Bartlow on a 1 in 854
falling gradient to the junction points on the Haverhill to Shelford Junction line,
49 m. 15 ch. from Liverpool Street.

The Saffron Walden branch station at Bartlow, 7 m. 21 ch. from Audley End,
was a simple structure situated three chains short of the junction. The platform
210 ft in length and constructed of raised earth and clinker with sleeper facing
was situated on the up side of the main single line. Passenger accommodation
was primitive and consisted of a wooden hut serving as a waiting shelter, whilst
post and hanging oil lamps provided illumination. Access to the Haverhill line
station was via tarmacadam footpath, 100 yards long and raised on an
embankment above dank wasteland.

The passenger waiting room at Ashdon Halt was formerly a five-compartment, second class coach built in October 1883 as GER No. 342. It was transferred from main line to suburban work in the 1890s following withdrawal of second class travel on the main line. The vehicle was widened from 8 ft to 9 ft sometime between 1902 and 1904 after which it re-entered traffic, and was subsequently withdrawn on 31st December, 1915. Early the next year the body was removed from the underframe and sent to Ashdon Halt as passenger accommodation where the compartment partitions were removed and replaced by wooden seats around the wall of the vehicle.   *Ken Paye*

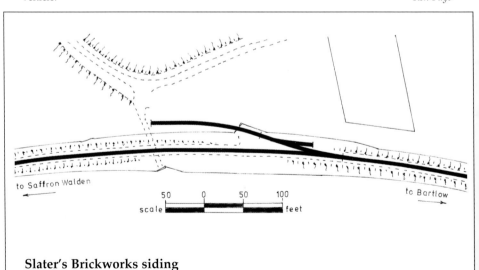

to Saffron Walden

to Bartlow

scale   50   0   50   100   feet

Slater's Brickworks siding

A general view of the main Stour Valley and Saffron Walden branch stations at Bartlow view looking south-east taken from the junction signal in 1910. The Bartlow tumuli are on the skyline whilst the Bartlow to Ashton road is in the middle ground.   *GERS/Windwood Collection*

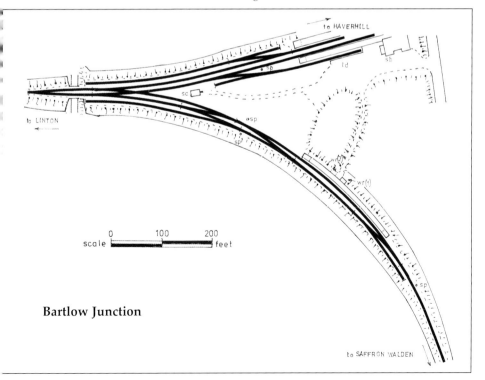

Bartlow Junction

Bartlow junction facing north with Bartlow Junction signal box in the 'V' of the lines from Audley End and Saffron Walden in the foreground and the route from Haverhill on the right in 1910. The latter continued to Shelford Junction on the Liverpool Street to Cambridge main line shown curving away in the far distance. A temporary possession of the branch single line is denoted by the red flag on the trolley in the foreground as permanent way staff appear to be putting finishing touches to newly ballasted track. *GERS/Windwood Collection*

Bartlow branch platform facing the junction. The low platform is part of the original structure, which has subsided. The remaining section was built up and refaced with new timbers. The points lead to the run-round loop, whilst to the left is the site of the former trap siding.

Author

Bartlow platform facing Audley End. The platform, which tended to subside away from the line, is timber faced. The simple wooden oil-lit hut provided the waiting accommodation. The run-round loop is to the right.   *Author*

Bartlow Stour Valley line station facing east towards Haverhill and Long Melford. The main station buildings and station master's house in the 1865 style of architecture are on the down side platform, whilst the up side is host to a waiting shed and porter's room.

Author's Collection

The abandoned Stour Valley line station at Bartlow after closure of the line and before the removal of the track.   *Author*

The abandoned branch platform at Bartlow in 1966 before the removal of the track.   *Author*

The track layout for the branch was essentially the same as at Audley End with a 260 ft-long run-round loop on the down side of the main single line opposite the platform. A double junction, later singled, was effected with the Haverhill line facing Shelford, to enable the through running of trains with the minimum of inconvenience. A short siding installed by the GER for the Saffron Walden Railway curved round alongside the Haverhill line, with access from facing points in the down loop line, which formed a continuation of the run-round loop. At the Saffron Walden end of the run-round loop was a short trap siding 35 ft in length, which was later removed.

Bartlow main station was a typical Stour Valley line crossing point with a long crossing loop served by two platforms, the main building of ornate structure, including the booking office, waiting rooms and station master's house, being on the Cambridge side platform. The goods reception roads with trailing connections from the loop lines and two sidings serving loading docks completed the layout. In addition to Bartlow Junction signal box containing a 39-lever Saxby & Farmer Duplex frame, which controlled all movements on the Saffron Walden branch, there was until 1926 Bartlow Station signal box containing a 20-lever Saxby & Farmer frame. This controlled all points and signals at the Haverhill end of the Stour Valley line station. From 1926, all such control was transferred to Bartlow Junction signal box.

The Bartlow Hills tumuli were seven large Roman mounds constructed by the Emporor Hadrian *circa* 120 AD, the highest 93 ft and the widest 147 ft. When the Haverhill to Shelford line was built and subsequently opened in 1865 the GER was compelled to run between the mounds and build an arch as well as retaining walls to protect the monuments. Initially the mounds dominated the view and were described as Roman burial places. Early preservationists attempted to stop the railway company demolishing 'Bartlow Hills' as they were then known, as they were a significant archaeological interest. Later they were barely visible and became covered in grass and trees.

When the Saffron Walden line first opened a speed limit of 20 mph was enforced but was reduced to 10 mph when the track formation deteriorated in 1866. After repairs the limit was again raised to 20 mph. On relaying with bullhead track the speed limit on the Audley End to Saffron Walden section was raised to 30 mph for passenger trains and 25 mph for goods trains. Thereafter for many years the line was treated almost as two branch lines, with priority always given to the short two miles section to the main line at Audley End.

The later GER *Appendix to the Working Timetable* showed the speed for passenger trains between Audley End and Saffron Walden as 40 mph and between Saffron Walden and Bartlow as 30 mph, whilst freight trains were restricted to 25 mph throughout. At Audley End down trains for the branch were restricted to 15 mph through the junction points, up trains to 5 mph through the connections leading from the single line to the up line at the branch station. Similar restrictions prevailed at Bartlow. These speed limits remained in operation until the closure of the line although the railbuses and railcars often exceeded the speed limit when descending Ashdon bank.

In GER days a platform bell was rung at Saffron Walden five minutes before the starting time and again when the train was due to depart.

Chapter Seven

Permanent Way, Signalling and Staff

Permanent Way

The original flat bottom track of the Saffron Walden Railway weighed 70 lb. per yard and was laid in 21 to 24 foot lengths. The rails were joined by fishplates weighing 22 lb. per pair connected by four $^7/_8$ inch screw bolts. The sleepers measuring 8 ft 10 in. by 9 in. by 4½ in., consisted of creosoted red pine laid 3 ft apart. The rails were fastened to the sleepers by fang bolts on either side of the rail joint and half fang bolts and half wood screws in the intermediate sleepers. Captain Tyler commented on inspecting the line in October 1865 that he would have preferred fang bolts throughout. On the Saffron Walden to Bartlow section the permanent way was again 70 lb. per yard flat-bottom rails in 21 to 24 ft lengths, fastened by fang bolts to sleepers 8 ft 10 in. by 9 in. by 4 in. spaced three feet apart, but two feet apart at the rail joints. As with the original section, the line was ballasted with chalk and gravel. Although satisfied with the layout Capt. Rich requested extra packing under the plain track and the points at Bartlow. He also stipulated the provision of stop blocks with a backing mound of chalk on the sidings at the junction.

The Audley End to Saffron Walden section of permanent way survived for 11 months, but within a week of the opening to Bartlow the formation came in for severe criticism. After additional packing with chalk and the replacement of undersized and rotten sleepers a detailed inspection of the line revealed more serious defects. As a result of the failure of Hanson, the contractor, to abide by the terms of his contract to maintain the permanent way for 12 months after the opening of the line to traffic, the GER was forced to step in and carry out the partial relaying of the line. The remedial work consisted of the removal of the worst of the chalk and gravel from the formation and replacing the deficiency with sound ballast. Further defective sleepers were replaced and, in accordance with the inspecting officer's wishes, the half fang bolts and half wood screws were removed from the intermediate sleepers and fully substituted with fang bolts.

Unfortunately this extensive remedial work lasted barely six years when the permanent way again came in for criticism. On 8th August, 1873 the GER Board was asked to rectify deficiencies between Audley End and Saffron Walden. On investigation it was found that this section of line carried the greater proportion of traffic. Whereas the original permanent way was wholly satisfactory on the Bartlow section with its two or three trains a day, exactly the opposite was the case between Audley End and Saffron Walden, where rails were wearing and sleepers splitting.

Although the section did not warrant relaying with heavier main line rails, traffic obviously required heavier rails and authority was later given to relay the two mile section with 75 lb. per yard bullhead track at a cost of £1,590 per single track mile. Work was completed in May 1874. These 75 lb. per yard rails survived until 1880 when the whole section was replaced by 80 lb. per yard bullhead track. Conversion was carried out at the same time as authority was given for permanent way alterations on both the main and branch lines at Audley End at a cost of £760.

In the meantime the replacement of the original track east of Saffron Walden had taken place with the section to Bartlow formed of 75 lb. per yard flat-bottom rail. By 1895 the Audley End to Saffron Walden section had been relaid with 85 lb. per yard 30 ft lengths of steel rail, whilst sleepers were increased in size to 8 ft 6 in. by 10 in. by 5 in., creosoted at the GER permanent way depots at Ponders End and Lowestoft.

In June 1902 the Way & Works Committee investigated the possibility of strengthening the permanent way on the branch to allow through running by main line trains, in the event of a mishap on the main line between Audley End and Shelford Junction. The GER Locomotive Committee duly advised it was desirable for the branch to take locomotives of classes '10', '1000', '1900' and '1150' with axle loads of up to 20 tons. After costing it was found that to convert the best section of the line, Audley End to Saffron Walden, would cost £420 and the lightly-laid section thence to Bartlow at £6,150.

The authority for the shorter section was readily agreed and merely consisted of the replacement of some 85 lb. per yard rails with new 87 lb. per yard track on the curved section at Audley End station and near Beechy Ride. Satisfied with this section, it was almost five years before the Bartlow section was tackled when 80 lb. per yard bullhead track replaced the remaining flat bottom section.

Soon after Grouping in 1923 the LNER began the protracted replacement of all remaining 24 ft length of rail on the branch with 30 ft lengths. By the outbreak of World War II nearly all the 30 ft rails were replaced by 45 and 60 ft lengths of bullhead track except for some sections near Ashdon and Bartlow. The rails weighing 85, 90 and 95 lb. per yard were of late GER and early LNER vintage. During the war only essential replacements were effected until 1946, when 60 ft lengths of rail replaced the remaining 30 ft length track. Further sections received 60 ft lengths as replacements became due but even so a considerable amount of 45 ft length sections remained when the branch closed. When the contractor removed the track examples of 80 to 97 lb. per yard rails existed.

Most of the bullhead rails, chairs and a proportion of sleepers used on the Saffron Walden branch were second-hand, having served initially on the main line. After nationalization a few British Standard rails of 93 and 95 lb. per yard were installed near Saffron Walden and Acrow. From takeover to closure, pointwork was constructed from standard GER and LNER components.

The chalk and gravel ballast used when the line opened was quickly replaced by ballast obtained from a local pit. Soon after the GER assumed full control of the branch, ashes and clinker were introduced. The GER found ashes were adequate for the ballasting on many of their branch lines and supplies were readily available from the motive power depots on the system. Ashes remained in use until the closure and when supplies were not available from locomotive sheds, wagon loads were obtained from Tate & Lyle's sugar refinery at Silvertown and the British Sugar Corporation's factories at Felsted and Ely.

The maintenance of the line from 22nd November, 1865 was covered as additional duties by the permanent way gang based at Audley End and when

Above: Audley End GER branch up distant signal. At one time this was operational but in later years the arm was fixed at caution.

Ken Paye

Top right: Bartlow down home signal (upper arm) and up starting signal (lower arm) of GER vintage on the same post.

Author

Right: Rear view of Audley End up fixed distant signal, which retained its decorative finial on the last day of passenger services, 6th September, 1964.

Ken Paye

the extension opened a small gang based at Bartlow maintained the section to Saffron Walden. When the SWR was taken over by the GER these arrangements were retained until about 1880 when a permanent way gang formed of one ganger and four platelayers was established at Saffron Walden. The gang covered the Audley End branch platform to the Bartlow branch platform inclusive. At the turn of the century the Saffron Walden gang took over full responsibility for the whole branch from the junction points at Audley End to the junction points at Bartlow and this arrangement persisted until closure. Retirements and transfers reduced staff numbers at the end and for heavy maintenance and renewals Audley End and Bartlow gangs assisted. In 1917 the call to arms had reduced the number of staff available for permanent way maintenance and the Bartlow gang, covering to Haverhill and also assisting on the minimal maintenance on the Saffron Walden branch, consisted of three men: W. Whiting, foreman platelayer, A. Mizen, second man and T. Atherton temporary platelayer. The Saffron Walden branch was included in the Cambridge District Engineer's area, and in 1891 J. Winbolt was district engineer and J. Tyler the district inspector.

Of the few individuals who worked on the branch, in October 1912 Charles Lofts was platelayer at Bartlow, Jabez Reeve ganger at Audley End in 1914 and Herbert Reeve, ganger at Audley End in 1924. W.W. Lees a platelayer at Bartlow died in May 1929 at the relatively early age of 35 years and W. Marsh, a retired ganger formerly employed at Saffron Walden, died on 10th March, 1930. Henry Bard, a ganger at Saffron Walden, retired on 28th August, 1931 whilst M. Law, a ganger at Audley End, retired on 9th February, 1933.

In addition to attending to day-to-day track maintenance, the Saffron Walden gang were responsible for cleaning toilets where no mains drainage existed. On hot and dry summer days especially during harvest times they patrolled the line, acting as beaters to extinguish small fires caused by stray sparks from passing locomotives.

Signalling

Signalling receives scant mention in the documents relating to the Saffron Walden Railway although Capt. Tyler in his first inspection of the line was notified of the single line being worked by the Train Staff principle. Certainly the inspector insisted on catch or trap points interlocked with the GER signals on the main line at Audley End. Train Staff & Ticket working was introduced from the outset as laid down by special order No. 1173 dated 16th October, 1865 with the Train Staff stations at Audley End and Saffron Walden. With the opening of the extension to Bartlow the Train Staff & Ticket arrangements were revised in accordance with special order No. 1402 of 15th June, 1870. The Train Staff stations were then Audley End, Saffron Walden and Bartlow. No engine or train was to run on the branch without a Train Staff or Train Staff Ticket.

The initial signals used on the line were supplied by Saxby & Farmer Ltd to the improved pattern originally introduced in 1856 with coloured aspect glasses rotating by the action of a connecting rod attached to bell crank levers, similar

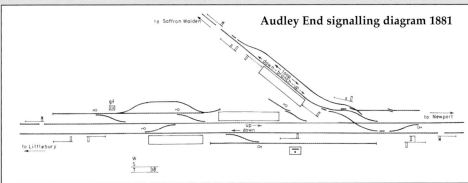

Audley End signalling diagram 1881

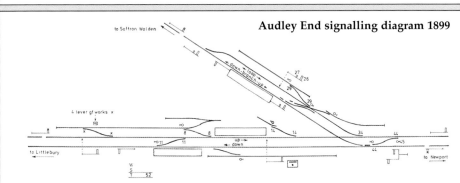

Audley End signalling diagram 1899

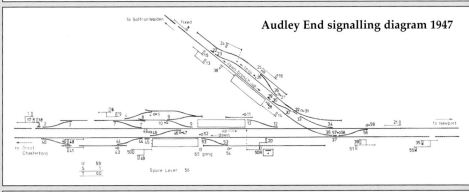

Audley End signalling diagram 1947

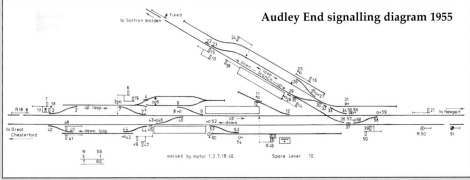

Audley End signalling diagram 1955

to those in use on the GER. Saffron Walden and Audley End stations were both equipped with a semaphore stop signal and one auxiliary or distant signal. When the extension opened, Bartlow received the same number of signals for the branch, whilst Saffron Walden was equipped with an additional auxiliary signal. The semaphore signals were some 15 to 20 ft tall and the arms conveyed danger at 90 degrees to the post, caution at 45 degrees and clear when slotted in the post. At night the revolving spectacles showed red for danger, green for caution and white for clear. The auxiliary signals were positioned 800 yards in the rear of the semaphore posts and kept at clear or 'all right' position unless required to protect a train standing between it and the semaphore signal.

Special instructions were issued regarding auxiliary signals. In the event of an auxiliary signal being at danger the driver of an approaching train had, after having brought his train to a stand, immediately to move his train forward with great care so far as the line was clear, so as to bring his train well within the protection of the signal. Drivers were especially cautioned that failure to carry out the regulation could result in an accident, which would otherwise be avoided. If it was not practical to draw the train far enough forward within the signal to afford sufficient protection from a follwing train, the guard was to go back at once with hand and percussion instruments to protect his train.

Audley End Junction signal box dating from 1881 had a 38-lever frame but was enlarged in 1899 and equipped with a 52-lever Saxby & Farmer frame with 4 inch centres. It was again enlarged to 60 levers in 1931 to cater for the installation of up and down loop lines parallel to the Cambridge main lines north of the station. The signal box was demolished on 27th November, 1983.   *Author*

A proposal was put forward in 1874 to interlock the points of the junction at Bartlow. After discussion by the Way & Works Committee, however, the scheme was dropped as it was considered the low density of the train service on the branch did not warrant the outlay, despite the danger of overrunning. In contrast in July 1876 a locking bar was installed on the branch junction points at Audley End. At the same time the branch signals at the junction station were replaced with lower quadrant signals.

Authorization for the extensive signalling alterations at Audley End was given in August 1880 at a cost of £950. The work, completed the following June, included the replacement of the old squat signal box located on the down side of the main line at the north end of the viaduct with a new structure 28 ft long by 11 ft wide with the signalman's working floor 12 ft above rail level, located 210 ft north of the original structure, at the back of the down reception siding. Other work included the fitting of facing point locks and locking bar on the points leading from the down main to the down branch and on the down branch to up branch crossover. The following branch signals were also re-sited: up branch distant, 800 yards from the signal box, up branch through home and up branch platform home located on the same post, on the down side of the main single line at the top of the embankment 17 ft from the nearest rail and 210 ft the Saffron Walden side of the branch platform. At the end of the platform was the down branch starter whilst at the south end guarding the entrance to the main line were the up branch starter for the through road and up branch starter from the platform road on the same post. Other work on this scheme involved the re-siting of signals and point locking bars on the main line. It is interesting to note that even at this early date the main line and branch distants were fitted with electric repeaters to tell the signalmen whether they were in the 'off' or 'on' position. At the same time all signals with the exception of the distants were lit by gas.

Despite the major renewal programme, trains on the branch continued to be worked by the ordinary single needle telegraph as the GER considered the amount of traffic handled did not justify the introduction of block signalling. Legislation on the safety of railways and signalling was approaching with the Regulation of Railways Act 1889. Anticipating the statute the GER Way & Works Committee authorized the installation of block working between Audley End and Saffron Walden on 18th October, 1887 employing Tyers single needle block instruments used in conjunction with the Train Staff & Ticket. This work was completed the following year just prior to the authority being given for block working between Saffron Walden and Bartlow Junction. The passing of the Act stipulated that block working was compulsory on all except single lines where Train Staff without tickets and 'one engine in steam' working existed and also for the interlocking of points and signals on running lines. The GER authorities decided to renew most of the equipment on the branch and by March 1890 the old semaphore signals were removed at Saffron Walden and Bartlow and replaced by conventional lower quadrant home and distant signals with pitch pine posts, cedar arms and cast- and wrought-iron fittings. In the same months block signalling was completed. Saxby & Farmer completed the interlocking of points and signals on the branch in August 1891 whilst new signal boxes to GER designs were erected at Saffron Walden and Bartlow Junction.

An up advanced starting signal was installed at Saffron Walden in November 1898 at a cost of £32 to facilitate shunting on the main single line within station limits, as the up starter stood at the end of the platform and in the rear of the exit points from the goods yard. Minor alterations were made at Audley End in July 1899 when the branch starting signal and up distant signal were re-sited, the latter 970 yards from the signal box.

The single line Train Staffs provided for single line working were: Audley End to Saffron Walden, hexagonal in shape and red in colour and Saffron Walden to Bartlow section, hexagonal, later triangular and blue, the paper and later metal tickets corresponding in colour with the respective Train Staff. In the latter years metal tickets were used.

In normal circumstances the Audley End signalman never saw the branch Train Staff as it was self-contained to the branch with the trains being worked by block signalling. When a goods train or other out of course working operated, a Train Staff Ticket was obtained by the use of the Train Staff from the locked box in the station master's office on the branch platform. Before push/pull operation was introduced in 1951 when an engine required to run round the train, lever No. 24, the starting signal from the branch loop, was always pulled 'off' as was No. 13 up branch home signal with the platform occupied to allow the engine to back onto the train. This was subject to the driver being in possession of the Train Staff. Although entering the section ahead from the run round loop, the move was never signalled on the block bell.

Saffron Walden station was provided with distant, home and starting signals in the down direction and distant, home, starter and advanced starter for up trains. Audley End was equipped with down starters on both the platform and loop roads and for up traffic a distant, later fixed, splitting homes for loop and platform roads and their associated starting signals. Bartlow branch signals included down fixed distant, home and starting signals with only a starting signal for up trains. The down home and up starter at Bartlow shared the same post.

The original Audley End Junction signal box controlling the main line and the branch was a small timber structure situated on the down side of the main line immediately north of the viaduct. It was replaced by a larger timber structure, sited 210 ft north of the original and behind the down refuge siding, which came into use in June 1881. This signal box originally had a 38-lever frame with all levers in use. The signal box was enlarged in 1899 and the structure measuring 28 ft by 11 ft with the operating floor 12 ft above rail level was equipped with a 52-lever Saxby & Farmer frame with 4 in. centres, with 51 working and one spare lever. In connection with the opening of the down and up loop lines north of the station in 1931, the box received a 60-lever second-hand Saxby & Farmer Duplex frame with 4 in. centres, originally with 59 working and one spare lever, and later with all levers working, before reverting to 59 working and one spare.

Saffron Walden signal box of timber construction measuring 24 ft by 11 ft 6 in. with operating floor 5 ft above rail level, controlled all points and signals at the station and possessed a 32-lever Saxby & Farmer Duplex frame with 4 in. centres, originally with 29 working and three spare levers and later with 26 working and six spares. Bartlow Junction signal box of all-timber construction measuring 28 ft by 11 ft with the operating floor 7 ft 10 in. above rail level had a 39-lever Saxby

Saffron Walden signal box, provided in 1892, was equipped with a 32-lever Saxby & Farmer Duplex frame with 4 in. centres originally with 29 working levers and three spare levers, later 26 working and six spare.
Author

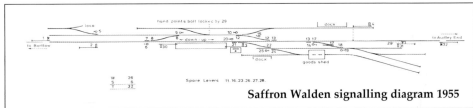

Saffron Walden signalling diagram 1955

Saffron Walden signal box controlled the majority of points and all signals at the station. Of timber construction it measured 24 ft by 11 ft 6 in. with operating floor 5 ft above rail level and possessed a 32-lever Saxby & Farmer Duplex frame with 4 in. centres. The box was abolished on 24th December, 1964.
R. Powell

& Farmer Duplex frame with 4 in. centres, originally with 37 working and two spare levers, later 33 working and six spare levers and then 32 working and 7 spare levers. Bartlow Station signal box of timber construction, measuring 20 ft by 11 ft 6 in. with operating floor 6 ft 6 in. above rail level had a 20-lever Saxby & Farmer frame with 4 in. centres, with 12 working and eight spares.

The Air Ministry siding at Saffron Walden, installed in 1939 but out of use by 1949 was controlled by a single-lever ground frame released by Annett's key on the Saffron Walden to Bartlow single line Train Staff. The sidings at Acrow, opened in November 1956, were controlled by a 2-lever ground frame, which was released by Annett's key attached to the Train Staff or to the metal tickets. The single-lever ground frame controlling the points to Slater's siding at 48 miles 17 chains was also released by Annett's key on the Train Staff, although the siding closed in 1931.

Specific instructions for block telegraph and signal working at Bartlow station were operative from 12th October, 1903. For down trains the Bartlow Junction signalman could give 'line clear' to the Station signalman if the line was clear to the Junction down starting signal, provided he had not given permission for a train to approach from the signal box in the rear in accordance with clause 4 of the Train Tablet block regulations. The Junction signalman was to maintain his slot on the Station signal box down home signal whenever there was occupation of the down line between the Station box home signal and his own starting signal. He was also required to place his slot on the Station box down home signal before giving permission for a train to leave the signal box in the rear. Whenever the disc in the Station signal box, worked from the Junction box in connection with the slot on the Station box down home signal, showed 'line blocked', the signalman at the Station box maintained his down home and distant signals at danger. For up trains the Station signalman could give 'line clear' to the Junction signalman if the line was clear to the Station up starting signal provided he had not given permission for a train to approach from the signal box in the rear under clause 4 of the single line block regulations. The Station box signalman was required to maintain his slot on the Junction up home signal for the Sudbury line, whenever there was any occupation of the up line between the Junction home signal and the Station up starting signal. He was also to place his slot on the Junction up home signal before giving permission for a train to leave Withersfield or Haverhill. Whenever the disc in the Junction signal box, worked from the Station signal box in connection with the slot on the Junction up home signal showed 'line blocked', the Station signalman was to maintain his up home and distant signals for the Sudbury line at danger.

In the event of a down train being brought to a stand at the Station down home signal, or an up train being brought to a stand at the Junction up home signal, waiting 'line clear', the signalman at whose box the train was detained was required to call the attention of the signalman at the box in advance, and having obtained it, give special bell signal 2 pause 2 pause 2. The signalman at the box in advance must, if the line was clear to the starting signal, acknowledge by shifting the needle to 'line clear', and then take his slot off the signal at the box in the rear. The signalman at the box in the rear was then to lower his home signal for the train to pass into the station as far as the line was clear.

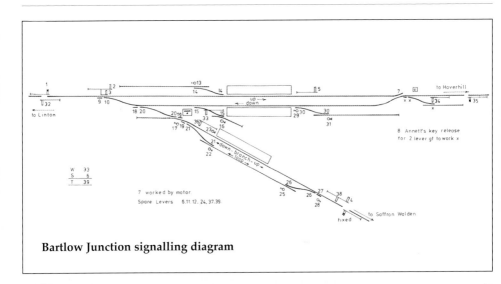

Bartlow Junction signalling diagram

A railbus forming a through Haverhill to Audley End train passing Bartlow Junction signal box before reversing to take the Saffron Walden branch on the right. These through workings only called at the branch platform on the outward and return journey. Bartlow Junction signal box opened in 1891 was equipped with a 39-lever Saxby & Farmer Duplex frame with 4 inch centres and after the abolition of Bartlow Station signal box in 1926 controlled all points and signals at the station.   *Dr I.C. Allen*

Special instructions were also issued on the same date for the shunting of vehicles on the main lines between Bartlow Station and Bartlow Junction signal boxes. In the event of an engine or vehicles being required to pass over the down or up main lines, the signalman who had let them on to the main lines but did not work the points by which they were to be shunted off the line, must if the engine or vehicles were proceeding in the right direction send a special bell signal 3 pause 3 pause 3 to the signalman in advance. If the signalman receiving the bell signal was in a position to accept them, he was to reply by repeating that bell code. If he was unable to accept the engine or vehicles he was not to acknowledge the call in any way, and until it was acknowledged the vehicles were not to leave. When the engine or vehicles had been shunted clear of the main line, the signalman controlling the operation was required to send the 'train out of section' signal 2 pause 1 to the signal box in the direction from which the vehicles came, which was to be acknowledged by one beat on the block bell.

If the engine or vehicles were travelling in the wrong direction along the down line, the signalman who required to pass them up the down line had first to send a special bell signal 2 pause 4 to the signal box in the rear. If the signalman receiving the call was in a position to accept the engine or vehicles he was to repeat the call 2 pause 4, but if he was not in a position to accept, he was not to acknowledge the signal in any way, and until the call was acknowledged, the engine or vehicles were not to be moved. When the engine or vehicles had arrived under the control of the signalman at the signal box in the rear, or had been shunted clear of the main lines, the signalman at the box in the rear was required to send special signal 4 pause 2 to the signal box in the direction from which the vehicles came, the call being acknowledged by repetition. If the engine of vehicles were travelling in the wrong direction along the *up* line the signalman who required to pass them down the line initially sent a special bell signal 2 pause 6 to the signal box in the rear.

When a shunter accompanied the engine or vehicles, the signalman who disposed of the vehicles was not to send the signal that the line was clear until the shunter or horseman in charge of the movement had informed him that the operation was completed. In the case of a light engine not accompanied by a shunter, the signalman was to ensure that the engine had passed clear of the main line before sending the appropriate bell signal. Each of the special bell signals was to be preceded by a 'call attention' signal.

From 19th March, 1908 specific instructions were issued regarding the special precautions to be taken for the working of the Saffron Walden branch at Audley End. In the event of fog or falling snow, if the men appointed to fog signal the up branch distant and home signals had not reported for duty, the signalman at Audley End was not to give permission for a train to leave Saffron Walden unless the up branch platform line was clear.

In connection with Electric Train Tablet Working introduced on the Shelford to Haverhill line from 7th January, 1909 the electric train tablet instrument in Bartlow Junction signal box was interlocked with the down advanced starting signal so that the signal could not be lowered until the Tablet for the single line section to Linton had been withdrawn.

During GER, LNER and early BR days Audley End Junction signal box was open continuously, whilst Saffron Walden and Bartlow Junction signal boxes were only open for trains shown in the working timetable and for trains specially advised. In World War I and World War II, however, Bartlow Junction signal box was open continuously for long periods to facilitate movements of troops, munitions, fuel and food. In 1952 Audley End signal box was open continuously whilst Saffron Walden and Bartlow signal boxes had reverted to being open for the running of trains shown in the working timetable and for trains specially advised. By 1961 Saffron Walden signal box was open from 5.35 am until 11.05 pm on weekdays and 9.00 am until 9.00 pm on Sundays when services operated, whilst Bartlow signal box was open at 4.55 am (Mondays excepted) or 5.45 am (Mondays only) until 8.40 pm on weekdays and 8.45 am until 9.30 am and then from 3.40 pm until 7.45 pm on Sundays.

Around the turn of the century modifications were made to the operating distant signals on the branch. At that time the GER distants were painted the same red as the stop signals and showed the same red and green aspects to drivers at night. To avoid confusion with the home signals, the distant signals were fitted with Coligny-Welch lamps, which showed an additional white > at night. In common with GER practice each wooden signal arm was stamped on the reverse with the name of the controlling signal box. With the advent of the LNER the distant signals were gradually repainted the familiar yellow with the black > and the Coligny-Welch lamps removed or modified to serve as ordinary lamps. After World War II some of the signal posts on the branch were found to be rotting and were replaced by those of tubular steel. LNER or BR upper quadrant arms gradually replaced some of the lower quadrant signal arms usually mounted on the same post, including Saffron Walden's up and down starting signals.

After the withdrawal of passenger services on 7th September, 1964, a signalman was retained at Saffron Walden to operate the points for the freight service and goods shunting pilot. With the cessation of goods working, however, the signalman was withdrawn and Saffron Walden signal box was abolished on 24th December, 1964 and the Train Staff & Ticket working replaced by 'one engine in steam'. This method remained in use until contractor's demolition trains commenced work. Bartlow Junction signal box closed on 17th April, 1966 before the withdrawal of goods and passenger services on the Stour Valley line although the structure outlived the closing of the Haverhill to Shelford line by some years until the frame was removed and the building vandalized. Audley End signal box survived until 27th November, 1983, its powers greatly diminishing in the latter years. A block switch was provided from 27th April, 1969, whilst the up main loop line was taken out of use on 9th November, 1969. The down siding points were removed on 4th January, 1975, with the up siding being removed a year later. Rationalization continued with the trailing main line crossover at the north end being take out of use on 17th September, 1978, to be replaced by a new main line trailing crossover located north of the down goods loop connection. Finally two weeks before the abolition of the signal box the down loop line was taken out of use. Signalling on the Cambridge main line was taken over by the new power signal box at Cambridge on 27th November, 1983.

The maintenance of the signalling equipment on the branch was for many years the responsibility of signal fitters based at Audley End.

Station masters

When the SWR opened to traffic, the staff appointed to work the line were already on the establishment of the GER but additional manpower was recruited locally. The station master appointed to Saffron Walden in 1865 was fortunate to have a house provided adjacent to the station. Unfortunately the said gentleman's name is not known, but he earned the magnificent sum of £70 per annum. Throughout the life of the Saffron Walden branch, station masters and other traffic staff played an important role in the life of the local community, as well as fostering good relationships between the railway company and its customers. Many sat on parish councils or as chairmen of local social groups and organizations. For some men the stay was long but for others the service on the branch was only a stepping-stone in the line of promotion.

In 1914 James William Hook Wilson was station master at Audley End occupying the accommodation above the station at an annual rental of £21 0s. 0d. which increased to £22 0s. 0d. from 1st July, 1915. Frederick Ward was at some time station master at Bartlow. When station master William Brown retired from Saffron Walden in April 1910, after 36 years in similar positions at Linton and Bartlow, he was succeeded by Richard Carroll. The new man stayed only three years until 19th March, 1913, before promotion moved him to Haverhill. Carroll's place was taken by Ernest Blanchard, who transferred from neighbouring Newport and remained at Saffron Walden until 1922, dealing with troop trains arriving and departing through the grim days of World War I. In 1914 he was paying £20 0s. 0d. as annual rental for the station accommodation, which increased to £22 0s. 0d. from 1st July, 1915. When Blanchard was transferred to Histon on the Cambridge to St Ives line he was presented with a case of pipes, silver mounted walking stick and a fountain pen from railway staff and local businessmen and travellers. Blanchard's place was then taken by Herbert William Moore, who had previously been station master at Docking, including Stanhoe and Sedgeford on the Heacham to Wells branch in Norfolk. Also in 1922, station master Albert George Edward Marsh, who had paid an annual rent for station accommodation of £18 0s. 0d. in 1914, raised to £19 0s. 0d. from 1st July, 1915, was transferred from Bartlow to Elmswell and his place was taken by S.T. Beales, promoted to the junction station from Emneth, on the Wisbech to Magdalen Road line. Beales moved to Fulbourne at the end of 1926 and was presented with a briar pipe by signalman Adams as a token of appreciation by local staff. During his stay at Bartlow, Beales and his staff had earned a first class Best Kept Station award in 1926 following two second class and one third class certificates. When Wilson moved on from Audley End the new incumbent was Herbert Ashwell Willis, who in 1924 was paying an annual rental of £21 0s. 0d. for the station accommodation.

H.W. Moore, who was paying £23 0s. 0d. annual rental for accommodation at Saffron Walden in 1924, retired on 31st May, 1927. He had commenced his railway career as a lad clerk in July 1882 and was made station master at Bulford (later Cressing) in March 1903. He later served at Battlesbridge, Burnham Market and Docking including Stanhoe and Sedgeford, before transferring to Saffron Walden in September 1922. Moore was also a church chorister for over 50 years. He died on 9th January, 1945.

William George Wybrew, station master at Mildenhall, was transferred to take charge at Saffron Walden in June 1927 but in January 1931 when H.A. Willis, the station master at Audley End was promoted to a similar position at Braintree, the posts of station master at Audley End and Saffron Walden were amalgamated at the former place and Wybrew assumed charge of both stations. The station house at Saffron Walden was thus available for letting to other staff. The supervision of the branch remained under the control of the station master at Audley End until closure of the line.

Back at Bartlow station master A. Green retired on 2nd February, 1934 and was replaced by E. Hannant, formerly a clerk at North Walsham. The grading was the lowest for a station master and Hannant being ambitious soon earned promotion to Tivetshall on the Ipswich to Norwich main line. In February 1935 H. Scoffield, a clerk at Eastwood on the former Great Northern Railway Pinxton branch, was promoted to take charge at Bartlow.

W.G. Wybrew subsequently retired through ill health on 28th February, 1938. He had served as station master at Stretham on the Ely to St Ives branch in 1912 before moving to Burwell in 1920, Mildenhall in 1922 and subsequently to Saffron Walden in 1927. W. Duddell, station master at Elmswell, gained promotion to Audley End including Saffron Walden in July 1938. In February 1939 F. Spurgeon, a clerk at Brandon, was appointed station master at Bartlow. After World War II C.E. Cadman station master at Bartlow was promoted to Smeeth Road and was replaced by F.W. Jacobs, formerly clerk at Wivenhoe, in 1946.

CAMBRIDGE LINE BRANCHES.

Slater's Siding, near Bartlow, on the Saffron Walden Branch.

Trucks are worked to and from Bartlow Station and this Siding by the Branch Engine, the Driver of which is to have the "Saffron Walden & Bartlow" Train Staff in his possession and be accompanied by the Guard, and also when required by one of the Bartlow Porters.

The Guard must unlock the Points in the Main Single Line and the Points of the Turn-out Siding, and after the shunting operations are completed he must, before returning, take care to re-lock both pairs of points in their proper position, and, on arrival at the Station, deliver up the Keys to the Station Master, who must retain them in his possession until again required.

The Station Master at Bartlow is responsible for seeing these Instructions strictly carried out; and for selecting such hours for the working as will not interfere with the Ordinary Trains.

Instructions for shunting Slater's siding near Bartlow.
Extract from *Great Eastern Railway Appendix to Working Timetable.*

G. E. R.

From

TO

SAFFRON WALDEN

Traffic staff

Saffron Walden staff in 1912 included Bill Munden, shunt horse driver, Jim Auger, shunt horse lad, Alf Sutton, shunter, later promoted to passenger guard and clerk Frederick Goddard, who, after he left the railway, became twice mayor of the town. William J. Norman a guard for many years on the Saffron Walden line retired on 21st August, 1922 and passed away on 26th November of the same year aged 67 years. Station master Moore with others attended the funeral and floral tributes were received from the Audley End branch of the National Union of Railwaymen. Another Saffron Walden guard, John Emms, retired on 24th September, 1924 after 51 years' railway service, having transferred to the branch in 1904. His father had been station master at Parham on the Framlingham branch. Emms passed away on 12th August, 1938 aged 79 years. Henry Purkiss, a signalman at Ely who retired on 27th September, 1929, had started his railway career as a lad porter at Bartlow on 5th November, 1883.

Traffic staff at Audley End in 1914 included Benjamin Clement, porter; Arthur Spoore porter; Atholl Alfred Saville, signalman; Henry Fitness, station foreman; John Fall, signalman; Frederick Perry, station foreman and Henry Willmott, station foreman. By 1924 additional staff included Fred Pluck, goods porter; Walter Law, signalman and John Pinnock, station foreman. All lived in the railway company station cottages, each paying an annual rent of £6 10s. 0d. in 1914.

The establishment of staff at Saffron Walden for many years was

Station master	4 goods porters
3 booking clerks	1 goods foreman
2 porters	3 goods clerks
2 signalmen	2 motor van drivers
1 station foreman	2 shunters

From the mid-1920s until the late 1950s, the complement was increased at certain times by four goods clerks and two motor drivers.

The comradeship between staff, working on the branch is evident by the many social gatherings arranged for their benefit. As an example, Audley End station and Saffron Walden branch staff held their annual dinner at the Neville Arms, Audley End on the evenings of 13th and 20th January, 1922, the two dinners enabling all staff on shift work to attend one or the other. Station master H.A. Willis of Audley End presided at both dinners.

Chapter Eight

Timetables and Traffic

With the building of the railway to Saffron Walden the developers were led to believe that an increase in population would occur as the line encouraged business. Unfortunately for the SWR and its successors the drift of population was only halted and it took nearly 100 years for numbers to increase by a thousand. Even then the increase within the last few years of the branch railway's existence came as part of the London commuter overspill.

The policy adopted by the GER of working of the line purely as a self-contained branch and not as a through route to the Suffolk towns via the Cambridge to Colchester line effectively hindered development of traffic, and the expected rewards never materialized. The branch, however, supported a through service to London for some years prior to World War I but during the 1930s such luxuries were not justified and all too soon the impact of the internal combustion engine was felt. Local industry was almost self-sufficient and therefore travel by rail to and from work was minimal. Only after World War II was there regular commuting to Cambridge and London.

It is thus surprising to find this seven mile branch line supporting a service of up to 22 weekday trains in each direction when the population of Saffron Walden was less than 8,000:

	1851	1861	1871	1881	1891	1901	1911	1921	1931	1951	1961
Saffron Walden	5,911	5,474	5,718	6,060	6,104	5,914	6,811	5,874	5,930	6,826	7,817
Ashdon	1,238	1,235	1,174	1,030	965	800	594	553	476	676	686
Bartlow	101	120	93	115	123	82	90	94	80	73	68
Total	*7,250*	*6,829*	*6,985*	*7,205*	*7,192*	*6,796*	*7,495*	*6,521*	*6,486*	*7,575*	*8,571*

The initial train service between Audley End and Saffron Walden consisted of six trains in each way, two designated 'Parliamentary' whilst the last train of the day also conveyed third class passengers. The remaining three trains in each direction were for first and second class passengers only. The seven minutes time allowed for the slightly less than two mile journey was standard for all trains. This timetable remained in operation during the winter months.

		1,2	Parl.	Parl.	1, 2	1,2	1, 2, 3
Up		am	am	am	pm	pm	pm
Saffron Walden	dep.	7.30	8.50	10.20	12.15	1.45	5.30
Audley End	arr.	7.37	8.57	10.27	12.22	1.52	5.37
Down		am	am	am	pm	pm	pm
Audley End	dep.	7.48	9.33	10.38	12.33	2.08	5.53
Saffron Walden	arr.	7.55	9.40	10.45	12.40	2.15	6.00

In the spring of 1866 slight adjustments were made to the timing of some afternoon trains and an additional later train in each direction was introduced departing Saffron Walden at 7.20 and returning from Audley End at 7.38 pm.

The working timetable for 1866 showed seven passenger trains in each direction on weekdays only. In the up direction the 8.50 and 10.20 am services ex-Saffron Walden conveyed first, second and third class passengers as well as Parliamentary fare paying passengers. The 5.30 and 7.20 pm ex-Saffron Walden also conveyed first, second and third class passengers whilst all other trains carried first and second class passengers only. In the down direction the 9.33, 10.38 am and 7.43 pm ex-Audley End conveyed first, second and third class passengers, the morning train also conveying Parliamentary fare paying passengers, with the remaining trains only conveying first and second class clientele. Goods traffic was worked by passenger train and by the branch engine making special trips when necessary.

The opening of the line to Bartlow engendered very little traffic and initially this section was served by only two trains in each direction and even they were in the afternoon, as may be noted from the accompanying timetable. The seven train service remained between Audley End and Saffron Walden with two trains being extended to and starting back from Bartlow. Again speed was of no consequence for 30 minutes were generously allowed for the five mile run. Only three trains in each direction made connections with London trains at Audley End, the fastest time between Bishopsgate and Saffron Walden being 1 hr 40 mins by the connection off the 8.00 am ex-Bishopsgate and 1 hr 50 mins in the up direction off the 7.20 pm ex-Saffron Walden.

Up		*am*	*am*	*am*	*pm*	*pm*	*pm*	*pm*
Bartlow	*dep.*					1.18		6.45
Saffron Walden	*dep.*	7.30	8.50	10.20	12.15	1.48	5.30	7.20
Audley End	*arr.*	7.37	8.57	10.27	12.22	1.55	5.37	7.27
Bishopsgate	*arr.*				12.50		3.40		9.10

Down		*am*	*am*	*am*	*am*	*pm*	*pm*	*pm*
Bishopsgate	*dep.*		8.00		11.00		4.05	
Audley End	*dep.*	8.03	9.33	10.38	12.38	2.08	5.53	7.38
Saffron Walden	*dep.*	8.10	9.40	10.45	12.45	2.15	6.00	7.45
Bartlow	*arr.*				1.15		6.30	

The working timetable for October 1870 showed a weekday-only service of seven passenger trains and one mixed train in each direction. All services ran between Audley End and Saffron Walden with the exception of the 12.53 pm ex-Audley End which ran through to Bartlow returning from there at 1.20 pm, with an additional Saturdays-only service running from Saffron Walden to Bartlow and return departing Saffron Walden at 6.05 and returning from Bartlow at 6.30 pm. The mixed trains ran as the first services of the day, 7.30 ex-Saffron Walden, returning from Audley End at 7.58 am.

Parliamentary fare paying passengers were conveyed by the 8.45 and 10.10 am ex-Saffron Walden and the 9.40 and 10.28 am return from Audley End. All other trains conveyed first, second and third class passengers with the exception of the 9.15 am, 12.35 and 5.25 pm up trains ex-Saffron Walden and the 1.20 pm ex-Bartlow, and in the down direction the 12.53 pm ex-Audley End to Bartlow and 1.53 and 5.50 pm Audley End to Saffron Walden. As before goods traffic was worked by passenger train and by the branch engine making special trips when necesssary.

SAFFRON WALDEN LINE.

Junction with Main Line at Audley End.

WEEK DAYS.

DOWN TRAINS.

Miles from Audley End.	FROM	morn	morn	morn	morn	even	morn	morn	even	morn	morn	even	even	even	even	even	even	even	even	even
	LONDON {Lpool St....dep.	6 0	...	...	8 45	...	10 32	...	2 32	2 50	...	4 32	...	5 15	...	7 32				
	{St. Pancras "	---	...	7 15	...	...	10 25	...	2 35	2 35	...	...	5 2	...	...	...				
	Broxbourne .... "	6 38	...	8 11	...	...	11 18	...	...	3 48	...	...	6 10	...	...	8 5				
	Bishop's Stortford ... "	7 14	...	9 32	...	...	12 5	...	8 33	4 23	...	...	6 37	...	...	8 36				
	Audley End ....arr.	7 44	...	9 46	...	...	12 33	...	8 49	4 53	...	...	...	...	...	9 2				
	Norwich ....dep.	...	...	...	8 32	8 32	...	...	...	2 7	...	...	...	4 40	...	...				
	Peterborough .... "	...	...	7 10	9 30	9 30	11 30	...	...	3 26	...	...	...	4 50	...	...				
	Ely .... "	...	...	8 30	10 56	10 56	12 55	...	...	4 32	...	...	...	7 22	...	...				
	Cambridge............ "	...	8 18	9 11	11 30	11 30	1 45	...	...	5 10	...	...	...	7 55	...	...				
	Audley End ....arr.	...	8 48	9 39	12 3	12 3	2 17	...	...	5 41	...	...	...	8 28	...	...				
2	Audley End ....dep.	7 50	8 55	9 12	12 6	12 6	2 20	3 53	4 55	5 48	6 39	...	8 35	9 5						
7¼	Saffron Walden ...... "	8 2	9 2	9 58	12 13	12 13	2 27	4 0	5 2	5 55	6 47	...	8 42	9 12						
	Bartlow ....arr.	8 14	...	...	12 56	12 56	...	...	5 14	...	7 0	...	...	...						

WEEK DAYS

UP TRAINS.

Miles from Bartlow.	FROM	morn	morn	morn	morn	even	even	even	even	even	even	even	even	even	even	even	even
							D	**E**									
	Bartlow ....dep.	7 30	8 20	...	...	12 20	1 8	1 45	...	...	5 20	...	6 20	...	7 50	...	8 50
5¼	Saffron Walden ...... "	7 37	8 35	9 25	11 55	12 20	2 3	2 3	3 10	...	5 23	...	6 26	...	8 10	...	8 56
7¼	Audley End ....arr.	7 37	8 42	9 32	11 58	12 27	2 10	2 10	3 17	...	5 39	...	6 26	6 37	8 17	...	9 2
	Audley End ....dep.	7 44	8 19	...	...	12 33	...	...	...	4 58	5 30	...	6 37	7 7	...	9 32	
21¾	Cambridge ....arr.	8 19	...	...	...	1 7	...	...	...	5 30	6 10	...	7 7				
35½	Ely .... "	8 52	...	...	...	1 58	...	...	...	6 10							
65¾	Peterborough .... "	10 18	...	...	...	3 22	...	...	...	7 35							
87¾	Norwich .... "	10 48	...	...	...	3 53	...	...	...	6 48							
	Audley End ....dep.	8 48	9 39	12 3	...	2 17	...	...	...	5 41	...	...	...	8 28			
19	Bishop's Stortford ...arr.	9 13	10 12	12 29	...	2 43	...	...	...	6 7	...	...	...	8 54			
31¼	Broxbourne .... "	10 23	11 15	12 57	...	3 20	...	...	...	6 43	...	...	...	9 29			
49¼	LONDON {St. Pancras "	10 22	11 14	1 35	...	4 0	...	...	...	7 28	...	...	...	10 5			
	{Lpool St.... "	10 15	11 10	1 30	...	4 0	...	...	...	...	...	...	...	10 5			

D Saturdays only. **E** Not on Saturdays.

Great Eastern Railway public timetable, November 1884.

As a result of investigations into traffic returns the GER notified the Saffron Walden Directors on 12th April, 1871 of proposed timetable changes. The 7.58 am ex-Audley End was to be extended to Bartlow returning at 8.55 am, whilst the 8.45 am ex-Saffron Walden and the 9.04 am ex-Audley End trains were to be withdrawn. Similarly the 9.33 am and 10.28 am trains were to be extended to Bartlow. On Thursdays it was considered certain trains could run through to Bishop's Stortford for market days as an experiment.

By 1872 the Bartlow extension had received a welcome increase in trains when the service consisted of eight journeys in each direction between Audley End and Saffron Walden, of which six were extended to Bartlow, although the 4.48 pm ex-Audley End and the 5.12 pm return only ran through on Thursdays. The fastest timings to and from London were 1 hour 42 minutes by the 8.00 am train ex-Bishopsgate and 1 hour 48 minutes by the 1.48 pm ex-Saffron Walden, passengers changing at Audley End.

Evidently the service to Bartlow received little support and was over generous for by 1874 only three trains ran through: the 8.05 am, 12.22 and 5.55 pm ex-Audley End, which returned from Bartlow at 8.55 am, 1.43 and 6.45 pm. Four other trains ran between Audley End and Saffron Walden with an additional train running on Thursdays only for the Bishop's Stortford market. The 10.10 am ex-Saffron Walden and the 10.28 am return working from Audley End were the only designated Parliamentary trains. The fastest journey from London was taking 1 hour 45 minutes on the 6.00 pm ex-Bishopsgate, whilst the slowest journey was 2 hours 20 minutes by the 10.10 am Parliamentary train ex-Saffron Walden, passengers again changing at Audley End in both directions.

The working timetable for 1875 showed a weekday-only service of six passenger, and one mixed train in each direction. The first up train of the day, 7.30 ex-Saffron Walden ran as a mixed train returning from Audley End at 8.05 am as a mixed train to Bartlow. The train then returned from Bartlow at 8.55 am as a passenger train to Audley End. By now all trains conveyed first, second and third class passengers with Parliamentary fares only available on the 10.10 am ex-Saffron Walden and 10.28 am return from Audley End. Bartlow was also served by an early afternoon return working departing Audley End at 12.22 returning from Bartlow at 1.43 pm. An additional market day train ran on Thursdays only departing Saffron Walden at 4.30 returning from Audley End at 4.50 pm, essentially to convey pasengers returning from Bishop's Stortford market. Goods traffic was worked by passenger train and by the branch engine making a special trip when necessary.

In July 1883 the branch services consisted of 12 down passenger trains, including four mixed, with four running through to Bartlow. Goods traffic was handled by the four mixed trains, the first of which, the 7.50 am ex-Audley End, was also a Parliamentary service. The up service also consisted of 12 passenger trains including four from Bartlow, one of which was Parliamentary and four of which were mixed trains. Running time of seven minutes was allowed for all trains between Audley End and Saffron Walden, whilst between Saffron Walden and Bartlow passenger trains were allowed 12 minutes and mixed trains 15 minutes. If freight traffic was beyond the scope of the mixed trains, the working timetable allowed for a special train to run a round trip between Saffron Walden and Audley End to clear the goods traffic. The journey time to and from Liverpool Street had improved with a timing of 1 hr 8 mins for passengers travelling by the 8.45 am ex-Liverpool Street. In the up direction, however, 1 hr 40 mins was the fastest timing by the 8.35 am and 11.52 am ex-Saffron Walden, all with changes at Audley End. Other passengers could take as long as 2 hrs 12 mins by the 2.50 pm from Liverpool Street and 1 hr 57 mins by the 2.03 pm ex-Saffron Walden.

The attractions of market towns in the surrounding area tempted many people to travel from Saffron Walden and nearby villages. Bishop's Stortford was relatively easy to reach by catching the branch train to Audley End and changing on to the connecting main line service. Haverhill was more difficult to reach as often the branch trains arriving at Bartlow only connected with Stour Valley line trains going to Cambridge. The GER rectified this shortcoming in the May 1890 timetable with the introduction of a train departing Saffron Walden at 12.43 pm arriving at Haverhill at 1.10 pm and returning at 4.05 pm with arrival at Saffron Walden at 5.33 pm.

By 1897 the down service consisted of 10 passenger trains and three mixed trains, one of which ran between Saffron Walden and Bartlow only. Only three trains ran to Bartlow with an additional train on Tuesdays, for Saffron Walden market day. The timing allowed between Audley End and Saffron Walden remained at seven minutes whilst between Saffron Walden and Bartlow the mixed train timing was accelerated to correspond with the passenger timing of 12 minutes. In the up direction there were 11 passenger trains and two mixed trains. The up working from Bartlow consisted of two passenger and one mixed train, the latter terminating at Saffron Walden, augmented by an additional train on Tuesdays. By this time the through trains were running to and from Liverpool Street at 7.40 am ex-Saffron Walden and returning at 6.02 pm ex-Liverpool Street, both with a 1 hr 30 mins timing. On Fridays the 12.33 pm ran through to Haverhill for the market, returning from there at 1.23 pm with a reversal at Bartlow. The working timetable showed paths for three goods trains in each direction between Audley End and Saffron Walden but these ran conditionally, arranged as required by the Audley End station master. Mixed trains working on the branch were restricted to a limit of 10 wagons. The down passenger trains between Audley End and Saffron Walden were now only allowed five minutes for the journey with seven minutes for mixed and goods trains. In the up direction passenger trains were allowed one minute extra running time between the two points.

In November 1897 the 5.25 pm ex-Liverpool Street train to Saffron Walden was withdrawn and replaced by a slip portion attached to the 4.30 pm ex-Liverpool Street. These through coaches were detached at Bishop's Stortford to be worked forward by an all-stations train to Saffron Walden arriving at 5.50 pm.

A decade later mandatory goods trains had been established and no longer ran as required. In the down direction two ran between Audley End and Saffron Walden, whilst the third ran through to Bartlow. In the up direction three goods trains ran from Saffron Walden to Audley End whilst the 2.45 pm ex-Bartlow terminated at Saffron Walden.

By now mixed trains ran at 7.55 am from Saffron Walden to Bartlow, 9.45 pm Audley End to Saffron Walden and 7.45 pm Bartlow to Saffron Walden. The through trains to London, Liverpool Street ran in slightly adjusted timings departing Saffron Walden at 7.43 am and returning from Liverpool Street at 6.01 pm. The 12.14 pm ex-Audley End continued to run through to Haverhill on Fridays returning at 1.23 pm. The passenger service consisted of 12 down trains and two running between Saffron Walden and Bartlow only, whilst two ran through from Audley End to Bartlow, augmented by the 4.55 pm ex-Audley End on Tuesdays only, the remainder running only between the junction and Saffron Walden. In the up direction 13 passenger trains were booked, two running the complete length of the line, one between Bartlow and Saffron Walden only, whilst the 5.26 pm ex-Bartlow ran on Tuesdays only. An innovation was a daily through train to Bishop's Stortford and return, departing Saffron Walden at 4.28 pm and returning from the Hertfordshire town at 5.22 pm, calling at all stations to Saffron Walden arriving there at 5.52 pm.

The working timetable for 1913 showed the following service on the branch:

	Passenger	Goods	Mixed
Audley End-Saffron Walden	10 Tues. only, 11 Tues. excepted	3	1
Audley End-Bartlow	1 Tues. excepted, 2 Tues. only	–	–
Saffron Walden-Bartlow	–	–	1
Bartlow-Saffron Walden	1	–	–
Bartlow-Audley End	2 Tues. excepted, 3 Tues. only	–	–
Saffron Walden-Audley End	11 Tues. only, 12 Tues. excepted	3	–

When goods traffic from London arrived at Audley End too late to be conveyed by the 6.33 am Mondays only (MO), 6.35 am Mondays excepted (MX) goods train to Saffron Walden, the 8.56 am Audley End to Saffron Walden passenger train was permitted to take wagons forward and run as a mixed train, departing the junction station at 9.05 am and arriving at Saffron Walden at 9.11 am. The 5.47 pm ex-Audley End was the through train from Bishop's Stortford departing the Hertfordshire town at 5.22 pm, whilst the 5.55 pm ex-Audley End on Mondays ran as a mixed train arriving at Saffron Walden at 6.01 pm. The 6.00 pm through train from Liverpool Street departed Audley End at 7.28 pm arriving at Saffron Walden four minutes later. In the up direction the 7.37 am ex-Saffron Walden was the through train to Liverpool Street arriving in the capital at 9.13 am, whilst the 4.28 pm ex-Saffron Walden was a through train to Bishop's Stortford arriving at 4.57 pm. This train was not to convey horseboxes for stations beyond Bishop's Stortford. The 7.45 pm train from Bartlow to Saffron Walden was permitted to convey three trucks of goods or cattle if the wagons were fitted with Westinghouse brake pipes.

The timetable for 5th October, 1914 showed acceleration in the journey times between London and Saffron Walden to 1 hr 13 mins by the 5.52 pm and 1 hr 6 mins by the 8.58 pm ex-Liverpool Street. In 1916 the through trains from Saffron Walden to Liverpool Street and Bishop's Stortford were starting from and terminating at Cambridge. The 7.19 am ex-Cambridge ran via Linton and departed from Bartlow at 7.45 am, with arrival at Liverpool Street at 9.46 am. A 5.38 pm return working from Liverpool Street followed the same route. An additional train departed from Liverpool Street at 2.05 pm on Saturdays only (SO), arriving at Bartlow at 4.17 pm and Cambridge at 4.43 pm. In the same

AUDLEY END, SAFFRON WALDEN AND BARTLOW.

Great Eastern Railway public timetable 1915.

timetable the through service to Bishop's Stortford departed Cambridge at 2.42 pm and travelled via the branch line with arrival at the Hertfordshire town at 4.08 pm. The return working followed a similar path. Two other interesting workings were the 3.05 pm Saturdays excepted (SX) Saffron Walden to Newport train and its return working at 3.42 pm SX, and an unbalanced 10.08 pm SX Newport to Saffron Walden train.

By 1917 the 7.17 am from Cambridge was the only daily train through to Liverpool Street whilst the 2.05 pm return working ran on Saturdays only. Freight facilities were improved by the addition of the 2.20 am express goods from Temple Mills to Cambridge, which ran via the branch. This train picked up wagons for Cambridge at Saffron Walden between 4.42 am and 4.58 am. Similar traffic was shunted at Bartlow between 5.05 am and 5.10 am before the train continued its journey to Cambridge. The 7.17 am train called all stations via Shelford, Bartlow, Saffron Walden and Audley End calling at Newport in the up loop platform at 8.10 am to await the 6.24 am express from Peterborough to Liverpool Street which called at Newport 8.18 to 8.19 am. The 7.17 am train then departed Newport at 8.33 am calling all stations to Sawbridgeworth and then Waltham Cross before arriving at Liverpool Street at 9.46 am. From 1st October, 1919 the train departed Cambridge at 7.35 am and ran main line throughout.

Services were reduced slightly during World War I to allow additional troop train paths to be included in the timetable but after hostilities the number of trains reverted to pre-war levels. One of the services withdrawn during this period was the through train to Liverpool Street, which was never re-instated. Another facility withdrawn as a result of the continuing miners strike in 1921 was the working of slip coaches to Audley End for attaching to the Saffron Walden branch train. The facility was first introduced back in May 1877 when a slip coach was attached to the 2.40 pm Liverpool Street to Norwich service. By 1897 two main line trains were slipping coaches at Audley End and this continued until the summer of 1914. In October of that year the new GER General Manager, H.W. Thornton, introduced his 'Radical Alterations' to the timetables and the Saffron Walden coaches were slipped at Newport and collected by the branch locomotive. By 1916 two down trains were slipping coaches at Newport and one at Audley End. The Newport slip coaches were later withdrawn and on 20th March, 1920 the 8.35 am Liverpool Street to Yarmouth Vauxhall train was slipping a coach at Audley End. The last slip coach service for Saffron Walden was withdrawn on and from 15th April, 1921.

The initial service offered by the LNER in January 1923 followed the post-war pattern of the GER timetables. In the down direction there were 10 passenger SX, 11 SO, two goods and one mixed between Audley End and Saffron Walden. Four passenger trains ran from Audley End to Bartlow and one passenger and one mixed train between Saffron Walden and Bartlow. In the up direction there were two passenger trains from Bartlow to Saffron Walden, four passenger trains running through from Bartlow to Audley End leaving 10 SX and 11 SO passenger trains together with three goods trains between Saffron Walden and Audley End. If there was no goods traffic the freight path was occupied by a light engine movement so that the locomotive could take up its next booked working. The above service still included the one through afternoon passenger train from Saffron Walden to Bishop's Stortford and return.

The LNER passenger timetable for 1928 showed the following weekdays only service with connections to and from Liverpool Street and Cambridge:

Down		am	am	am	am	am	am	am	am	am	SO pm
Liverpool Street	dep.		6.45	7.18		8.30			10.05	11.50	12.29
Audley End	dep.		7.40	8.16		9.18	9.44	10.07	11.38	1.04	1.54
Saffron Walden	arr.		7.44	8.20		9.22	9.48	10.11	11.42	1.08	1.58
	dep.	7.12			8.42			10.15		1.10	
Ashdon Halt	dep.	7.21			8.51			10.24		1.19	
Bartlow	arr.	7.26			8.56			10.29		1.24	
Cambridge	arr.	8.05						11.07			

Down (cont.)		pm	pm	T pm	pm	pm	pm	pm	pm
Liverpool Street	dep.	12.48	2.34	2.48	4.15	4.45	5.49	7.10	8.22
Audley End	dep.	3.02	3.45	4.38	5.39	5.39	7.14	8.22	9.38
Saffron Walden	arr.	3.06	3.49	4.42	5.43	5.43	7.18	8.28	9.42
	dep.			4.44			7.20		
Ashdon Halt	dep.			4.53			7.29		
Bartlow	arr.			4.58			7.43		
Cambridge	arr.			5.42			8.06		

Up		am	am	am	am	am	am	pm	SO pm	pm	SO pm
Cambridge	dep.				8.40						1.05
Bartlow	dep.		7.41		9.14		10.45				1.38
Ashdon Halt	dep.		7.47		9.20		10.51				1.44
Saffron Walden	arr.		7.55		9.28		10.59				1.52
	dep.	7.06	8.00	8.52	9.30	9.53	11.08	12.15	1.34		2.30
Audley End	arr.	7.10	8.04	8.56	9.34	9.57	11.12	12.19	1.38		2.34
Liverpool Street	arr.	8.57	9.27	10.17		11.27		2.07	3.18		5.09

Up (cont.)		SX pm	pm	pm	pm	pm	pm	pm	pm
Cambridge	dep.					4.57		7.22	
Bartlow	dep.					5.37		7.55	
Ashdon Halt	dep.					5.43		8.01	
Saffron Walden	arr.					5.51		8.09	
	dep.	2.42	3.25	3.35	4.20	5.55	6.50		9.18
Audley End	arr.	2.46	3.29	3.40	4.24	5.59	6.54		9.22
Liverpool Street	arr.	5.08		5.17	6.10	7.58	8.35		10.29

T – On Tuesdays departs Saffron Walden 4.55 pm, Ashdon Halt 5.04 pm, Bartlow arrive 5.09 pm.

The 1930 branch timetable showed the same number of trains but with slightly adjusted timings. By this date, however, the 6.00 pm Cambridge to Northumberland Park goods train was booked to run via Linton, Bartlow and Saffron Walden where stops were made to pick up wagons for up road destinations. Sixteen minutes were allowed for shunting at Bartlow and 15 minutes at Saffron Walden. This train ran regularly until 3rd July, 1939. The goods engine which had been booked for shunting at Saffron Walden from 10.00 am since the turn of the century continued to be shown in the timetable.

The working timetable for 1937 showed the following service.

	Passenger	Goods	Mixed	Light engine
Audley End-Saffron Walden	13 SX, 14 SO	2	–	–
Audley End-Bartlow	4 SX, 5 SO	–	–	–
Saffron Walden-Bartlow	1	–	1	–
Bartlow-Saffron Walden	2 SX, 3 SO	–	–	–
Bartlow-Audley End	4	–	–	–
Saffron Walden-Audley End	12 SX, 16 SO	3 SX, 2 SO	–	1 SX

The 6.35 am down goods train conveyed newspapers off the 4.35 am ex-Liverpool Street train, whilst the 9.14 am ex-Audley End to Saffron Walden passenger train was downgraded to run as a mixed train if freight traffic arrived at Audley End too late to be attached to the 6.35 am goods train. The 6.30 pm Audley End to Saffron Walden train could be held up to 15 minutes waiting connection with the 5.20 pm train ex-Liverpool Street, whilst the 8.13 pm Audley End to Saffron Walden passenger train ran as a mixed train when required SX. In the up direction the 7.55 pm Bartlow to Saffron Walden passenger train could work not exceeding three piped wagons of goods or

cattle. By now the through Cambridge to Northumberland Park yard freight train was withdrawn leaving all freight to be worked to Audley End to be picked up there. The goods engine arrived half and hour earlier at 9.30 am to perform shunting at Saffron Walden whilst several mixed trains were still restricted to tail loads of 10 wagons. The working timetable for 3rd July, 1939 showed the same service with minor adjustments in some of the timings.

Despite the reduction of trains on the outbreak of war a reasonable service was maintained, withdrawal of some of the local buses being the prime reason for the retention of the service. In May 1941 first class facilities were withdrawn from branch trains, a feature which remained in force for a decade.

In 1942 the following passenger services operated weekdays only:

Audley End-Saffron Walden	Audley End-Bartlow	Saffron Walden-Bartlow
7.35 am	11.10 am	7.22 am
8.05 am	1.08 pm	3.20 pm
8.44 am	7.00 pm	5.16 pm
9.40 am		
12.20 pm		
2.05 pm SO		
2.45 pm SX		
3.01 pm SO		
3.40 pm		

Audley End-Saffron Walden	Audley End-Bartlow	Saffron Walden-Bartlow
4.20 pm SX		
5.33 pm		
6.20 pm		
7.56 pm SX		
8.10 pm SO		
9.48 pm		

Saffron Walden-Audley End	Bartlow-Audley End	Bartlow-Saffron Walden
7.10 am	8.05 am	1.42 pm
7.50 am	11.48 am	3.40 pm
9.15 am	5.46 pm	7.31 pm
10.55 am		
12.50 pm		
1.50 pm SO		
2.26 pm SX		
2.46 pm SO		
4.06 pm SX		
5.03 pm		
6.40 pm SX		
6.45 pm SO		
7.20 pm		
9.34 pm		

At the end of hostilities the train service gradually recovered to that of pre-war timetable despite the worn out state of the locomotives and rolling stock. The timetable operated from 6th May, 1946 showed the following trains:

AUDLEY END, SAFFRON WALDEN AND BARTLOW

Single Line

DOWN   WEEKDAYS

Miles from Audley End (M.C.)	Station	No. 1	2	3	4	5	6	7	8	9	10	11	12	13	14	15
	Description		OP		OP	OP		OP	OP		OP		OP			
	Class															
	Audley End (S)	6 10 am			7 25 am	8 5 am		8 44 am	9 43 am		10 25 am		11 20 am			
1 67	Saffron Walden (S)	6 17			7 29	8 9		8 48	9 47		10 30		11 24			
	Saffron Walden			7 13										11 26		
5 11	Ashdon Halt			7 22										11 35		
7 21	Bartlow (S)			7 27										11 40		

1   To convey also Newspapers off 4.30 a.m. ex Liverpool Street.

Station	No. 16	17	18	19	20	21	22	23	24	25	26	27	28	29	30	31
Description	OP		OP	OP					OP		OP			OP	OP	
Class			SX	SO			SX		SO		SX	SO		SO		
Audley End (S)	12 23 PM		1 7 PM	1 12 PM			2 8 PM		2 12 PM		2 45 PM	2 55 PM		3 7 PM	3 40 PM	
Saffron Walden (S)	12 27		1 11	1 16			2 15		2 16		2 49	3 2		3 11	3 44	
Saffron Walden			1 14	1 19						2 20	3 10			3 20		
Ashdon Halt			1 23	1 28							3 19			3 29		
Bartlow (S)			1 28	1 33					2 40		3 24			3 34		

25   To Cambridge.
30   When 2.28 p.m. relief ex Liverpool Street runs, to start at 3.50 p.m., due Saffron Walden 3.54 p.m.

Station	No. 32	33	34	35	36	37	38	39	40	41	42	43	44	45	46	47
Description		OP		OP	OP	OP	OP	OP		OP	OP	OP	OP	OP	OP	
Class				SX	SO		SX			SO						
Audley End (S)		4 22 PM		5 11 PM	5 18 PM	5 42 PM	6 20 PM	6 49 PM		7 8 PM	7 40 PM	8 0 PM	8 26 PM	9 15 PM	9 56 PM	
Saffron Walden (S)		4 26		5 15	5 22	5 46	6 24	6 53		7 12	7 44	8 4	8 30	9 22	10 0	
Saffron Walden				5 18	5 24					7 15						
Ashdon Halt				5 27	5 33					7 24						
Bartlow (S)				5 32	5 38					7 29						

London & North Eastern Railway working timetable, 6th May, 1946 - down trains

BARTLOW, SAFFRON WALDEN AND AUDLEY END

Single Line

WEEKDAYS

UP

Miles from Bartlow	No.	1	2	3	4	5	6	7	8	9	10	11	12	13	14	15
	Description	E & V	OP		OP	OP		OP	OP		OP		OP		OP	LE
	Class															
		am	am		am	am		am	am		am		am		PM	PM
M. C.	Bartlow ....(S)				8 5								11 51			12 45
2 10	Ashdon Halt				8 11								11 57			
5 34	Saffron Walden ...(S)				8 19								12 5			1 0
	Saffron Walden ...	5 40	7 6		7 47	8 30		9 16	10 5		11 0		12 6		12 46	
7 21	Audley End ....(S)	5 47	7 10		7 51	8 34		9 20	10 9		11 5		12 10		12 50	

1 May run as a goods train.

No.	16	17	18	19	20	21	22	23	24	25	26	27	28	29	30	31
Description				OP			OP	OP		OP	OP	OP		OP		OP
Class			SX	SO		SO	SX	SO		SX	SO	SO		SX		SO
			PM	PM		PM	PM	PM		PM	PM	PM		PM		PM
Bartlow ....(S)							1 58	1 58						3 40		4 0
Ashdon Halt							2 4	2 4						3 47		4 7
Saffron Walden ...(S)							2 12	2 12						4 0		4 20
Saffron Walden ...			1 35	1 50		2 17	2 26	2 47		3 12	3 15	4 5		4 5		
Audley End ....(S)			1 42	1 54		2 27	2 30	2 51		3 16	3 19	4 9		4 9		

26 Advertised to leave Saffron Walden 3.12 p.m.

No.	32	33	34	35	36	37	38	39	40	41	42	43	44	45	46	47
Description		OP		OP	OP	OP	OP	OP	OP	Mxd	ECS	OP	OP		OP	
Class		SX		SO		SX	SO	SX			SO					
		PM		PM	PM	PM	PM	PM	PM	PM	PM	PM	PM	PM	PM	
Bartlow ....(S)						5 46						8 20				
Ashdon Halt						5 52						8 26				
Saffron Walden ...(S)						6 0						8 34				
Saffron Walden ...		4 55		5 2	5 30	6 6	6 35	6 50	6 58	7 23	7 50	8 13		8 40	9 28	
Audley End ....(S)		4 59		5 6	5 34	6 10	6 39	6 54	7 2	7 30	7 54	8 17		8 47	9 32	

40 Advertised Audley End arr. 7.4 p.m. Not in connection with 5.49 p.m. ex Liverpool Street.

41 To be ordinary passenger train on Saturdays.

London & North Eastern Railway working timetable, 6th May, 1946 - up trains.

'G5' class 0-4-4T No. 67269 with the Saffron Walden branch train at Audley End on 26th May, 1956. The push-pull stock is driving brake/composite No. E63423 and third No. E61441. Alongside the platform road is the run-round loop and outside that the long storage siding. To the left is the ornate frontage of Audley End main line station and beyond that the goods shed, unusually placed at right angles to the main line sidings because of restricted space.

H.C. Casserley

Two-coach push-and-pull set at Bartlow with 'G5' class 0-4-4T No. 67269. By this date the trap siding off the run-round loop had been replaced by catch points. In the background is Bartlow Junction signal box. *H.C. Casserley*

	Passenger	Goods	Mixed	Light engine	Empty stock
Audley End-Saffron Walden	14 SX, 15 SO	3	–	–	–
Audley End-Bartlow	5	–	–	–	–
Saffron Walden-Bartlow	1	1	–	1	–
Bartlow-Saffron Walden	1 SX, 2 SO	–	–	–	–
Bartlow-Audley End	5 SX, 4 SO	–	–	–	–
Saffron Walden-Audley End	13 SX, 16 SO	3	1 SX	–	1 SO

The point to point running times for passenger trains on the branch in 1949 were: Audley End to Saffron Walden five minutes; Saffron Walden to Ashdon Halt eight minutes; Ashdon Halt to Bartlow five minutes; Bartlow to Ashdon Halt five minutes; Ashdon Halt to Saffron Walden eight minutes and Saffron Walden to Audley End five minutes.

By now the through service to Bishop's Stortford had ceased and the branch became self-contained. With the demise of many mixed trains throughout the country it is interesting to note that the branch retained one mixed train running SX between Saffron Walden and Audley End departing at 7.23 pm. The mixed train was finally withdrawn on the introduction of push-and-pull working in 1951. The summer 1952 timetable commencing 30th June showed few changes other than adjustments of timing. Freight services were reduced by one train in each direction and the total number of trains using the line was as follows:

	Passenger	Goods	Empty stock	Engine and brake van
Audley End-Saffron Walden	16 SX, 15 SO	2	–	–
Audley End-Bartlow	5	–	–	–
Saffron Walden-Bartlow	1	–	–	–
Bartlow-Saffron Walden	1	–	–	–
Bartlow-Audley End	5	–	–	–
Saffron Walden-Audley End	15	1	1	1 SX

The point to point running times of the class 'H', 'J' or 'K' freight trains across the branch in 1952 were: Audley End to Saffron Walden seven minutes; Saffron Walden to Bartlow 18 minutes, Bartlow to Saffron Walden 20 minutes and Saffron Walden to Audley End seven minutes.

The winter 1956 timetable showed the following trains:

Audley End-Saffron Walden		*Audley End-Bartlow*	*Saffron Walden-Bartlow*
7.33 am	5.44 pm SX	10.10 am SO	7.02 am
8.09 am	5.52 pm SO	11.15 am	10.22 am SX
8.41 am	6.20 pm	1.14 pm SO	
9.35 am	6.37 pm SX	1.38 pm SX	
11.38 am SO	7.40 pm SX	3.36 pm	
12.41 pm	7.47 pm SO	4.52 pm	
1.50 pm SO	8.05 pm SX	6.56 pm SX	
2.48 pm SO	8.31 pm	7.02 pm	
3.02 pm SX	9.51 pm		
4.12 pm	10.07 pm		

'G5' class 0-4-4T No. 67322 propels her train near Thicko's farm between Bartlow and Ashdon Halt in 1956.   *Dr I.C. Allen*

'N7/3' class 0-6-2T No. 69690 standing at Bartlow branch platform after arrival from Saffron Walden on 14th June, 1958, shortly before diesel railbuses were introduced on the route.
                                                                                          G.R. Mortimer

Saffron Walden-Audley End		Bartlow-Audley End	Bartlow-Saffron Walden
7.04 am	5.25 pm SX	7.28 am	8.09 pm
9.00 am	6.28 pm SX	8.05 am	
9.50 am SO	6.43 pm SO	10.48 am	
11.24 am SO	6.48 pm SX	11.55 am	
12.55 pm SO	7.22 pm	2.07 pm SO	
1.10 pm SX	7.50 pm SX	2.18 pm SX	
1.24 pm SO	8.15 pm	4.06 pm	
3.15 pm	9.37 pm	5.43 pm	
3.55 pm	9.59 pm		

The running time allowed for trains was five minutes between Audley End and Saffron Walden and 14 minutes between Saffron Walden and Bartlow including the stop at Ashdon Halt. The fastest time between Liverpool Street and Saffron Walden was afforded by the 5.54 pm ex-Liverpool Street, which connected with the 6.56 pm from Audley End giving an arrival time at Saffron Walden at 7.01 pm, an overall time of 1 hour 7 minutes. An even quicker time of 1 hr 4 mins was possible in the up direction on the 12.55 pm SO from Saffron Walden which connected with the 12.36 pm ex-Cambridge; this departed Audley End at 1.05 pm and ran non stop to Liverpool Street arriving at 1.59 pm.

Through journeys to Haverhill were reintroduced after many years on 3rd February, 1958, with the 'N7'-powered push-and-pull trains. The 9.35 am Audley End to Saffron Walden was extended to Haverhill, whilst the return working 10.17 am ex-Haverhill replaced the 10.48 am Bartlow to Audley End service. In the evenings the 6.57 pm SX and 7.02 pm SO Audley End to Bartlow trains were similarly extended to Haverhill. These ran back empty stock to Bartlow for the next up working. The through trains to Haverhill remained a feature of the line until closure. Steam workings remained for only a few months and on 7th July, 1958 diesel railbuses took over the passenger workings on the branch when Sunday services were introduced.

The timetable introduced in November 1960 allowed the following service, all worked by railbus:

	Weekday passenger	Empty stock	Sundays passenger
Audley End to Saffron Walden	13 SX, 12 SO	–	3
Audley End to Bartlow	7	–	2
Saffron Walden to Bartlow	1	–	–
Bartlow to Saffron Walden	1	–	–
Bartlow to Audley End	7	–	2
Saffron Walden to Audley End	12	1 SX	3

On weekdays the 8.07 am from Audley End was extended through to Acrow Halt, returning at 8.18 am to pick up its booked timing of 8.21½ am from Saffron Walden. Other trains called at Acrow Halt only if required. The 9.38 am train from Audley End was extended beyond Bartlow to Haverhill arriving at 10.10 and returning at 10.22 am as a through train to Audley End. On Sundays two afternoon trains ran through to Haverhill. Both omitted calling at Ashdon Halt and stopped only at Bartlow to exchange the single line Train Staff. If there were passengers for Ashdon and Bartlow unofficial calls were made to set down passengers. The railbus was allowed 3½ minutes between Audley End and Saffron Walden and 12 minutes from Saffron Walden when calling at Acrow and Ashdon halts.

WEEKDAYS AUDLEY END, BARTLOW AND HAVERHILL

All trains are Diesel Railbuses—Calls at Acrow Halt not advertised

DOWN

Mileage M	C	Station		2-15	2-15	2-15	2-15	2-15	2-15	2-15	2-15	2-15	2-15	2-15	2-15	2-15	2-15	2-15	2-15
												‡ 9 50		‡ 11 50		‡ 13 50			
						SX	SO	SX	SO	SX									
0	0	AUDLEY END	dep	7 00	7 44	7 57	8 00	8 11	8 24	8 34	9 00	9 34	11 02	11 34	13 02	13 34	15 02	15 34	16 00
1	67	Saffron Walden	arr	7 03½	7 47½	8 00½	8 03½	8 14½	8 27½	8 37½	9 03½	9 37½	11 05½	11 37½	13 05½	13 37½	15 05½	15 37½	16 03½
			dep	7 04				8Q15				9 38		11 38		13 38			16 04
2	73	Acrow Halt		7 07				8Q17½				9 41		11 41		13 41			16 07
5	11	Ashdon Halt		7 12								9 46		11 46		13 46			16 12
7	21	BARTLOW	arr	7 16								9 50		11 50		13 50			16 16
			dep									9‡54½		11‡54½		13‡54½			
		HAVERHILL	arr									10 04½		12 04½		14 04½			

DOWN

Station		2-15	2-15	2-15	2-15	2-15	2-15	2-15	2-15	2-15	2-15	2-15	2-15
					SX	SO	SX				SO		
AUDLEY END	dep	16 50	17 06	17 32	18 30	18 34	18 43	19 10	19 40	20 50	21 38	21 54	22 20
Saffron Walden	arr	16 53½	17 09½	17 35½	18 33½	18 37½	18 46½	19 13½	19 43½	20 53½	21 41½	21 57½	22 23½
	dep			17 36					19 44				
Acrow Halt				17 39									
Ashdon Halt				17 44					19 52				
BARTLOW	arr			17 48					19 56				
	dep												
HAVERHILL	arr												

SUNDAYS

DOWN

Station		2-15	2-15	2-15	2-15	2-15	2-15
AUDLEY END	dep	13 16	13 56	15 02	15 56	18 02	19 56
Saffron Walden	arr	13 19½	13 59½	15 05½	15 59½	18 05½	19 59½
	dep				16 00	18 06	
Acrow Halt							
Ashdon Halt							
BARTLOW	arr				16c09	18c15	
	dep				16 12	18 18	
HAVERHILL	arr				16 21	18 27	

WEEKDAYS HAVERHILL, BARTLOW AND AUDLEY END

All trains are Diesel Railbuses—Calls at Acrow Halt not advertised

UP

Mileage M	C	Station		2-15	2-15	2-15	2-15	2-15	2-15	2-15	2-15	2-15	2-15	2-15	2-15	2-15	2-15	2-15
						SX	SO	SX	SO	SX	SX	SO						
		HAVERHILL	dep											10 22		12 22		14 22
0	0	BARTLOW	arr											10 32		12 32		14 32
			dep		7 25									10 38		12 38		14 38
2	10	Ashdon Halt			7 30									10 43		12 43		14 43
4	28	Acrow Halt			7 34					8Q20½								
5	34	Saffron Walden	arr		7 36½					8Q23				10 49½		12 49½		14 49½
			dep	6 53	7 37½	7 50½	7 53	8 03½	8 12½	8 23½	8 45	8 53	9 09½	10 50½	11 20½	12 50½	13 20½	14 50½
7	21	AUDLEY END	arr	6 56½	7 41	7 54	7 56½	8 07	8 16	8 27	8 48½	8 56½	9 13	10 54	11 24	12 54	13 24	14 54

UP

Station		2-15	2-15	2-15	2-15	2-15	2-15	2-15	2-15	2-15	2-15	2-15	2-15	2-15	2-15
								SX				SO	SX	SO	
HAVERHILL	dep														
BARTLOW	arr														
	dep			16 24			17 57½				20 26				
Ashdon Halt				16 29			18 02½				20 31				
Acrow Halt							18 06½								
Saffron Walden	arr			16 35½			18 09				20 37½				
	dep	15 20½	15 50½	16 36½	16 58½	17 16½	18 09½	18 36½	18 49½	19 20½	20 38½	21 20½	21 39½	21 47½	22 00½
AUDLEY END	arr	15 24	15 54	16 40	17 02	17 20	18 13	18 40	18 53	19 24	20 42	21 24	21 43	21 51	22 04

SUNDAYS

UP

Station		3-15	2-15	2-15	2-15	2-15	2-15
		ECS					
HAVERHILL	dep					17 20	19 00
BARTLOW	arr					17c29½	19c09½
	dep					17 32½	19 12½
Ashdon Halt							
Acrow Halt							
Saffron Walden	arr					17 40	19 20
	dep	13†01	13 27½	14 47½	15 27½	17 40½	19 20½
AUDLEY END	arr	13†04½	13 31	14 51	15 31	17 44	19 24

The final British Railways (Eastern Region) passenger working timetable, 1964.

After the introduction of diesel services the branch freight traffic was worked between Audley End and Saffron Walden and by 1961 the following paths were available in the working timetable; all trains running as class 'K' except the first up working which was class 'G', engine and brake van:

Down		am	pm	Up		am	am
Audley End	dep.	6.20	1.48	Saffron Walden	dep.	5.50	11.50
Saffron Walden	arr.	6.27	1.55	Audley End	arr.	5.57	11.57

The final timetable, operative in 1964 showed little alteration and the following passenger service operated:

	Weekdays		Sundays
	SX	SO	
Audley End to Saffron Walden	15	16	4
Audley End to Acrow Halt	1*	–	–
Audley End to Bartlow	4	4	–
Audley End to Haverhill	3	3	2
Haverhill To Audley End	3	3	2
Bartlow to Audley End	4	4	–
Acrow Halt to Audley End	1*	–	–
Saffron Walden to Audley End	15	16	4 †

* Extended beyond Saffron Walden to and from Acrow Halt only if required.
† Three passenger and one empty coaching stock.
On weekdays the 7.40 pm ex-Audley End, 8.26 pm ex-Bartlow and the three up services from Haverhill omitted calling at Acrow Halt. No services called at Ashdon Halt and Acrow Halt on Sundays.

The open expanse of Essex countryside forms a backcloth as railbus No. E79962 trundles past the Audley End fixed distant signal with a Saffron Walden train on 5th September, 1964.   *Author*

Fares

In the first years of operation first, second, third and Parliamentary class fares were offered. The latter meant third class travel at 1*d*. per mile, which had to be provided on every line by at least one train in each direction on weekdays under the Act of 1844. The full local fare structure on the opening of the line was as follows:

Audley End to Saffron Walden

	First	Second	Third	Parliamentary
Single	3*d*.	2*d*.	1½*d*.	1*d*.
Return	6*d*.	4*d*.	3*d*.	2*d*.

Bishopsgate to	Audley End		Saffron Walden	
	s.	d.	s.	d.
First class	9	0	9	6
Second class	7	3	7	7
Third class	5	6	5	9
Parliamentary	3	7½	3	9½

By 1884 fares from Liverpool Street to stations on the branch were:

	Audley End				Saffron Walden				Bartlow			
	Single		Return		Single		Return		Single		Return	
	s.	d.	s.	d.	s.	d.	s.	d.	s.	d.	s.	d.
First class	8	0	12	0	8	6	12	9	9	6	14	2
Second class	6	0	9	6	6	4	10	0	7	2	11	5
Third class	3	6½	7	1	3	8½	7	5	4	2	8	4

Local fares were:

Audley End to	Saffron Walden				Bartlow			
	Single		Return		Single		Return	
	s.	d.	s.	d.	s.	d.	s.	d.
First class	0	6	0	9	1	6	2	2
Second class	0	4	0	6	1	2	1	11
Third class	0	2	0	4	0	7½	1	3

The fare table from Liverpool Street in 1947, the last year of LNER ownership was:

	First single		First monthly return		Third single		Third monthly return	
	s.	d.	s.	d.	s.	d.	s.	d.
Audley End	12	7	15	2	7	7	10	1
Saffron Walden	13	1	15	11	7	9	10	7
Ashdon Halt	13	10	16	11	8	3	11	3
Bartlow	14	7	17	11	8	9	11	11

In 1955 fares from Liverpool Street were as follows:

	First single		First return			Third single		Third return	
	s.	d.	£	s.	d.	s.	d.	s.	d.
Audley End	10	0	1	0	0	6	8	13	4
Saffron Walden	10	5	1	0	10	6	11	13	10
Bartlow via Saffron Walden	11	8	1	3	4	7	9	15	6

Local fares on the branch were Audley End to:

	First single		First return		Third single		Third return	
	s.	d.	s.	d.	s.	d.	s.	d.
Saffron Walden	0	5	0	10	0	3	0	6
Bartlow	1	8	3	4	1	1	2	0

The final fare table for the branch stations from Liverpool Street in 1964 when the railbuses conveyed second class accommodation only was:

	First single		First return			Second single		Second return		
	s.	d.	£	s.	d.	s.	d.	£	s.	d.
Audley End	15	9	1	11	6	10	6	1	1	0
Saffron Walden						11	0	1	2	0
Ashdon Halt						11	9	1	3	3
Bartlow via Saffron Walden						12	3 *	1	4	6 *

* Higher fares were charged when travelling via Shelford or Cambridge; first class fares were also available by these routes.

Excursions

The excursion and special traffic offered by the GER to the Saffron Walden branch cannot be compared with the programme enjoyed by lines serving holiday centres. Special traffic was slow to materialize and patronage on excursions varied considerably according to the time of year, destination and not the least the weather. When the line opened agricultural and other manual workers wages were low and it was to the middle and upper classes of the town that the railway excursion appealed to most of all. Gradually alterations came and the introduction of paid holidays and additional leisure periods brought the price of the railway excursion within the pockets of almost all townspeople.

For example on 13th August, 1866, the GER ran an excursion from Saffron Walden to Hunstanton for the modest fare of 3s. 6d. and Saffron Walden passengers changed to the through train at Audley End. Despite the relatively low fare only 32 tickets were sold. In contrast, an excursion to Yarmouth on 7th August, 1869 attracted 142 passengers from Saffron Walden and 99 from Audley End.

In June 1890 an excursion from the town for a cricket tournament at Cambridge attracted 62 passengers, whilst the special for the Chelmsford Show sold only 32 tickets. The last seaside excursion of the year to Yarmouth on 5th September carried 150 passengers from the town including the Union School children, Sunday schools and members of the Change Ringing Association. The GER also issued, during that year, special excursion fares at 4s. 6d. for the Lord

Mayor's Show, tickets being available from Saturday to Monday inclusive. On Wednesday 17th June, 1896, 112 passengers travelled from Saffron Walden on an excursion to Lowestoft. Of this total 95 were members of the Society of Friends Adult Sunday School.

Queen Victoria's Diamond Jubilee on Tuesday 22nd June, 1897 was declared a public holiday and the GER entered into the spirit of the occasion by making it possible for as many people to visit London by issuing return tickets to Liverpool Street. These were available on 22nd June and also from branch stations having a local train after departure of the normal connection to London so that passengers could wait at Audley End for the last up main line train on 21st June. The tickets were available for return on 22nd June or at any time up to 8.00 am on 23rd June. For the event a train departed Shelford at 4.20 am calling at all stations to Broxbourne connecting at Audley End with a special early train from Saffron Walden. A return service departed Liverpool Street at 2.25 am on 23rd June for Roydon and all stations to Shelford, with a connection from Audley End to Saffron Walden.

Two excursions during July 1901 to Clacton attracted 54 and 195 passengers but only 5 and 20 from Bartlow, the lower figures indicating an overcast day. The halcyon days continued and in August 1910, 35 people booked from Saffron Walden for the excursion to Felixstowe. In contrast, two weeks later 326 passengers booked tickets to Yarmouth.

Between the two World Wars the excursion programme available to residents of Saffron Walden included the usual East Anglian destinations and in addition Spalding, Lincoln and York. During World War II the excursion programme was abandoned and after hostilities the number of trips and variety of destinations were cut back severely. The final destinations afforded to the branch passengers were Southend, Clacton, Walton and Hunstanton but trippers had to change at Audley End or Bartlow to join the special trains for the onward journey.

Goods traffic

After the commencement of freight traffic on the line, from 27th November, 1865, the forecast made by Pierce proved to be correct for barley, wheat, hay, straw and vegetables formed the basic commodities conveyed by rail. Although these items were responsible for the highest receipts in the early years, fruit traffic gradually increased with considerable loadings at Bartlow. Most of the London fruit traffic was at one time routed over the branch but then wagons were conveyed via Shelford to Cambridge for outsorting for the onward journey. Sugar beet was occasionally dispatched from Saffron Walden to the British Sugar Corporation factories at Ely and Felsted after their opening in the late 1920s, but as the area for sugar beet cultivation was well to the south of the town, it was usually sent via Sibley's on the Thaxted branch. Despite the coming of the railway the malting industry in Saffron Walden was on the decline and by the 1870s only three maltsters were trading in the town compared with over a dozen in the first half of the century. However the largest brewery, the Anchor Brewery latterly run by J.W. and J.L. Taylor in the High Street, which had a malt house attached, and another built near the station, still required supplies of barley brought by rail in the late

19th and early 20th century. As well as being used for malting in the town, barley was also conveyed to the maltings at Bishop's Stortford, Sawbridgeworth and Ware. With the rationalization and closure of these maltings the commodity was later sent further afield to Bury St Edmunds, Godmanchester and Scotland.

Watercress was grown near Bartlow station for a short while and was conveyed by train to Saffron Walden and Cambridge markets but this traffic, although small, ceased when the stream became polluted. Milk was at one time sent from Bartlow and Audley End to Saffron Walden in the familiar 17 gallon churns. Sometimes the churns were sent further afield to Cambridge but in both instances two loads were dispatched daily, the first by the early morning train and the second late in the afternoon. Only one load was sent in the winter months.

Of the more specific items handled on the branch, Acrow Engineering Ltd and the Railway Foundry at Saffron Walden regularly dispatched machinery by rail. When Acrow's moved their premises a mile east of the town in 1953 they sent a greater tonnage than before by rail, including important equipment used in the construction of the Kariba Dam which was routed via Avonmouth Docks. The siding alongside Acrow's Coronation Works was on the down side of the line on the Bartlow side of Acrow Halt at 44 miles 52 chains from Liverpool Street. The points were in a trailing direction for down trains and the layout consisted of three sidings. In the latter years it was customary to use two mobile cranes for lifting pipework and other equipment on and off wagons. Acrow was developed by William A. de Vigier, a Swiss national, and the company was named after Arthur Crow, the solicitor who formed the company, with the aim of appearing at the top of every alphabetical list of industrial firms.

Special authority was given for a locomotive to propel 30 tank wagons from Saffron Walden to the Air Ministry siding or other wagons to Acrow siding. The following instruction regarding Acrow's siding appeared in the 1960 GE line Appendix:

> This siding is situated on the down side of the single line between Saffron Walden and Bartlow. Access to the siding is controlled by a two lever ground frame locked by an Annett's key on the Train Staff and Metal tickets.
> Owing to the steep falling gradient in the direction of Saffron Walden vehicles must not be left on the single line when the siding is being shunted.

The largest commodity by far received in the goods yard at Saffron Walden was coal. Even before the line opened a Mr Sawyer of Oxford Street, Sheffield wrote to Gibson in April 1864, requesting a site for a coal wharf at Saffron Walden station as he wished to set up a distribution centre for fuel in the area. Each October from 1866 an annual coal fair was held at Saffron Walden goods yard organized by John Stokes, a local coal and corn merchant. Special trains ran from Audley End to convey businessmen from surrounding areas to the event. Visitors were invited to inspect the seven or eight piles of coal stacked in the coal staithes whist being serenaded by the Volunteer Band. For customers ordering one ton or over of coal, free beer was supplied and this practice remained in force until 1914, although by then on a much reduced scale under the organization of Stoke's successor, G.H. Barnard. It is interesting to note that before the advent of the telephone in the town, Billy Bird, the coal foreman, had a 'blower' electric

'G4' class 0-4-4T No. 8105 pulls off long siding into the engine shed road with two wagons of locomotive coal on 27th June, 1936.   *H.C. Casserley*

'G5' class 0-4-4T No 67269 shunting Dix's siding at Saffron Walden on 2nd October, 1954.
                                                                                    Author's Collection

telephone direct from the office in the station yard to the company's coal office in the High Street. Other coal merchants at Saffron Walden were Mayhill & Sons, G.J. Horton and Barnard Brothers Ltd. Later additions were Coote & Warren and the Co-operative Wholesale Society. Coote and Warren were also at Bartlow. Additional imports received at Saffron Walden included seed potatoes from Scotland, animal foodstuffs and fertilizers for local farms, agricultural machinery and 'smalls' traffic for local shops and warehouses.

Livestock handled by the freight services was two-way traffic and in the early years horse traffic was often conveyed in wagons attached to passenger trains. Horse traffic was also generated by the Essex or Puckeridge Foxhounds, which often met in the area, and, on rare occasions, by the West Suffolk Hunt. At the turn of the century this traffic declined and with the advent of motor vehicles after World War I, horseboxes were rarely seen on the branch. The one exception was regular traffic provided by a local family who bred horses and used the yard at Saffron Walden for conveyance of animals from the stud in the late 1920s until 1939. Cattle wagons were a common feature until the early 1950s for the regular conveyance of livestock to and from Saffron Walden market. Outgoing cattle were regularly sent to Bishop's Stortford market on Thursdays, Haverhill and sometimes Bury St Edmunds and Cambridge. Although livestock was handled, the area served by the branch was essentially arable farming and therefore crops provided a greater proportion of goods receipts.

Brief reference has already been made of the importance the branch played in the two world wars. World War I saw the arrival and departure of thousands of army personnel to and from the various training camps in the area. As well as handling the many troop trains, the station and goods yard staff offloaded and loaded thousands of tons of provisions, equipment and heavy arms together with army horses which arrived from all parts of Britain. World War II was entirely the opposite for instead of men and materials, fuel oil was the essential traffic.

Oil storage sidings for the Air Ministry were installed early in 1939 to serve underground pipelines to various military establishments. Situated on the up side of the line at 44 miles 22 chains, entry was via facing points in the down direction. The fuel depot contained two sidings capable of taking six wagons each alongside the discharge platforms. During World War II 498 trains were handled in the sidings, but by 1949 they were out of use.

Mention must be made of the railway horses allocated to Saffron Walden goods yard for shunting and haulage of delivery carts. For many years they were stabled at the Railway Arms as the railway possessed no stables of its own. A small rental was paid by the Great Eastern to the licensee for the use of the facility. The shunting horse finally disappeared from Saffron Walden in 1920.

The only mechanical aids available to goods staff at Saffron Walden were the fixed cranes of 1 ton 10 cwt capacity located on the loading dock served by Dix's siding and another in the goods shed. After World War II assistance was given by a road mobile crane, which was joined by a second in 1957 when it was often used at Acrow sidings. In addition to the 15 tons wagon weighbridge in the yard, there was a 6 tons cart weighbridge. Cartage in the area was the responsibility of the railway company, latterly in LNER and BR days using four road motors and eight road trailers.

The following goods facilities were available at the branch stations:

Audley End   Loading gauge
                                Loading dock
                                2 paved cattle pens
                                Water supply for animals in transit
                                Goods shed with storage capacity for 300 quarters of grain
                                2 x fixed cranes, 1 ton capacity each
                                Weighing machine 1 ton 2 cwt capacity
                                3 wagon turntables (later reduced to 2)
                                Facility for dealing with furniture vans on wheels
                                Facility for lifting vans by crane power

Saffron Walden   Loading gauge
                                Loading dock, restricted to 14 ft in length
                                2 paved cattle pens
                                Water supply for animals in transit
                                Goods shed with storage capacity for 250 quarters of grain
                                2 x fixed cranes 1 ton 10 cwt capacity each
                                Wagon weighbridge 15 tons capacity
                                Cart weighbridge 6 tons capacity
                                Weighing machine 1 ton 2 cwt capacity
                                4 wagon turntables (later reduced to 3)
                                Company cartage
                                Facility for dealing with furniture vans on wheels
                                Facility for loading round timber by arrangement
                                Siding capacity for 112 wagons

Bartlow   Loading gauge
                                Loading dock
                                Paved cattle pen
                                Weighing machine 5 cwt capacity
                                Lock-up for small packages
                                Facility for dealing with furniture vans on wheels

The latest time for loading goods for delivery the next day was 6.00 pm Mondays to Fridays and 3.00 pm Saturdays, later amended to 5.00 pm and 12.30 pm respectively.

The authorized loading of goods trains in 1870 was:

Class of locomotive	Goods trucks		Coal trucks		
	Down	Up	Down	Up	
First class*	25	25	21	21	382 tons gross, 250 tons nett
Second class	21	21	18	18	300 tons gross, 200 tons nett
Third class	16	16	14	14	252 tons gross, 160 tons nett
Fourth class	14	14	12	12	220 tons gross, 140 tons nett

* Including '417' class 0-6-0s.

The 1891 GER *Appendix to the Working Timetable* showed the following engine loads for freight traffic:

Class of locomotive	Goods trucks		Coal trucks	
	Down	Up	Down	Up
First class	25	25	21	21
Second class	21	21	18	18
Third class	16	16	14	14

The following classes were designated:

First class engines	477	0-6-0
	Y14	0-6-0
Second class engines	T26	2-4-0
	E10	0-4-4T
	M15	2-4-2T
Third class engines	'Little Sharpie'	2-4-0
	E22	0-6-0T
	140	0-4-2T

The later GER *Appendix to the Working Timetable* showed the following loads for freight traffic on the branch and the undermentioned locomotives regularly allocated to the line were classified as follows:

GER class	LNER class	Type	Classified
Y65	F7	2-4-2T	E
E22	J65	0-6-0T	H
Y14	J15	0-6-0	C
T26	E4	2-4-0	F
M15	F4	2-4-2T	D
S44	G4	0-4-4T	B

	Audley End-Saffron Walden				**Saffron Walden-Bartlow**			
Class of	*Down*		*Up*		*Down*		*Up*	
locomotive	*Mineral goods*		*Mineral goods*		*Mineral goods*		*Mineral goods*	
A	40	40	38	40	30	30	30	30
B	29	40	25	35	23	30	22	30
C	25	35	22	31	20	28	20	28
D	23	33	20	28	18	26	18	26
E	20	28	18	26	16	23	16	23
F	20	28	17	24	15	21	15	21
G	18	26	15	21	13	18	13	18
H	18	26	15	21	13	18	13	18

By 1942 the wagon limit of trains on the Saffron Walden branch was 50 vehicles, although trains of this length were never hauled. The full list of the authorized loads permitted was:

Audley End to Saffron Walden and Saffron Walden to Audley End			
	Minerals	*Goods*	*Empties*
No. 1 class goods engine	27	40	40
2	30	45	50
3	33	49	50
4	37	50	50
5	41	50	50
6	45	50	50

Saffron Walden to Bartlow and Bartlow to Saffron Walden			
	Minerals	*Goods*	*Empties*
No. 1 goods engine	18	27	36
2	20	30	40
3	22	33	44
4	24	36	48
5	27	40	50
6	30	45	50

Between Saffron Walden and Bartlow the 'C12' passenger tank engines could work 25 mixed wagons, of which not more than 10 were to be fully loaded.

Where passenger locomotives regularly hauled freight services, as at Saffron Walden, the 'C12', 'F7' and 'J65' classes were restricted to loads of eight mineral wagons less than a No. 1 goods engine. The 'E4', 'F4', 'F5', 'F6', 'G4' and 'G5' classes were to convey six mineral wagons, or equivalent, less than a No. 1 goods engine. The 'N7' class was equivalent to a No. 2 goods engine.

British Railways Eastern Region later amended the loads of class 'J' and 'K' freight trains, in most cases reducing the permitted loading.

Audley End to Saffron Walden and Saffron Walden to Audley End

	Heavy	Goods	Empties
No. 1 group engine	22	39	44
No. 2 group engine	25	44	50
No. 3 group engine	24	44	50
No. 4 group engine	31	50	50
No. 5 group engine	34	50	50
No. 6 group engine	39	50	50

Saffron Walden to Bartlow and Bartlow to Saffron Walden

No. 1 group engine	13	23	26
No. 2 group engine	17	30	34
No. 3 group engine	17	30	34
No. 4 group engine	20	35	40
No. 5 group engine	22	39	44
No. 6 group engine	24	42	48

The groups of engines which regularly worked over the branch were:

No. 1 group engine	E4 class	2-4-0
	C12 class	4-4-2T
	F4 class	2-4-2T
	F5 class	2-4-2T
	F6 class	2-4-2T
	J65 class	0-6-0T
	G5 class	0-4-4T
No. 2 group engine	J15 class	0-6-0
No. 3 group engine	N7 class	0-6-2T

The 'E4', 'F4', 'F5' and 'F6' classes were to convey five heavy wagons, or equivalent, less than the loads shown, whilst the 'J65' class conveyed seven wagons or equivalent less.

After the introduction of diesel traction Brush type '2' locomotives were restricted to a load of 44 wagons and the 204 hp diesel-mechanical shunting locomotives to 10 wagons between Audley End and Saffron Walden only.

Chapter Nine

Locomotives and Rolling Stock

The light construction of the SWR with its steep gradients and numerous curves restricted, to some degree, the choice of motive power. Fortunately the GER was endowed with suitable traction units for use on this and many other branch lines, and over the years a number of locomotives spent their last operational days working from Saffron Walden depot. From the 1880s until World War I only locomotives of 40 tons weight and under were permitted on the branch.

The LNER Engine Route Availability book permitted the following classes of tender locomotives on the branch: 'B12', for occasional working subject to a speed restriction of 30 mph, 'E4', 'J15', 'J19', 'J20' subject to speed restriction of 25 mph, 'J21' and 'K2' conforming to LNER loading gauge. Tank engine classes allowed on the line were 'C12', 'G5', 'J65' to 'J70' inclusive, 'N5', 'N7', 'Y1', 'Y3', 'Y5', 'Y6' and 'Y10'. Later the LNER and British Railways designated the line to Route Availability group 5 (RA5) then RA6, although RA5 locomotives were restricted to 30 mph and RA6 locomotives to 20 mph throughout. The introduction of main line diesel locomotives found authority for classes '12/2', '13/2', '16/2' and '17/3', later '31/0', '31/1' and '37' to work across the branch, subject to an additional restriction of 20 mph when passing over bridge No. 2107 between Audley End and Saffron Walden.

The first locomotive to run on the line was the *Little Eastern*, a small outside cylinder 0-4-0 saddle tank built by Manning, Wardle & Co. of Leeds and delivered on Hanson, the contractor's orders, to Saffron Walden in January 1865. She was immediately pressed into service hauling spoil and material trains alongside the horse-drawn wagons. *Little Eastern* also hauled the first through train of contractor's wagons on both the Audley End to Saffron Walden and Saffron Walden to Bartlow sections of line. Her principal dimensions were:

Cylinders	9½ in. x 14 in.
Motion	Stephenson with slide valves
Boiler pressure	140 psi
Coupled wheels	2 ft 9 in.
Wheelbase	4 ft 9 in
Weight	10 tons 10 cwt
Water capacity	250 gallons

Services on the opening of the line on 23rd November, 1865 were hauled by a Sinclair 'W' class 2-2-2 main line locomotive No. 60 in charge of driver Duce. Built by Slaughter, Gruning & Co. (Works No. 550) and delivered to the GER in June 1864, this relatively modern locomotive, one of the celebrated 'W' class, was obviously taken off important express work for the day to provide some prestige for the occasion and to give local officials and townspeople a first-hand inspection of one of the GER's latest main line engines. The engine was one of 31 express passenger locomotives, built by Fairburn & Co., Slaughter, Gruning

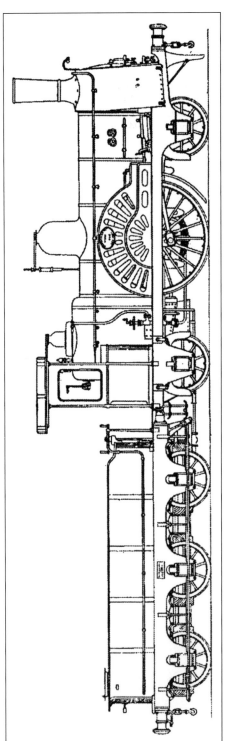

Above: Sinclair 'W' class 2-2-2 tender locomotive.

Right: Sinclair's famous 'W' class 2-2-2s were associated with the branch. No. 60 worked the first public train whilst Nos. 0290 and 0295 finished their working career from Saffron Walden. No. 0297 is an example of the locomotive used on the first through trains from Saffron Walden to Liverpool Street.
Author's Collection

& Co., Kitson & Co. and Schneider et Cie. No. 60 was renumbered 283 in 1870 and was rebuilt in May 1873. By coincidence two locomotives of the same class built by Kitson, and the last to remain in service Nos. 0290 and 0295 (Works Nos. 1205 and 1195 and built in September and August 1865 respectively) later ended their days on the line before being withdrawn in 1894. As Nos. 290 and 295 they had been rebuilt in October and November 1881 and were placed on the duplicate list by having an '0' prefix added to their running number in 1886. The leading dimensions of No. 60 as working on the Saffron Walden branch were:

Cylinders		16 in. x 24 in.
Motion		Stephenson with slide valves
Boiler	*Max. diameter*	3 ft 11^1/$_8$ in.
	Length	11 ft 9 in.
Firebox		5 ft 2 in.
Heating surface		
	Tubes 190 x 1^7/$_8$ in.	969.0 sq. ft
	Firebox	82.3 sq. ft
	Total	1,051.3 sq. ft
Grate area		15.7 sq. ft
Boiler pressure		120 psi
Leading wheels		3 ft 7 in.
Driving wheels		7 ft 1 in.
Trailing wheels		3 ft 7 in.
Tender wheels		3 ft 7 in.
Wheelbase		
	Engine	15 ft 0 in.
	Tender	11 ft 5 in.
Weight in working order		
	Engine	29 tons 5 cwt
	Tender	21 tons 15 cwt
	Total	51 tons 0 cwt
Water capacity		1,600 gallons

The detailed differences of Nos. 0290 and 0295 from the above were:

Max. axle loading		13 tons 13 cwt
Weight in working order		
	Engine	32 tons 0 cwt
	Tender	23 tons 16 cwt
Water capacity		2,000 gallons

Certainly in the early years one of the diminutive 'X' class 2-4-0Ts was working the branch, in 1865 and 1866 No. 121 was the regular engine outbased at Saffron Walden, together with No. 123 which was transferred from Buntingford to Saffron Walden to take over the branch workings. No. 123 was followed by sister engines No. 120 and 122 the following year. Designed by Robert Sinclair, the total class of five locomotives was built at Stratford Works and originally put to service on the North Woolwich branch in December 1862. The engines were responsible for handling the branch services until 1880 when No. 121 was transferred to March for use on the construction trains on the Great Northern & Great Eastern

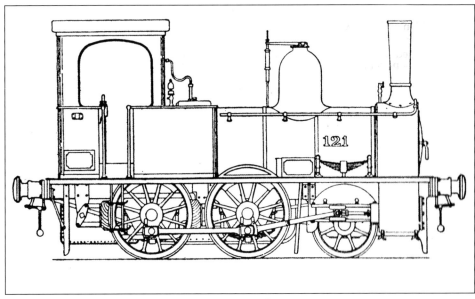

GER 'X' class 2-4-0T No. 121 designed by Robert Sinclair.

E.B. Wilson 'Jenny Lind' class 2-2-2 tender locomotive Nos. 105 and 107.

Joint Railway between Spalding and Sleaford. No. 120 remained at Saffron Walden and was withdrawn for scrapping in October 1880, whilst No. 121 was condemned in July 1882. No. 123 was scrapped in April 1882 after being badly damaged in a collision with a Great Northern Railway tank locomotive on the Victoria Park branch in East London. In 1884 No. 122 was renumbered 1220 and after being withdrawn from service in July 1885 it was sent to Peterborough and converted to a stationary boiler for the repair shops where it survived until 1907. The principal dimensions of the 'X' class were:

Cylinders	*2 outside*	12 in. x 18 in.
Motion		Stephenson with slide valves
Boiler	*Max. diameter*	3 ft 1½ in.
	Length	7 ft 7½ in.
	Firebox	3 ft 0 in.
Heating surface		
	Tubes 80 x 2 in.	288.13 sq. ft
	Firebox	44.70 sq. ft
	Total	332.83 sq. ft
Grate area		6.4 sq. ft
Boiler pressure		120 psi
Leading wheels		3 ft 1 in.
Coupled wheels		4 ft 1 in.
Length of frame		18 ft 9¼ in.
Weight in working order		21 tons 8 cwt
Max axle loading		7 tons 15 cwt
Water capacity		545 gallons

In 1865 and 1866 'Jenny Lind' 2-2-2s Nos. 103, 105 and 107 were working some of the branch services. The use of the 'Jenny Lind' class in the Cambridge District alternated between the Saffron Walden and Sutton branches. Built by E. B. Wilson & Co., No. 103 appeared in June 1847 and 104 in September of the same year. Three further locomotives with slightly larger dimensions No. 105, 106 and 107 were built in October, November and December 1848 respectively. The class had an eventful career for No. 103 was derailed on 20th February, 1860 when approaching Tottenham with the 7.00 am train from Cambridge, the leading tyre on the locomotive fractured and derailed the train. Six people lost their lives including driver Rowell and fireman Cornwell. After they were relegated to branch line work, No. 103 appears to have been the regular branch locomotive but at times of maintenance was replaced by Nos. 105 and 107. No 107 collided with a horse on the Sutton branch on 16th July, 1866, the animal being killed but the locomotive tender sustained damage, which required repairs at Cambridge the following day. On 18th July, 1866 George MacAllan, the Cambridge district locomotive superintendent attended a meeting at Stratford to discuss the type of engines required to work the Sudbury, Saffron Walden and Sutton branches and presumably the '103' class were considered suitable for the latter branches for they continued to work the services. No 107 was again in trouble on 6th August, 1866 when working with the tender off No. 103, she derailed at Ely Sutton Branch Junction with the 8.10 am Sutton to Ely train. The class however, had an uneventful career when working the Saffron Walden branch. No. 103 was withdrawn from traffic in June 1874, 104 in July

1868, 105, in November 1867, 106 in October 1869 and No. 107 in April 1869. The leading dimensions were:

Cylinders		15 in. x 20 in.
Motion		Stephenson with slide valves
Boiler	Max. diameter	3 ft 6 in.
	Length	10 ft 6½ in.
		11 ft 0 in.*
	Firebox	4 ft 3 in.
		4 ft 6 in.*
Heating surface		
	Tubes 124 x 2 in.	720.0 sq. ft
	148 x 2 in.	920.0 sq. ft*
	Firebox	80.0 sq. ft
	Total	800 sq. ft
		1,000.0 sq. ft*
Grate area		12.7 sq. ft
Boiler pressure		120 psi
Leading wheels		4 ft 0 in.
Driving wheels		6 ft 0 in.
Trailing wheels		4 ft 0 in.
Wheelbase	Engine	14 ft 6 in.
		14 ft 7 in.*
Weight	Engine	23 tons 11 cwt
Max. axle weight		10 tons 19 cwt
Tender	Wheels	3 ft 6 in.

* Nos. 105 to 107

In the event of the non-availability of the 'X' class tank engines Gooch 'A' class 2-2-2Ts were used, including No. 22 which spent some time at Saffron Walden in 1866. Nos. 20 to 25 were built by the ECR between September 1851 and May 1852, whilst Longridge & Co., of Bedlington constructed Nos. 4, 5 and 6 and introduced them into traffic between April and October 1852. The engines had their water tanks placed under the barrel of the boiler. No. 22 was transferred to the duplicate list and renumbered 022 in January 1878 and was withdrawn from traffic in December 1879. The leading dimensions of the class were:

Cylinders		12 in. x 22 in.
Motion		Stephenson with slide valves
Boiler	Max. diameter	3 ft 1½ in.
	Length	10 ft 0 in.
	Firebox	3 ft 6 in.
Heating surface		
	Tubes 114 x 1⁷/₈ in.	554.0 sq. ft
	Firebox	70.0 sq. ft
	Total	624.0 sq. ft
Grate area		9.75 sq. ft
Boiler pressure		110 psi
Leading wheels		3 ft 8 in.
Driving wheels		6 ft 6 in.
Trailing wheels		3 ft 8 in.
Wheelbase		14 ft 0 in.
Max. axle loading		8 tons 10 cwt
Weight in working order		23 tons 17 cwt

Another class to cover the branch duties was E.B. Wilson 2-4-0s of the '193' class. Eight locomotives were introduced into service, Nos. 193 to 196 in December 1848, Nos. 197 and 198 in January 1849 and Nos. 199 and 200 in February 1849. They were supplied with six-wheel tenders and certainly Nos. 193, 195 and 196 spent some time working the Saffron Walden branch in 1866 and 1867. The principal dimensions of the class were:

Cylinders		15 in. x 22 in.
Motion		Stephenson with slide valves
Boiler	*Max. diameter*	3 ft 8 in.
	Length	10 ft 10 in.
	Firebox	4 ft 2¾ in.
Heating surface		
	Tubes 150 x 1⁷/₈ in.	863.8 sq. ft
	Firebox	81.3 sq. ft
	Total	945.1 sq. ft
Grate area		12.6 sq. ft
Leading wheels		3 ft 8 in.
Coupled wheels		5 ft 0 in.
Max. axle loading		10 tons 15 cwt
Wheelbase		
	Engine	14 ft 8½ in.
Weight in working order		
	Engine	24 tons 3 cwt

Yet another veteran was 2-2-2 No. 65, which was sent to Saffron Walden on 10th July, 1866 to replace No 193. She was one of seven members of the '61' class express passenger engines built by Stothert & Slaughter and introduced as follows; Nos. 61 and 62 in February 1846, Nos. 63 and 64 in June 1846, Nos. 65 and 66 in August 1846 and No 67 in September 1846. By 1865 the class had been relegated from top link passenger work and were employed on cross-country and branch line duties. No. 65 was rebuilt in July 1868, placed on the duplicate list and renumbered 650 in 1875 before being withdrawn in June 1878. The leading dimensions of the '61' class were:

Cylinders		15 in. x 22 in.
Motion		Stephenson with slide valves
Boiler	*Max. diameter*	3 ft 9 in.
	Length	11 ft 3½ in.
Firebox		4 ft 8 in.
Heating surface		
	Tubes 152 x 1⁷/₈ in.	736.0 sq. ft
	Firebox	73.5 sq. ft
	Total	809.5 sq. ft
Grate area		13.82 sq. ft
Boiler pressure		90 psi
Leading wheels		3 ft 6 in.
Driving wheels		6 ft 0 in.
Trailing wheels		3 ft 6 in.
Wheelbase	*Engine*	12 ft 0 in.
Tender water capacity		1,350 gallons

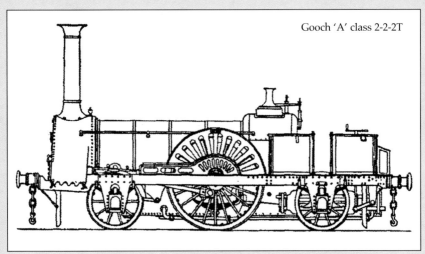

Gooch 'A' class 2-2-2T

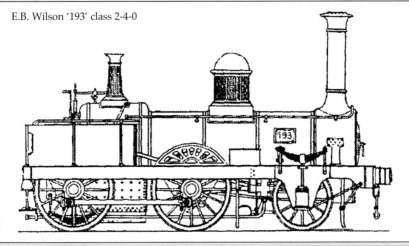

E.B. Wilson '193' class 2-4-0

Stothert & Slaughter '61' class 2-2-2 No. 65

With the transfer of 'X' class locomotives their place was taken by 'T7' class 0-4-2Ts, initially No. 12. Built between 1871 and 1875 especially for light branch traffic and designed by Samuel W. Johnson, the class totalled 15 in number. Later No. 16 replaced No. 12 and thereafter until about 1886 two members of the class were working the Saffron Walden branch services. The first three locomotives Nos. 81 to 83 were prototypes of the 'T7s' but were included in the class, differing from others in that their tanks held only 500 gallons of water and consequently the weight in working order was reduced to 30 tons 19 cwt. The last batch No. 15 to 19 built during the reign of William Adams at Stratford in 1875 had larger side tanks and only 148 tubes, which reduced the heating surface to 711.12 sq. ft. Instead of the Johnson fluted chimney Nos. 15 and 16 were fitted with the Adams plain taper chimney. Nos. 17 to 19 had round top dome covers and Ramsbottom safety valves over the firebox instead of the spring balance safety valves on the dome. As on the Buntingford branch the straight weatherboard originally fitted to the 'T7' class proved unpopular with footplate staff after the covered cabs of the 'X' class 2-4-0Ts. No. 12 was withdrawn in 1892 and No. 16 in 1894. The principal dimensions of the 'T7' class were:

Cylinders		15 in. x 20 in.
Motion		Stephenson with slide valves
Boiler	Max. diameter	3 ft 10 in.
	Barrel length	9 ft 1 in.
	Firebox	4 ft 4¾ in.
Heating surface		
	Tubes 204 x 1½ in.	754.0 sq. ft
	Firebox	76.0 sq. ft
	Total	830.0 sq. ft
Grate area		12.75 sq. ft
Boiler pressure		140 psi
Driving wheels		5 ft 3 in.
Trailing wheels		3 ft 7 in.
Wheelbase		14 ft 6 in.
Weight in working order		33 tons 12 cwt
		30 tons 19 cwt*
Max. axle loading		11 tons 8 cwt
		11 tons 7 cwt*
Water capacity		750 gallons
		500 gallons^

* Nos. 81 to 83

The absence of water supplies at Bartlow and Audley End meant delays were incurred regularly topping up the meagre tanks on the 'T7' class locomotives at Saffron Walden and in 1886 the GER decided to replace the tank engines on the branch. To this end, the two former Thetford & Watton Railway 0-4-2s Nos. 6 and 7, by now on the duplicate list and numbered 0806 and 0807, were transferred to Saffron Walden shed. The pair were built by Sharp, Stewart & Co. in 1876 (Works Nos. 2595 and 2596) for through train working between Bury St

'T7' class 0-4-2T designed by S.W. Johnson for light branch duties. No. 16 was one of the class which was outbased at Saffron Walden.   *LPC*

Former Thetford & Watton Railway 0-4-2 GER No. 0806, which with sister engine No. 0807 worked the Saffron Walden branch in the late 1880s.   *Author's Collection*

Edmunds and Swaffham. When the Thetford & Watton line was taken over by the GER, the pair were renumbered 806 and 807 and were transferred to Cambridge and Lynn respectively. Subsequently both were overhauled at Stratford Works and fitted with the Westinghouse brake and Ramsbottom safety valves in place of the spring balance type originally fitted. Painted in GER royal blue, the pair then worked the Saffron Walden branch satisfactorily until No. 0807 was withdrawn for scrapping in December 1890. No. 0806 lasted another year being withdrawn in December 1891. Former footplate staff who remember the men who worked on these locomotives, said the four-wheel tenders rode roughly and whenever possible the locomotives ran boiler first. The leading dimension of the former Thetford & Watton locomotives were:

Cylinders	2 inside	16 in. x 22 in.
Motion		Stephenson with slide valves
Boiler	Max. diameter	3 ft 10¾ in.
	Length	10 ft 0 in.
Firebox		4 ft 1¹/₈ in.
Heating surface		
	Tubes 192 x 1¾ in.	901.0 sq. ft
	Firebox	74.0 sq. ft
	Total	975.0 sq. ft
Grate area		11.5 sq. ft
Coupled wheels		5 ft 0 in.
Trailing wheels		3 ft 6 in.
Tender wheels		3 ft 6 in.
Wheelbase		
	Engine	13 ft 3 in.
	Tender	9 ft 6 in.
Weight in working order		
	Engine	25 tons 5 cwt
	Tender	14 tons 0 cwt
	Total	39 tons 5 cwt
Max. axle loading		10 tons 6 cwt
Water capacity		1,200 gallons

From time to time occasional visits were made by representatives of Samuel Johnson's No. 1 class, nicknamed 'Little Sharpies', as between October 1867 and August 1872 30 of the total of 40 locomotives were built by Sharp, Stewart. During the years 1889 and 1893 the whole class was rebuilt and most were then allocated to cross-country and branch line duties. Cambridge depot was host to 12 of the class for many years and although their allocated diagrams included workings to Norwich, Ipswich, Lynn, Peterborough and Colchester from the university city, they also covered branch line duties, either in the absence of the regular branch locomotive or when on high mileage and ready for shops. It was under these conditions that the Saffron Walden shed used the locomotives on the branch. In their final years most were drafted away to branch lines in Norfolk from where they were withdrawn from service between 1901 and 1913. The following were outbased at Saffron Walden at sometime during their career:

Thetford & Watton Railway 0-4-2 No. 807

Johnson 'Little Sharpie' 2-4-0 tender locomotive

GER No	GER duplicate No.	Date duplicated	Withdrawn
1	01	1911	1913
3			1904
27			1910
32			1901
36			1901
47			1908
48			1911
104	0104	1905	1911
106			1903
118			1903
160	0160	1901	1902
161	0161	1901	1901

The leading dimensions of the 'Little Sharpies' were:

Cylinders		16 in. x 22 in.
Motion		Stephenson with slide valves
Boiler	Max. diameter	4 ft 2 in.
	Length	9 ft 1 in.
Firebox		4 ft 6 in.
Heating surface		
	Tubes 223 x 1⅝ in.	881.24 sq. ft
	Firebox	78.00 sq. ft
	Total	959.24 sq. ft
Grate area		12.4 sq. ft
Boiler pressure		140 psi
Leading wheels		3 ft 8 in.
Coupled wheels		5 ft 8 in.
Tender wheels		3 ft 8 in.
Weight in working order		
	Engine	30 tons 15 cwt
	Tender	18 tons 6 cwt
	Total	49 tons 1 cwt
Max. axle loading		10 tons 10 cwt
Water capacity		1,184 gallons

The next class introduced to the branch had a long association of over 25 years of almost continuous service at Saffron Walden. In 1889 James Holden produced ten 6-coupled passenger tank engines for light branch line duties and classified the locomotives 'E22'. A further 10 with detailed differences were added in 1893. Many of the locomotives were sent to work on the Fenchurch Street to Blackwall line with the result they were quickly nicknamed the 'Blackwall Tanks'. The remaining locomotives were sent to lightly-laid branch lines on the GER system, including Stoke Ferry and Eye. By 1894 Cambridge depot had an allocation of three of the class and the policy of working the Saffron Walden branch with tender locomotives was partially superseded, with one of the trio sub-shedded at the Essex town. The little tank locomotives easily handled the two- or three-coach branch trains and were very popular with footplate staff. No. 150 the first of the class, and No. 152 had long sessions on

Holden 'E22' class 0-6-0T No. 152 worked alternatively between the Stoke Ferry branch and Saffron Walden. No. 152 is shown with front coupling rods removed running as a 2-4-0T.
LCGB/Ken Nunn Collection

The 12 members of the 'Y65' class 2-4-2Ts introduced in 1909/10 were the least successful of S.D. Holden's designs. Originally intended to replace the 'E22' class 0-6-0Ts on light branch duties they saw service on many lines but proved unpopular on all but a few. No. 1307 in full GER blue livery at Mildenhall was allocated to Cambridge and saw service on the Saffron Walden, Mildenhall and Ramsey High Street branches.   *Author's Collection*

the branch but not at the same time as they alternated between Stoke Ferry and Saffron Walden. In 1920 No. 152 was on branch duties but three years later was transferred to Stoke Ferry to take the place of No. 150, which then worked from Saffron Walden. Sister engines Nos. 151 and 158 were also known to have spent time on the branch services. The long-standing connections ceased in 1925 when the 'E22s', now classified 'J65' by the LNER departed to fresh pastures to make way for larger locomotives.

GER No.	LNER 1924 No.	Withdrawn
150	7150	June 1937
151	7151	July 1937
152	7152	October 1935
158	7158	March 1932

The principal dimensions of the class were:

Cylinders	2 inside	14 in. x 20 in.
Motion		Stephenson with slide valves
Boiler	Max. diameter	4 ft 2 in.
	Barrel length	9 ft 1 in.
	Firebox	4 ft 6 in.
Heating surface		
	Tubes 227 x $1^5/_8$ in.	909.4 sq. ft
	Firebox	78.0 sq. ft
	Total	987.4 sq. ft
Grate area		12.4 sq. ft
Boiler pressure		160 psi
Coupled wheels		4 ft 0 in.
Tractive effort		11,106 lb.
Length over buffers		27 ft 2 in.
Wheelbase		13 ft 4 in.
Weight in working order		36 tons 11 cwt
Max. axle loading		13 tons 3 cwt
Water capacity		650 gallons
Coal capacity		2 tons 10 cwt

The next locomotives associated with the Saffron Walden branch were the 'Y65' class 2-4-2Ts designed by S.D. Holden and introduced into service 1909/10. Built for light branch work to replace the 'E22' 0-6-0Ts, they were the least successful of Holden's 2-4-2 tank classes and after a time were relegated to auto-train working and other menial tasks. Twelve locomotives, Nos. 1300 to 1311, were constructed at Stratford Works and their small boilers and enormous cabs soon earned then the nickname of 'Crystal Palaces'. No. 1301 after a short spell at Buntingford transferred to Saffron Walden in December 1909 to work alongside the 'E22' class. The stay was short however, and it was later transferred to Walton-on-Naze. From time to time other locomotives of the class worked on the Saffron Walden branch but at no time did they gain the monopoly, for they usually worked alongside an 'E22' or other classes. Four other engines, utilized on the branch, were Nos. 1302, 1306, 1307 and 1308. No. 1306 was the regular locomotive around Grouping. By 1928 the class had left

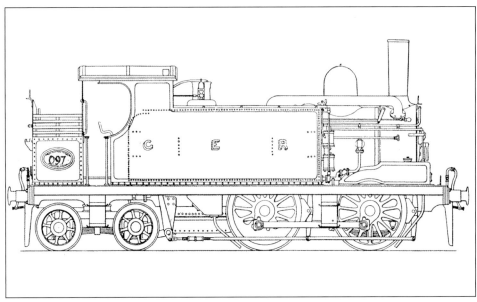

Massey Bromley 'E10' class 0-4-4T No. 097.

Massey Bromley 'E10' class 0-4-4T No. 097 ended its working life on Saffron Walden branch duties between 1901 and 1912.   *Author's Collection*

and been replaced by the 'G4' class 0-4-4Ts. The LNER redesignated the 'Y65s' to class 'F7' and renumbered them 8300 to 8311. No. 8301 and 8303 were sent to Scotland in 1931 to work on the Gifford, Lauder and Selkirk branches and the Galashiels to Peebles line. The last of the ex-Saffron Walden 'F7s' was condemned in November 1948 as No. 7093 from St Margarets depot, Edinburgh.

GER No.	LNER 1924 No.	LNER 1942 No.	LNER 1946 No.	Withdrawn
1301	8301	7593	–	April 1943
1302	8302	–	–	May 1931
1306	8306	–	–	April 1931
1307	8307	7596	–	June 1943
1308	8308	7597	7093	November 1948

The leading dimensions of the 'F7' class were:

Cylinders	2 inside	15 in. x 22 in.
Motion		Stephenson with slide valves
Boiler	Max. diameter	3 ft 11½ in.
	Length	9 ft 1 in.
	Firebox	4 ft 6 in.
Heating surface		
	Tubes 199 x 1⅝ in.	797.2 sq. ft
	Firebox	75.7 sq. ft
	Total	872.9 sq. ft
Grate area		12.2 sq. ft
Boiler pressure		160 psi
Leading wheels		3 ft 6 in.
Coupled wheels		4 ft 10 in.
Trailing wheels		3 ft 6 in.
Tractive effort		11,607 lb.
Length over buffers		30 ft 11 in.
Wheelbase		19 ft 6 in.
Weight in working order		45 tons 14 cwt
Max. axle load		14 tons 3 cwt
Water capacity		1,000 gallons
Coal capacity		2 tons

Interspersed with the comings and goings of the 'E22' and 'Y65' classes, the GER sent a Massey Bromley 0-4-4T to end its working life at Saffron Walden on relatively light duties. No. 097, which had been placed on the GER duplicate list in 1905, was built at Stratford Works in 1879 as one of 60 class 'E10' passenger tank locomotives. The class was employed on the intensive suburban services from Liverpool Street and Fenchurch Street and after displacement by larger locomotives, some later emigrated to country sheds. From 1887 to 1896 locomotives were rebuilt with a new boiler and other detailed differences. The railway company was evidently short of locomotives and the 'E10s' additional power compared with the 'E22' and 'Y65' classes meant that during its stay on the branch from 1910 to 1912 it was invariably booked on the mixed passenger and freight diagram. As No. 97 the locomotive had hardly distinguished itself

'F4' class 2-4-2T No. 7580 was regularly outbased at Saffron Walden shed for the branch workings in the 1930s. Here she is shown with stove pipe chimney at Stratford in 1930.

Author's Collection

'F4' class 2-4-2T No. 7174 at Saffron Walden on 27th June, 1936.   *H.C. Casserley*

in its career for it had twice derailed, once on 30th August, 1882 near Leiston on the Aldeburgh branch and again on 15th May, 1883 between Wrabness and Parkeston. She was also experimentally fitted in 1901 with Holden's patent apparatus for burning liquid fuel but this was later removed. The leading dimensions of No. 097 were:

Cylinders		16½ in. x 22 in.
Motion		Stephenson with slide valves
Boiler	Max. diameter	4 ft 2 in.
	Length	9 ft 1 in.
	Firebox	4 ft 11³/₈ in.
Heating surface		
	Tubes 223 x 1⁵/₈ in.	881.24 sq. ft
	Firebox	84.81 sq. ft
	Total	966.05 sq. ft
Grate area		13.9 sq ft
Boiler pressure		160 psi
Wheelbase		20 ft 2 in.
Frame length		26 ft 6 in.
Coupled wheels		4 ft 10 in.
Trailing wheels		2 ft 10 in.
Max. axle loading		15 tons 13 cwt
Weight in working order		44 tons 17 cwt
Water capacity		1,000 gallons

The strengthening of the permanent way on the branch allowed the GER motive power superintendent to relieve the regular branch locomotive undergoing repairs or washout with the 'M15' and later 'M15R' rebuilds on Saffron Walden branch services. Initially designed by T.W. Worsdell the first locomotive entered service in 1884. Three years later 40 were working but they proved troublesome and their excessive fuel consumption, partly caused by the incorrect setting of the Joy's valve gear, led to the nickname 'Gobblers'. When James Holden became mechanical engineer of the GER he removed the Joy's valve gear and fitted the more conventional Stephenson's valve gear. Between 1903 and 1909 a further 120 locomotives were built and put to service on the London suburban services. From 1911 until 1923 the GER rebuilt 30 locomotives with boilers of 180 psi pressure and brass-rimmed parallel chimneys and classified them 'M15R'. Withdrawal of the 1884 to 1887 batch commenced in 1913 and the remainder were later condemned by the LNER, the final locomotive going in 1929. Some of Holden's 1903 to 1909 series were withdrawn in the same year although it was 1956 before the 'F4s', as they were reclassified by the LNER, were extinct. The 'M15' ('F4') and 'M15R' ('F5') made spasmodic appearances at Saffron Walden after World War I when Cambridge sent a locomotive down as relief. By 1921 one locomotive was regularly allocated to the branch to be followed by a second in 1924. Four years later they were displaced by the 'G4' class 0-4-4Ts after which they took up the role of relief engine until the early 1950s. The 'F4s' and 'F5s' were not popular on the Saffron Walden branch as they were prone to slipping on Ashdon bank with even the lightest of loads. The wear and tear on the flanges caused by the curvature of the line was a problem, which appears not to have troubled other four-coupled tank locomotives. Locomotives known to have worked from Saffron Walden included:

GER No.	LNER 1924 No.	LNER 1946 No.	BR No.	Withdrawn
F4 class				
79	7079	7187	67187	August 1955
93	7093	–	–	May 1932
105	7105	–	–	March 1935
174	7174	7170	–	April 1948
573	7573	7153	–	July 1951
580	7580	–	–	July 1937
799	7799	–	–	March 1926
F5 class				
790	7790	7219	67219	November 1956

The leading dimensions of the 'F4' class were:

Cylinders	2 inside	17½ in. x 24 in.
Motion		Stephenson with slide valves
Boiler	Max. diameter	4 ft 2 in.
	Barrel length	10 ft 2½ in.
	Firebox	5 ft 5 in.
Heating surface		
	Tubes 227 x 1⁵/₈ in.	1,018.0 sq. ft
	Firebox	98.4 sq. ft
	Total	1,116.4 sq. ft
Grate area		15.3 sq. ft
Boiler pressure		160 psi
Leading wheels		3 ft 9 in.
Coupled wheels		5 ft 4 in.
Trailing wheels		3 ft 9 in.
Tractive effort		15,618 lb.
Length over buffers		34 ft 10 in.
Weight in working order		51 tons 11 cwt
Max. axle loading		14 tons 18 cwt
Water capacity		1,200 gallons
Coal capacity		3 tons 10 cwt

The detailed differences of the 'F5' class were:

Heating surface		
	Tubes 227 x 1⁵/₈ in.	1,018.0 sq ft
	Firebox	96.7 sq. ft
	Total	1,114.7 sq ft
Grate area		15.2 sq. ft
Boiler pressure		180 psi
Tractive effort		17,571 lb.
Weight in working order		53 tons 19 cwt
Max. axle loading		16 tons 0 cwt

In 1928 the GER 'S44' class, reclassified 'G4' by the LNER displaced the 'Gobblers' at Saffron Walden. Forty locomotives were built to the design of James Holden between 1898 and 1901 at Stratford, especially for handling the heavy suburban trains on the Enfield and Chingford lines. At one time they were rostered for a Saturday-only working from Liverpool Street to Audley End. By the late 1920s they were struggling with the heavy suburban trains and were subsequently replaced by the 'F4', 'F5' and 'F6' class 2-4-2s and 'N7' class 0-6-2Ts. Withdrawal of the class began in 1929 by which time Nos. 8105, 8114, 8122 and 8139 had arrived at Cambridge, with two out-based at Saffron Walden. They remained the regular branch locomotives for almost a decade, performing all that was asked of them, although on occasions an 'F4' 2-4-2T deputized including No. 7105 in 1934. No. 8139 transferred away to March depot in January 1938, where she was employed as last of the class on carriage shunting duties prior to withdrawal at the end of the year.

GER No.	LNER 1924 No.	Withdrawn
1105	8105	January 1938
1114	8114	September 1931
1122	8122	December 1932
1139	8139	December 1938

The principal dimensions of the 'G4' class were:

Cylinders	2 inside	17 in. x 24 in.
Motion		Stephenson with slide valves
Boiler	Max. diameter	4 ft 2 in.
	Barrel length	10 ft 0 in.
	Firebox	5 ft 5 in.
Heating surface		
	Tubes 225 x 1⅝ in.	989.1 sq. ft
	Firebox	94.9 sq. ft
	Total	1,084.0 sq. ft
Grate area		15.3 sq. ft
Boiler pressure		160 psi
Coupled wheels		4 ft 11 in.
Trailing wheels		3 ft 1 in.
Tractive effort		15,988 lb.
Length over buffers		32 ft 8 in.
Wheelbase		22 ft 4 in.
Weight in working order		53 tons 8 cwt
Max. axle loading		17 tons 1 cwt
Water capacity		1,349 gallons
Coal capacity		2 tons 10 cwt

In September 1931 the LNER authorities arranged for a twin-engine 6-cylinder gear-driven 200 hp Sentinel steam railcar to work trials over the Mildenhall and Saffron Walden branches, with a view to possible replacement of steam locomotives and hauled coaches on lightly-used services and thereby effecting economies. The vehicle chosen was No. 2283 *Old Blue* (Works No. 7823) built to diagram 98, which had entered service on 17th October, 1930,

In 1928 James Holden's GER 'S44' class 0-4-4Ts, then reclassified 'G4' by the LNER commenced working the Saffron Walden branch services. A total of 40 locomotives were built between 1898 and 1901at Stratford for handling heavy suburban trains on the Enfield and Chingford lines. At one time they were rostered for a Saturday-only working from Liverpool Street to Saffron Walden. No. 1122 shown at Stratford in GER grey livery was one of four to work the Essex branch and was renumbered 8122 before withdrawal from traffic in December 1932.

LCGB/Ken Nunn Collection

James Holden GER class 'S44' 0-4-4T later classified 'G4' by the LNER. Members of this class were used on the Saffron Walden branch in the early 1930s.

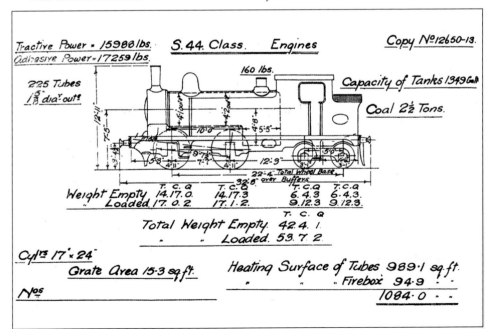

Sentinel twin-engine 6-cylinder gear-driven 200 hp steam railcar No. 2283 *Old Blue* built to diagram 98 (Sentinel Works No. 7823) standing at Middlesbrough in 1932. This car ran trials on East Anglian branch lines, including the Saffron Walden line in September 1931. *J. Armstrong*

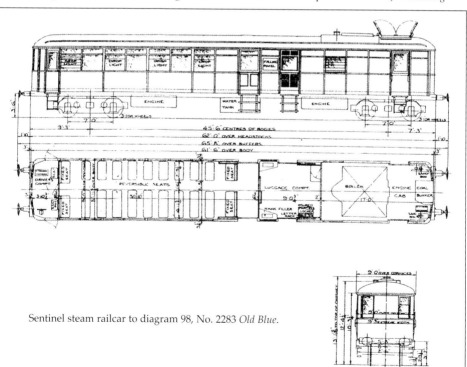

Sentinel steam railcar to diagram 98, No. 2283 *Old Blue*.

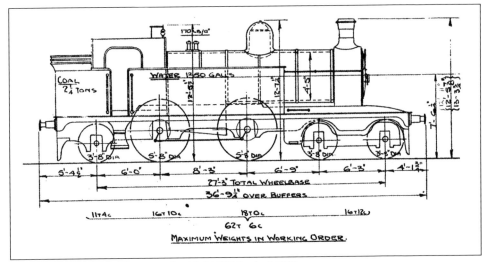

Ivatt GNR 'C2' class 4-4-2T, reclassified 'C12' by the LNER.

'C12' class 4-4-2T No. 4509 at Saffron Walden on 24th June, 1938. To the left permanent way staff appear to be discussing a problem with the track. No. 4509 was one of four members of the class which worked on the Saffron Walden branch and although being of GNR lineage and thus 'foreign' to local enginemen proved popular as they handled both passenger and freight services with ease, despite their 5 ft 8 in. driving wheels. No. 4509 was built as GNR No. 1509, before being renumbered by the LNER 4509. She was later renumbered in the 1946 scheme to 7367 and subsequently by BR to 67367 before being withdrawn from traffic in August 1958.

Author's Collection

painted green and cream. Initially allocated to Guisborough on the former North Eastern section of the LNER, the car then spent six months at St Margarets, Edinburgh before working five days of trials at Norwich from 14th to 19th September, 1931 and then at Ipswich on 19th and 20th of the month. *Old Blue* then took up trial duties at Cambridge from 21st to 25th September before heading back to Guisborough from where she was withdrawn on 8th September, 1941. Evidently the trials from Cambridge were unsuccessful for its suitability was questionable, as mixed trains ran on both the Mildenhall and Saffron Walden branches and also between Huntingdon and St Ives, and no further attempt was made to introduce the steam railcars.

After the withdrawal of the 'G4' class 0-4-4Ts the LNER appeared loath to re-employ the 'F4' and 'F5' class 2-4-2Ts for any lengthy period and subsequently three Ivatt 'C12' class 4-4-2Ts were allocated to Cambridge in 1938 with two sub-shedded at Saffron Walden to work the branch. They were originally introduced between 1898 and 1907 for use on Great Northern Railway services in the London suburban area and also in the West Riding of Yorkshire. The trio Nos. 4509, 4520 and 4534, although 'foreign' motive power to local enginemen proved worthy of their easy task and despite their 5 ft 8 in. diameter driving wheels rarely slipped on Ashdon bank, even with freight trains. By 1943 No. 4502 had joined her sisters after working on the Midland & Great Northern line from Yarmouth Beach. Typical duties in July of that year showed Nos. 4502 and 4534 working the branch passenger and goods diagrams, No. 4509 on the Cambridge to Saffron Walden freight train, whilst No. 4520 was spare at Cambridge. Because of increased oil traffic passing over the branch to the Air Ministry siding the whole line was reballasted; No. 4534 was used extensively on this job and saw little passenger work. Under the 1946 LNER renumbering scheme the 'C12s' were renumbered, 4502 becoming 7360, 4509 to 7367, 4520 to 7375 and 4534 to 7385 although it was November 1946 before the latter received her new number. Under nationalization, former LNER locomotives had 60,000 added to their numbers and the four Saffron Walden stalwarts became Nos. 67360, 67367, 67375 and 67385. The combination of the war years with consequential reduction in maintenance left the 'C12' class engine rather the worse for wear. On Saffron Walden's hard water they tended to prime, despite the addition of molasses in the tanks but remained popular with footplate staff. Their days were numbered on the branch, however, for after investigation the decision was taken to introduce push-and-pull trains in 1951. After their removal from the Saffron Walden line, Nos. 67360, 67367 and 67385 were retained at Cambridge and worked on the Stour Valley line to Sudbury and Marks Tey, whilst No. 67375 was transferred to March. By 1953 the quartet were based at Bury St Edmunds and working to Long Melford and Cambridge. Three locomotives were withdrawn in 1955 but No. 67367 remained in service until August 1958, when she was withdrawn from her home territory at Grantham. As No. 4509, this locomotive had worked the last train on the former Great Northern Railway (GNR) Stamford to Wansford branch on 29th June, 1929.

GNR No.	LNER 1924 No.	LNER 1946 No.	BR No.	Withdrawn
1502	4502	7360	67360	January 1955
1509	4509	7367	67367	August 1958
1520	4520	7375	67375	April 1955
1534	4534	7385	67385	April 1955

The leading dimensions of the 'C12' class were:

Cylinders	2 inside		18 in. x 26 in.
Motion			Stephenson with slide valves
Boiler	Max. diameter		4 ft 5 in.
	Barrel length		10 ft 1 in.
	Firebox		5 ft 6 in.
Heating surface			
	Tubes 213 x 1¾ in.		1,016.0 sq. ft
	Firebox		103.0 sq. ft
	Total		1,119.0 sq. ft
Grate area			16.25 sq. ft
Boiler pressure			170 psi
Leading wheels			3 ft 8 in.
Coupled wheels			5 ft 8 in.
Trailing wheels			3 ft 8 in.
Tractive effort			17,900 lb.
Length over buffers			36 ft 9¼ in.
Wheelbase			27 ft 3 in.
Weight in working order			62 tons 6 cwt
Water capacity			1,350 gallons
Coal capacity			2 tons 5 cwt

The GER 'G69' class, later designated 'F6' by the LNER, represented the final development of the 2-4-2Ts designed by S.D. Holden. Built at Stratford Works in 1911 and 1912 the class was readily distinguishable from the 'M15' and 'M15R' classes because of the windows in the cab side sheets. Soon after Grouping the entire class was fitted with vacuum ejectors and their wooden cab roofs replaced by roofs of steel incorporating a sliding ventilator. Representatives of the class only appeared on the Saffron Walden branch after World War II when one or two displaced from the London suburban services were transferred to Cambridge. As with the 'F4' and 'F5' classes they only appeared on the branch in the event of the non-availability of a 'C12' class 4-4-2T or a 'G5' class 0-4-4T. Locomotive known to have deputized included No. 67221, 67222, 67227 and 67237. In most cases the stay at Cambridge was not prolonged and they were soon transferred to other depots in East Anglia.

GER No.	LNER 1924 No.	LNER 1946 No.	BR No.	Withdrawn
62	7062	7221	67221	October 1957
63	7063	7222	67222	August 1955
68	7068	7227	67227	May 1958
8	7008	7237	67237	August 1955

The principal dimensions of the 'F6' class were:

Cylinders	2 inside	17½ in. x 24 in.
Motion		Stephenson with slide valves
Boiler	Max. diameter	4 ft 2 in.
	Barrel length	10 ft 2½ in.
	Firebox	5 ft 5 in.
Heating surface		
	Tubes 227 x 1⅝ in.	1,018.0 sq. ft
	Firebox	96.7 sq. ft
	Total	1,114.7 sq. ft
Grate area		15.2 sq. ft
Boiler pressure		180 psi
Leading wheels		3 ft 9 in.
Coupled wheels		5 ft 4 in.
Trailing wheels		3 ft 9 in.
Tractive effort		17,571 lb.
Length over buffers		34 ft 10 in.
Wheelbase		23 ft 0 in.
Weight in working order		56 tons 9 cwt
Max. axle loading		17 tons 3 cwt
Water capacity		1,450 gallons
Coal capacity		3 tons

Push-and-pull services commenced in July 1951 with motive power supplied by three 'G5' class 0-4-4Ts. The transformation took over a week to complete and during that time the 'G5s' shared duties with a 'C12' class locomotive. Wilson Worsdell designed the locomotives for the North Eastern Railway (NER) and 110 of these class 'O' engines were built between 1894 and 1901. On Grouping they were re-designated class 'G5' by the LNER and in August 1938 No. 2093 was transferred from its native North-East to Stratford to work the Seven Sisters to Palace Gates branch service, to be followed by No. 1882 the following January. The two were subsequently fitted with compressed air-operated push-and-pull gear in January and February 1939 respectively and replaced the 'F7' class 2-4-2Ts on that service. No. 1780 joined the other two at Stratford in May 1944 and after fitting for auto-train working, took up duties on the Epping to Ongar service. Nos. 1780 and 1882 returned to the North-East from November 1947 until May 1948 when they again took up duties at Stratford. Under the LNER renumbering scheme No. 1780 became 7269 in January 1946, No. 1882 became 7279 in June and No. 2093 became 7322 in November of the same year. By the time the trio transferred to Cambridge, they had received BR numbers 67269, 67279 and 67322.

As with the 'C12' class it was normal for two locomotives to cover the branch duties, whilst the third received maintenance or was spare at Cambridge. The 'G5s' found the two-coach push-and-pull sets well within their capabilities but during their six years reign on the branch the footplate staff viewed them with mixed feelings. When propelling the train, the locomotive could only run with the regulator shut or fully open which made the speed of the train difficult to control, especially when the fireman, as well as his normal duties, had to alter

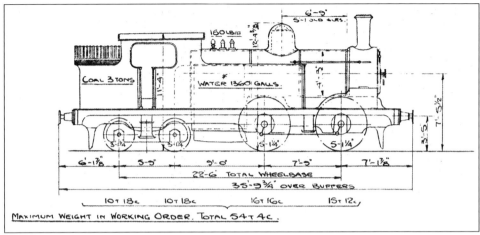

Wilson Worsdell NER 'O' class 0-4-4T, later reclassified 'G5' by the LNER.

'G5' class 0-4-4T No. 67279 at Audley End preparing to leave with a train for Saffron Walden in 1955. One of the 110 class 'O' locomotives introduced by Wilson Worsdell for the North Eastern Railway between 1894 and 1901, No. 1882 now designated to class 'G5' by the LNER was transferred from her native territory in January 1939 to work with sister locomotive No. 2093 on the Seven Sisters to Palace Gates service, where the pair were equipped with compressed air push-and-pull gear. Joined by a third member of the class the trio later worked on the Epping to Ongar branch before No. 1882, by now renumbered by the LNER to 7279, briefly returned north from November 1947 to May 1948. No. 7279 renumbered by BR to 67279 was withdrawn from service in November 1956.   *Author's Collection*

the cut-off to compensate. The local crews decided to overcome the problem by installing a bolt to stop the regulator from opening beyond first port. The bolt solved the problem for a short time and then unfortunately had the habit of shearing off. After various modifications this procedure was abandoned when one day a bolt sheared off and flew across the cab just missing the fireman. The 'G5s' also had a habit of throwing out big end cotter pins. The local permanent way staff made quite a collection of them before presenting the remnants back to their motive power colleagues. The period the 'G5s' were at Saffron Walden was not without incident. In March 1954 No. 67269 sustained a damaged buffer beam and frame after being in collision with No. 67322 in the shed. No. 67322 was in trouble later in the year when working a Saffron Walden to Audley End train. The push-and-pull control failed and the train ran through the branch platform at Audley End and almost finished up running through the trap siding and down the embankment. With the arrival of the 'N7' class 0-6-2Ts the 'G5s' were immediately displaced from the branch and placed in store at Cambridge shed before being withdrawn.

NER No.	LNER 1924 No.	LNER 1946 No.	BR No.	Withdrawn
1780	1780	7269	67269	October 1956
1882	1882	7279	67279	November 1956
2093	2093	7322	67322	November 1956

The principal dimensions of the 'G5' class were:

Cylinders	2 inside		18 in. x 24 in.
Motion			Stephenson with slide valves
Boiler	Max diameter		4 ft 3 in.
	Barrel length		10 ft 3 in.
	Firebox		5 ft 6 in.
Heating surface			
	Tubes 205 x 1¾ in.		995.0 sq. ft
	Firebox		98.0 sq. ft
	Total		1,093.0 sq. ft
Grate area			15.6 sq. ft
Boiler pressure			160 psi
Coupled wheels			5 ft 1¼ in.
Trailing wheels			3 ft 1¼ in.
Tractive effort			17,200 lb.
Length over buffers			35 ft 9¾ in.
Wheelbase			22 ft 6 in.
Weight in working order			54 tons 4 cwt
Max. axle loading			16 tons 16 cwt
Water capacity			1,360 gallons
Coal capacity			3 tons

During August 1956 'N7/3' class 0-6-2T No. 69720, built at Doncaster in April 1928 (Works No. 1687) was borrowed from Stratford shed to conduct clearance trials over the Saffron Walden branch. The outcome was successful for in October 1956 'N7/5' class 0-6-2T No. 69651, built at Gorton in February 1927, and 'N7/3' class Nos. 69690 and 69692, built by William Beardmore & Co. in

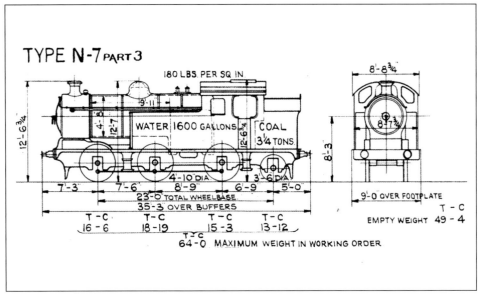

LNER 'N7/3' class 0-6-2T.

LNER 'N7/5' class 0-6-2T.

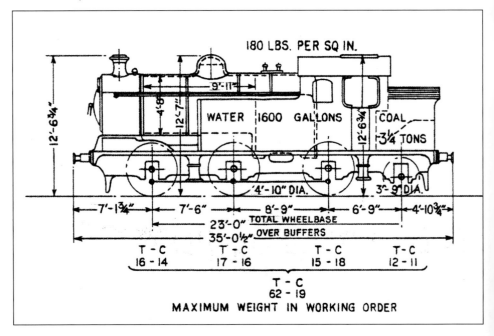

August 1927 (Works Nos. 313 and 315 respectively), fitted with vacuum control gear, were transferred to Cambridge for push-and-pull working on the Saffron Walden branch and the 'G5' class 0-4-4Ts were immediately displaced. Before transfer to Cambridge the 'N7s' had worked from Annesley, Kings Cross and Neasden sheds. As with the 'G5s' it was usual to keep two locomotives out-based at Saffron Walden with the other undergoing maintenance or spare at Cambridge. With their superior tractive effort, the 'N7s' were masters of any task required on the branch. Footplate crews were enthusiastic with their new acquisitions and considered them the best tank locomotives to work from Saffron Walden. The three were kept in excellent condition and performed admirably. The reign of the 'N7s' was unfortunately shortened for on 7th July, 1958 diesel railbuses replaced steam traction on passenger services. One 'N7' and a push-and-pull unit, however, covered failures in the following week after which diesel traction reigned supreme. Their push-and-pull days over the trio were transferred to Stratford, from where Nos. 69651 and 69690 were withdrawn on 13th January, 1961. No. 69692 was one of the last of the class to be withdrawn on 9th September, 1962, the last day of steam working on the former GER lines south of March.

LNER 1924 No.	LNER 1946 No.	BR No.	Withdrawn
873	9651	69651	January 1961
2618	9720	69720	November 1960
2650	9690	69690	January 1961
2652	9692	69692	September 1962

The principal dimensions of the 'N7/3' and 'N7/5' classes as working on the Saffron Walden branch were:

Cylinders	2 inside	18 in. x 24 in.
Motion		Walschaerts with 9 in. piston valves
Boiler	Max. diameter	4 ft 8 in.
	Barrel length	9 ft 7 in.
	Firebox	6 ft 0 in.
Heating surface		
	Tubes 132 x 1¾ in.	599.6 sq. ft
	Flues 18 x 5 in.	231.2 sq. in.
	Firebox	107.3 sq. in.
	Total evaporative	938.1 sq. ft
	Superheater	
	elements 18 x 1³/₃₂ in.	134.2 sq. ft
	Total	1,072.3 sq ft
Grate area		17.7 sq. ft
Boiler pressure		180 psi
Coupled wheels		4 ft 10 in.
Trailing wheels		3 ft 6 in.*
		3 ft 9 in.†
Length over buffers		35 ft 3 in.*
		35 ft 0½ in.†
Tractive effort		20,512 lb.
Wheelbase		23 ft 0 in.

'N7/3' class 0-6-2T No. 69690 hauling the 11.15 am Saturdays-only Audley End to Bartlow train approaching Bartlow on 14th June, 1958.   *G.R. Mortimer*

Audley End to Saffron Walden train arriving at Saffron Walden behind 'N7/5' class 0-6-2T No. 69651 on 14th June, 1958.   *G.R. Mortimer*

Weight in working order	64 tons 0 cwt*
	62 tons 19 cwt†
Max. axle loading	18 tons 19 cwt*
	17 tons 16 cwt†
Water capacity	1,600 gallons
Coal capacity	3 tons 5 cwt

* N7/3 class. † N7/5 class.

One of the most celebrated classes of locomotives to work on the Saffron Walden branch was the GER 'T26' class, nicknamed 'Intermediates'. A total of 100 were built to the design of James Holden between 1891 and 1902. Most were assigned to mixed traffic duties, long cross-country routes and slower traffic on the main lines. From about the turn of the century until Grouping a member of the class was allocated to Saffron Walden, and during this period worked the through train to and from Liverpool Street. This included the haulage of the 6.00 pm train from London, which was formed of 14 coaches, the first six for Saffron Walden, the next six for Hertford and two for Buntingford, the last eight coaches being dropped off at Broxbourne. On Saturdays the Saffron Walden portion was one composite coach less. The LNER classified the class 'E4' but in the late 1920s and early 1930s many were scrapped. By 1936 Cambridge only had an allocation of two and their visits to the branch were infrequent. In 1942 the class was reduced to 18 in total, of which 11 were at Cambridge. From then until their final demise representatives of the 'E4' class occasionally worked on the Saffron Walden line deputizing for a failed 'C12' or 'G5' class tank engine. The last locomotive to be withdrawn No. 62785, condemned in December 1959, was restored to its former glory as GER No. 490 and is now part of the National Railway Collection. The following locomotives are known to have worked across the Saffron Walden branch when allocated to Cambridge depot:

GER No	LNER 1924 No.	LNER 1946 No.	BR No.	Withdrawn
409	7409	2794	62794	August 1955
417	7417	–	–	January 1930
424	7424	–	–	January 1929
427	7427	2780	62780	September 1955
430	7430	–	–	April 1926
432	7432	–	–	July 1929
433	7433	–	–	April 1927
434	7434	–	–	December 1933
436	7436	–	–	June 1929
438	7438	–	–	May 1926
454	7454	–	–	June 1928
455	7455	–	–	March 1934
456	7456	–	–	December 1928
457	7457	–	–	June 1931
458	7458	–	–	August 1937
459	7459	–	–	March 1935
460	7460	–	–	April 1929
461	7461	–	–	September 1931
463	7463	2781	62781	January 1956
477	7477	2783	62783	December 1954

'E4' class 2-4-0 No. 62788 waits at Audley End with the branch train on 8th September, 1956. To the left is long siding and the run-round loop.   *R.C. Riley*

'E4' class 2-4-0 No. 62788, fitted with side window cab when it worked the Darlington to Penrith and Tebay services, stands at Audley End with the branch train on 8th September, 1956.
                    R.C. Riley

GER No	LNER 1924 No.	LNER 1946 No.	BR No.	Withdrawn
478	7478	2784	62784	May 1955
479	7479	–	–	March 1938
482	7482	–	–	September 1929
490	7490	2785	62785	December 1959
494	7494	2787	62787	November 1956
496	7496	2788	62788	March 1958
500	7500	–	–	June 1936
501	7501	–	–	October 1938
502	7502	–	–	January 1939
503	7503	2790	62790	January 1956
504	7504	–	–	November 1938

The principal dimensions of the 'E4' class were:

Cylinders	2 inside	17½ in. x 24 in.
Motion		Stephenson with slide valves
Boiler	Max. diameter outside	4 ft 4 in.
	Barrel length	10 ft 0 in.
	Firebox	6 ft 0 in.
Heating surface		
	Tubes 242 x 1⁵/₈ in.	1,063.8 sq. ft
	Firebox	100.9 sq. ft
	Total	1,164.7 sq. ft
Grate area		18.0 sq. ft
Boiler pressure		160 psi
Leading wheels		4 ft 0 in.
Coupled wheels		5 ft 8 in.
Tractive effort		14,700 lb.
Length over buffers		48 ft 2 in.*
Wheelbase		16 ft 6 in.
Weight in working order		40 tons 6 cwt
Max. axle loading		14 tons 3 cwt
Tender		
	Wheelbase	12 ft 0 in.
	Wheel diameter	4 ft 1 in.
	Weight in working order	30 tons 13 cwt
	Water capacity	2,640 gallons
	Coal capacity	5 tons

* Engine and tender

In the 1880s Samuel Johnson's '417' class 0-6-0 tender locomotives regularly worked across the Saffron Walden branch with the goods service from Cambridge. Originally introduced between 1867 and 1869 and built by Neilson & Co. and the Worcester Engine Co., the 60 locomotives built were numbered 417 to 476 and initially worked main line goods trains, but on the introduction of the '477' and 'Y14' class 0-6-0s were relegated to pick-up freights and branch line work. The various members of the class allocated to the Cambridge District worked out their last years on the branch. The first of the class was withdrawn in 1888 and scrapping continued every year, with the exception of 1897, until 1899.

'417' class 0-6-0s introduced by Samuel Johnson after displacement from main line duties were employed on Saffron Walden branch freight workings to and from Cambridge. No. 446 built by the Worcester Engine Co. is typical of the class.   *Author's Collection*

The survivors after 1891 were placed on the duplicate list by having an '0' prefix added to their running number. The principal dimensions of the class were:

Cylinders	*2 inside*	16½ in. x 24 in.
Motion		Stephenson with slide valves
Boiler	*Max. diameter outside*	4 ft 2 in.
	Length	10 ft 0 in.
	Firebox	5 ft 5 in.
Heating surface		
	Tubes 203 x 1¾ in.	957.6 sq. ft
	Firebox	94.9 sq. ft
	Total	1,052.5 sq. ft
Grate area		15.27 sq. ft
Boiler pressure		140 psi
Driving wheels		5 ft 3 in.
Tender wheels		3 ft 7 in.
Wheelbase		
	Engine	15 ft 3 in.
	Tender	9 ft 0 in.
Weight in working order		
	Engine	30 tons 15 cwt
	Tender	21 tons 17 cwt
	Total	52 tons 12 cwt
Max. axle loading		11 tons 5 cwt
Water capacity		1,740 gallons

The next class to be associated with the Saffron Walden branch goods workings to Cambridge, was the '477' class 0-6-0s, designed by Samuel Johnson and dating from 1871 to 1873. Numbered in the series 477 to 526, the class came from a variety of builders: Beyer, Peacock; Robert Stephenson; Dübs; Nasmyth Wilson; and the Yorkshire Engine Co. All were rebuilt between 1888 and 1895. By the time they were used on the Saffron Walden branch, the engines had relinquished their main line goods turns and were relegated to branch line and secondary duties. Nos. 477 to 496 were placed on the duplicate list by having an '0' prefix added to the running number in 1894, whilst Nos. 497 to 506 were similarly treated in 1896. The remaining locomotives still in service were added to the duplicate list in 1899, and the survivors were withdrawn between 1897 and 1902. The leading dimensions of the class were:

Cylinders	2 inside		17 in. x 24 in.
Motion			Stephenson with slide valves
Boiler	Max. diameter outside		4 ft 2 in.
	Barrel length		10 ft 0 in.
	Firebox outside length		5 ft 5 in.
Heating surface			
	Tubes 223 x 1⅝ in.		980.0 sq. ft
	Firebox		94.9 sq. ft
	Total		1,074.9 sq. ft
Grate area			15.27 sq. ft
Boiler pressure			140 psi
Coupled wheels			5 ft 2 in.
Tender wheels			3 ft 8 in.
Wheelbase			
	Engine		15 ft 6 in.
	Tender		12 ft 0 in.
Weight in working order			
	Engine		32 tons 13 cwt
	Tender		26 tons 5 cwt
	Total		58 tons 18 cwt
Max. axle loading			12 tons 6 cwt
Water capacity			2,038 gallons

For many years special freight trains, ballast trains and the through Cambridge goods service were hauled by the GER 'Y14' class 0-6-0s designed by T.W. Worsdell and introduced into traffic in 1883. Such was the success of the design that building continued until 1913. All except 19 of the class totalling 289 were built at Stratford Works with the rest constructed by Sharp, Stewart. The LNER re-designated the class to 'J15' and the ubiquitous locomotives were occasionally sent to Saffron Walden to deputize for the regular branch locomotive provided they were fitted with the Westinghouse brake or, in later years, the vacuum brake. Locomotives known to have worked the branch included:

GER No.	LNER 1924 No.	LNER 1946 No.	BR No.	Withdrawn
508	7508	5428	–	August 1949
509	7509	5429	–	November 1950
510	7510	5430	65430	January 1956
511	7511	5431	65431	March 1951
516	7516	5435	65435	October 1956
520	7520	5437	–	September 1950
523	7523	5438	65438	June 1958
526	7526	5439	–	November 1951
527	7527	5354	–	February 1951
529	7529	–	–	December 1931

GER No.	LNER 1924 No.	LNER 1946 No.	BR No.	Withdrawn
530	7530	5355	–	April 1951
531	7531	–	–	August 1928
532	7532	5356	65356	April 1957
535	7535	–	–	March 1936
536	–	–	–	August 1923
546	7546	5474	65474	February 1960
547	7547	5475	65475	September 1959
548	7548	5476	65476	September 1962
549	7549	5477	65477	February 1960
553	7553	5451	65451	September 1959
555	7555	5453	65453	August 1962
559	7559	5457	65457	February 1962
563	7563	5461	65461	April 1960
570	7570	5468	65468	September 1959
571	7571	5469	65469	August 1962
642	7642	5442	65442	May 1958
645	7645	5445	65445	August 1962
646	7646	5446	65446	December 1960
805	7805	–	–	April 1928
806	7806	–	–	October 1939
813	7813	5350	–	February 1951
825	7825	5352	–	May 1948
826	7826	–	–	April 1929
831	7831	–	–	November 1936
832	–	–	–	August 1923
833	7833	5359	65359	December 1955
834	7834	5360	–	November 1947
835	7835	–	–	September 1936
836	7836	5361	65361	September 1962
837	7837	5362	–	July 1951
838	7838	–	–	July 1934
839	7839	–	–	July 1936
840	7840	5363	–	August 1949
842	7842	–	–	November 1934
843	7843	5364	–	June 1949
845	7845	–	–	December 1938
847	7847	5366	65366	June 1952
848	7848	5367	–	January 1950
849	7849	5368	–	May 1948
851	7851	–	–	October 1936
856	7856	–	–	October 1936
857	7857	5374	–	November 1950
887	7887	5390	65390	December 1958
888	7888	5391	65391	December 1958
897	7897	5396	–	March 1951
908	7908	5403	–	August 1947

GER No.	LNER 1924 No.	LNER 1946 No.	BR No.	Withdrawn
911	7911	5405	65405	August 1958
913	7913	5406	–	April 1951
920	7920	5410	–	February 1948
921	7921	5411	–	April 1948
924	7924	5413	–	November 1950
928	7928	5417	65417	August 1956
929	7929	5418	–	March 1948
942	7942	5425	65425	October 1956

The leading dimensions of the 'J15' class were:

Cylinders	2 inside		17½ in. x 24 in.
Motion			Stephenson with slide valves
Boiler	Max. diameter		4 ft 4 in.
	Barrel length		10 ft 0 in.
	Firebox outside length		6 ft 0 in.
Heating surface			
	Tubes 242 x 1⁵/₈ in.		1,063.8 sq. ft
	Firebox		105.5 sq. ft
	Total		1,169.3 sq. ft
Grate area			17.9 sq. ft
Boiler pressure			160 psi
Coupled wheels			4 ft 11 in.
Tender wheels			4 ft 1 in.
Tractive effort			16,942 lb.
Length over buffers			47 ft 3 in.*
Wheelbase			
	Engine		16 ft 1 in.
	Tender		12 ft 0 in.
	Total		35 ft 2 in.
Weight in working order			
	Engine		37 tons 2 cwt
	Tender		30 tons 13 cwt
	Total		67 tons 15 cwt
Max. axle loading			13 tons 0 cwt
Water capacity			2,640 gallons
Coal capacity			5 tons

* Engine and tender

The advent of eight-coupled heavy goods locomotives on the Whitemoor to Temple Mills and other ex-GER main line freight workings from the 1930s gradually released ex-GER tender engines for cross-country and branch line freight services. The LNER 'J17' class 0-6-0s built to the design of J. Holden were initially introduced from 1900 as GER class 'F48' with round-topped fireboxes. Another batch of 30 were built with Belpaire fireboxes as class 'G58' from 1905 to 1911. Thereafter some of the earlier locomotives were rebuilt with Belpaire fireboxes and reclassified. After Grouping the 'F48s' became LNER class 'J16' and the 'G58s' LNER class 'J17' but by 1932 all the round-top firebox locomotives had been rebuilt with a Belpaire firebox as class 'J17' and class 'J16' became extinct. The LNER authorities were initially reluctant to allow the 'J17' class on the Saffron Walden branch and they were officially banned before World War II but when during hostilities the fuel trains serving the depot east of Saffron Walden were sometimes too heavy for the branch tank engine or 'J15' class to handle, the motive power authorities resorted to using a 'J17' class engine. Thereafter the class made sporadic visits to the line on the branch freight and engineers trains. The following 'J17s' were known to have worked across the branch:

GER No	LNER 1924 No.	LNER 1946 No.	BR No.	Withdrawn
1152	8152	5502	65502	September 1959
1156	8156	5506	65506	August 1960
1167	8167	5517	65517	May 1955
1170	8170	5520	65520	February 1961
1182	8182	5532	65532	February 1962
1187	8187	5537	65537	January 1957
1211	8211	5561	65561	December 1959
1215	8215	5565	65565	April 1960
1225	8225	5575	65575	February 1958
1239	8239	5589	65589	January 1961

The leading dimensions of the 'J17' class were:

Cylinders	2 inside	19 in. x 26 in.
Motion		Stephenson with slide valves
Boiler	Max. diameter outside	4 ft 9 in.
	Barrel length	11 ft 9 in.
	Firebox outside length	7 ft 0 in.
Heating surface		
	Firebox	117.7 sq. ft
	Tubes	863.5 sq. ft
	Flues	282.7 sq. ft
	Total evaporative	1,263.9 sq. ft
	Superheater	154.8 sq. ft
	Total	1,418.7 sq. ft
Tubes		156 x 1¾ in.
Flues		18 x 5 in.
Elements		18 x 1³/₃₂ in.
Grate area		21.24 sq. ft
Boiler pressure		180 psi
Coupled wheels		4 ft 11 in.
Tender wheels		4 ft 1 in.
Tractive effort		24,340 lb.
Length over buffers		50 ft 6 in.*
Wheelbase	Engine	17 ft 8 in.
	Tender	12 ft 0 in.
	Total	38 ft 0 in.
Weight in working order		
	Engine	45 tons 8 cwt
	Tender	38 tons 5 cwt
	Total	83 tons 13 cwt
Max. axle loading		16 tons 11 cwt
Water capacity		3,500 gallons
Coal capacity		5 tons

* Engine and tender

A stranger to the line on 2nd July, 1954 was ex-London Midland Region (LMR) class '4MT' 2-6-0 No. 43161, allocated to Yarmouth Beach, working a train of oil tankers from Saffron Walden to Newport (Essex). It then returned light engine to Saffron Walden to work the freight train back to Cambridge via Bartlow, a diagram normally worked by a 'J15' class 0-6-0. The class was introduced in 1947 to the design of H.G. Ivatt, grandson of the former GNR Locomotive Engineer H.A. Ivatt and many were allocated to the former Midland & Great Northern Railway route from Peterborough to Yarmouth and Norwich. After closure of the majority of those lines in 1959 the locomotives were reallocated to former GER sheds.

As mentioned in Chapter Five the closure of the Cambridge main line at Great Chesterford between 2.00 am and 11.00 pm on Sunday 16th June, 1957 necessitated the diversion of main line trains via the Saffron Walden branch. For the first time BR Standard class '7MT' 4-6-2s were permitted including Nos. 70003 *John Bunyan*, 70009 *Alfred the Great* and 70042 *Lord Roberts.* Designed by R.A. Riddles, the class of 55 was built at Crewe Works and introduced into service between 1951 and 1954 for mixed traffic services. The locomotives were initially allocated to the Eastern, Western and London Midland regions with the last five going to the Scottish Region. They revolutionized the passenger services on the ex-GER Liverpool Street to Norwich services and later Clacton interval services until displaced by diesel traction in 1961. Between May and September 1951 No. 70009 *Alfred the Great* spent time allocated to Nine Elms shed on the Southern Region where she was used on Waterloo to Bournemouth services, almost exclusively on the 'Bournemouth Belle' Pullman train.

BR No.	Name	Withdrawn
70003	*John Bunyan*	25th March, 1967
70009	*Alfred the Great*	21st January, 1967
70042	*Lord Roberts*	13th May, 1967

Another visitor to the branch on the Sunday of diversions was BR Standard class '4MT' 2-6-0 No. 76034, allocated to Stratford. Several 'B1' class 4-6-0s, including Nos. 61286 and 61301, were given special dispensation to haul trains over the branch on the same day. In addition No. 61371 was provided as a pilot to down trains and a banker to up workings between Saffron Walden and Bartlow, because of the severe gradients. Built to the design of Edward Thompson, the class was introduced from December 1942 with the first 10 being delivered by June 1944. Construction resumed in November 1946 with completion in June 1950 when 409 were in service. No. 61057, wrecked in an accident at Witham in 1950, was not replaced. The 'B1s' were the LNER standard design of mixed traffic locomotive working over the entire system from London and East Anglia to the former Great North of Scotland lines radiating from Aberdeen. Long after steam traction was barred south of March from September 1962, 'B1' class 4-6-0 No. 61119 worked a VIP special train to Saffron Walden on 30th May, 1963 entering the branch via Bartlow.

On 16th June, 1957 at least four members of the 'B17' class 4-6-0s traversed the Saffron Walden branch on diverted main line trains. The 73 members of the class were introduced from 1928 to supplement the 'B12' class 4-6-0s on GE

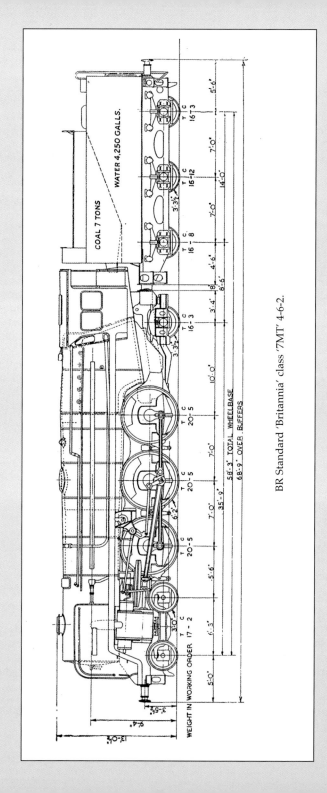

BR Standard 'Britannia' class '7MT' 4-6-2.

section express services and later locomotives were drafted to work heavy expresses on the Great Central section between Marylebone, Leicester, Nottingham, Sheffield and Manchester. In the last years they all returned to work in East Anglia. They were divided into sub-classes with minor differences in dimensions and those positively identified included:

LNER No.	Name	LNER 1946 No.	BR No.	Sub-class	Tender type	Withdrawn
2808	Gunton	1608	61608	B17/6	GE	March 1960
2827	Aske Hall	1627	61627	B17/6	GE	July 1959

Also on 16th June, 1957 class 'J20' 0-6-0 No. 64685, allocated to Bishop's Stortford depot, worked across the Saffron Walden branch with an engineering train. The largest of the ex-GER 0-6-0s the 'D81' class were designed by A.J. Hill and a total of 25 engines were introduced into traffic between 1920 and 1922. They were later classified 'J20' by the LNER. In accordance with the GE practice the new design had cylinders, valve gear, boiler and other parts interchangeable with the Holden '1500' class 4-6-0s. When introduced into traffic the 'J20s' were the most powerful 0-6-0 freight locomotives in Great Britain and retained this superiority until O.V.S. Bulleid introduced his 'Q1' class 0-6-0 s on the Southern Railway in 1942. Initially the 'D81s' and later 'J20s' worked the heavy Whitemoor to Temple Mills freight trains and although fitted with vacuum ejectors rarely worked passenger trains. However they were called to work excursion traffic in the 1930s including trains over the neighbouring Bishop's Stortford to Braintree branch.

Diesel traction

In 1957 British Railways placed orders with five manufacturers for the delivery of 22 lightweight diesel railbuses with a view to carrying out extensive trials on selected rural services. Five 150 hp 4-wheel diesel railbuses were built by Waggon und Maschinenbau GmbH at Donauworth, Germany, to lot No. 50482 for use on the Eastern Region routes. The first two, Nos. E79960 and E79961, travelled via the Zeebrugge to Harwich train ferry and were delivered to Stratford diesel depot on 31st March, 1958. The other three, Nos. E79962, E79963 and E79964, quickly followed and after trials on the Witham to Maldon East and Witham to Braintree branches were sent to Cambridge on 19th April to commence trials on the Saffron Walden, Mildenhall and Haverhill lines. Such was their success that they completely replaced steam traction on the Witham to Maldon East, Witham to Braintree and Saffron Walden branches from 7th July, 1958.

The bodies of these railbuses were designed to British Railways requirements and the underframe, power equipment, transmission and brake gear was similar to the Uerdingen type of railbuses then running on the German Federal Railway. The underframe consisted of channel-shaped cross beams welded to longitudinal girders whilst the body framing was of light steel structure. The side and roof panels were of light alloy sheets riveted to the body framing. The body of the railbus was suspended elastically and swung from four points of

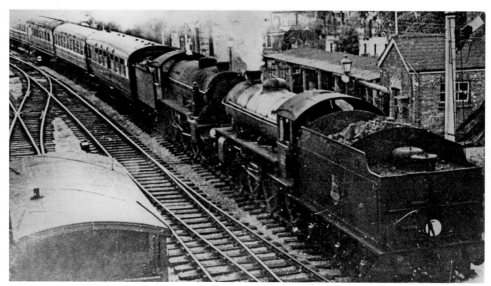

A poor quality view of a Liverpool Street to Cambridge main line train hauled by an unidentified 'B17' class 4-6-0 and piloted by 'B1' class 4-6-0 No. 61371 for the climb over the 1 in 75 of Ashdon bank awaits the 'right away' from Saffron Walden on Sunday 16th June, 1957.
D. Campbell

Another poor image taken on Sunday 16th June, 1957. Bridge renewal work at Great Chesterford resulted in the diversion of Liverpool Street to Cambridge main line trains across the Saffron Walden branch. An unidentified 'B17' class 4-6-0 pulls a train of mixed Gresley and Thompson coaches into Saffron Walden in the late afternoon. The fireman is preparing to hand over the Audley End to Saffron Walden Train Staff to the signalman.   *D. Campbell*

the running bogie frame. The floor, body, sides and roof were fitted with insulation materials against heat and sound. The interiors were lined with polished plywood panels while ceilings were painted ivory. The upper parts of the side windows were hinged to provide limited ventilation whilst curtains were also provided.

The centrally-situated doors on each side of the body were power operated and under the control of the driver. Push button operation for the guard or passengers was also used. In cases of emergency the doors were opened and closed by hand and once in service this appears to be the main method adopted by train crews to open and close doors at stations. Seating was arranged for 56 passengers in rows of two seats on one side of the car and three seats on the other in two saloons.

Initially the railbuses were unpopular at Saffron Walden; the limited seating capacity meant overcrowding during the morning and evening peak whilst riding on four wheels was uncomfortable and the swaying and bouncing at speeds over 30 mph was alarming. City commuters and others bemoaned the withdrawal of first class accommodation and many now motored to the railhead at Audley End instead of supporting the local branch line. At first the railbus failure rate was high and initially the 'N7' steam-hauled push-and-pull train was substituted, and on 14th July, 1958 diesel shunting locomotive No. D2010 hauling two coaches worked the first service of the day as the railbus had gearbox problems. Subsequent replacements came in the form of two-car diesel multiple units from Cambridge. These included Wickham, Craven and Metropolitan Cammell units.

After modification the railbuses settled down to work the branch, one working for two or three days before returning to Cambridge, Coldham Lane diesel depot for maintenance. The diagrams were:

Day 1 – 6.22 am Cambridge to Mildenhall, 7.36 am Mildenhall to Cambridge, thence to Chappel and Wakes Colne via the Colne Valley line, before working the Witham to Braintree branch. Stabled overnight at Braintree.
Day 2 – Worked the Braintree branch in the morning, then to the Witham to Maldon East branch. Stabled overnight at Maldon East.
Day 3 – Worked the Maldon East branch in the morning, then empty railbus to Marks Tey to work the 1.22 pm to Cambridge via the Colne Valley line. From Cambridge worked the 4.27 pm Cambridge to Mildenhall, 5.46 pm Mildenhall to Newmarket, 6.35 pm Newmarket to Mildenhall, 7.21 pm Mildenhall to Cambridge. Thence light diesel to Audley End and Saffron Walden. Stabled overnight at Saffron Walden.
Day 4 – Worked the Saffron Walden branch, then light diesel to Cambridge for maintenance.
Day 5 – Maintenance at Cambridge

The replacement railbus was brought to either Audley End or Bartlow by a Cambridge driver, who, after handing over to a Saffron Walden driver, returned with the relieved unit to Cambridge.

By the early 1960s traffic was reduced to such a degree that the railbus was adequate for all loadings and in off-peak times often ran empty between Saffron Walden and Bartlow. On market days and Saturdays, however, the central guard's compartment was overcrowded with prams, pushchairs, mail parcels

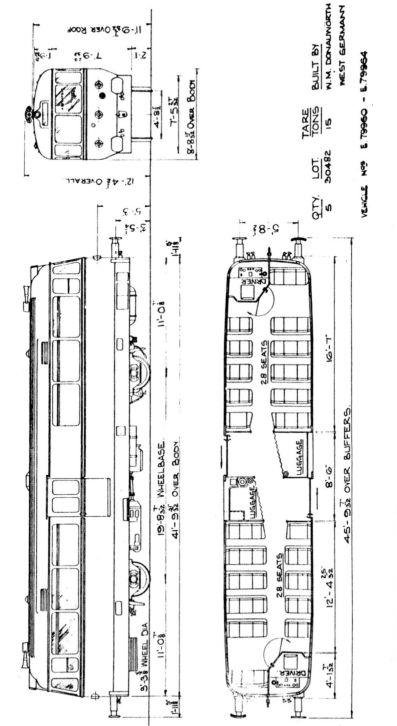

11'-9 23/32 OVER ROOF

7'-9 23/32

2:1

4'-8 7/8

8'-8 17/32 OVER BOOM

12'-4 7/8 OVERALL

1'-9 7/8

5'-3"

3'-5 5/8"

1'-8 5/8

11'-0 1/8

19'-8 7/8 WHEELBASE.

41'-9 3/8 OVER BODY.

3'-3 3/8 WHEEL DIA.

11'-0 1/8

1'-11 5/8

DRIVER

5'-8 1/2

28 SEATS

16'-7"

LUGGAGE

8'-6"

45'-9 5/32 OVER BUFFERS.

LUGGAGE

28 SEATS

12'-4 25/32

4'-1 5/32

DRIVER

2 SECONDS 56 SEATS

Waggon und Maschinenbau 150 hp 4 wheel railbus.

BUILT BY
N.M. DONAUWÖRTH
WEST GERMANN

TARE
TONS
15

QTY. LOT.
5   30482

VEHICLE Nos E.79960 - E.79964

SCALE

Feet

LOCOMOTIVES AND ROLLING STOCK 199

and even a pig or young calf being conveyed to market. The railbuses remained on the branch until the withdrawal of the passenger services and it fell to E79963 to operate the last Sunday service and the last passenger train on 6th September, 1964.

The closure of the Saffron Walden branch and the line from Witham to Maldon East, closed on the same day, rendered the German railbuses surplus to requirements. Their use on the Witham to Braintree branch was short-lived and they had been replaced by two-car diesel-multiple-units. All five railbuses were placed in store at Cambridge diesel depot until June 1965 when No. E79964 was sent north for trials on the Haltwhistle to Alston branch on the North Eastern Region. After failing dismally it joined 79961 then pre-fixed 'M' at Buxton, and both worked the Buxton branch. Nos. E79960, E79962 and E79963 were withdrawn from Cambridge in November 1966. No. M79961 was withdrawn from Buxton depot on 29th October, 1966, whilst M79964 lasted until April 1967, also being withdrawn from Buxton. Four of the five railbuses survived for further service on preserved railways, Nos. 79960 and 79963 going to the North Norfolk Railway at Sheringham and Nos. 79962 and 79964 to the Keighley & Worth Valley Railway.

The leading dimensions of the railbuses were:

Type	2-2 (1-A)
Weight in working order	18 tons
Wheelbase	19 ft 8¼ in.
Wheel diameter	3 ft 3½ in.
Length over buffers	45 ft 9¼ in.
Length over body	41 ft 10 in.
Width over body	8 ft 8½ in.
Inside width	8 ft 4 in.
Overall height from rail	11 ft 9 in.
Floor height from rail	4 ft 0 in.
Interior height floor to ceiling	7 ft 8 ¼ in.
Power weight ratio	10 hp/ton
Maximum speed, equivalent engine speed and gear ratio	*1st gear:* 8 mph, 1,800 rpm, 5.54
	2nd gear: 14 mph, 1,800 rpm, 2.99
	3rd gear: 24 mph, 1,850 rpm, 1.85
	4th gear: 33 mph, 1,800 rpm, 1.34
	5th gear: 45 mph, 1,850 rpm, 1.00
	6th gear: 55 mph, 1,600 rpm, 0.72
Fuel oil capacity	44 gallons
Fuel oil capacity for pre-heat unit	5½ gallons
Cooling water system	22 gallons
Control system	Pneumatic and electro-pneumatic
Brake	Compressed air – disc brakes
*Engine**	One horizontal 6-cylinder diesel 4-stroke engine underfloor Bussing Braunschweig 150 hp at 1,900 rpm
Transmission	Bussing type F K 9-2
Fluid coupling	Oil capacity 17½ to 18½ pints
Heating equipment	Dreiha hot water heating type W604, connected 6-cylinder engine cooling water system

* Three of the railbuses, Nos. E79961, E79963 and E79964 were later fitted with AEC A220X-type engines, which proved more reliable in service.

Railbus No. E79963 departing from Saffron Walden past the up home signal en route to Haverhill on 6th September, 1964. To the right of the main single line are long siding and the points to the former engine shed.   *Ken Paye*

Railbus No. E79963 departing from Saffron Walden in September 1963, and passing the goods yard. To the left is Dix's road and the adjacent loading dock.   *Ken Paye*

Saffron Walden station with a four-wheel 150 hp railbus at the platform. No E79963 was one of five used on Saffron Walden branch services from 7th July, 1958 until the branch closed to passenger traffic on 6th September, 1964.   *Ken Paye*

Railbus No. E79963 running between Audley End and Saffron Walden on the last day of passenger service, 6th September, 1964. Audley End up fixed distant signal is in the background.   *Ken Paye*

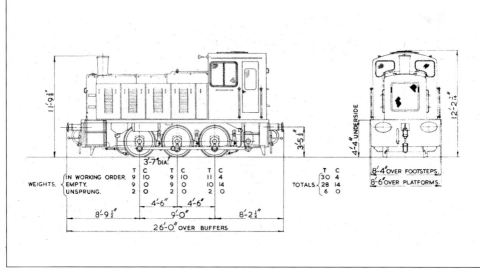

BR class '03' 204 hp 0-6-0 diesel-mechanical shunting locomotive.

Class '03' 0-6-0 diesel-mechanical shunting locomotive No. D2018 making for Saffron Walden after a goods trip working to Audley End in September 1964.   *Ken Paye*

With the withdrawal of steam traction from the line, a BR class '03' 204 hp diesel-mechanical shunting locomotive was allocated to Saffron Walden to work freight trips to either Audley End or Bartlow conveying outgoing wagons to be picked up by main line or cross-country goods services. Similarly incoming wagons were collected and worked to Saffron Walden. To achieve this, the shunting locomotive's diagram commenced at 6.53 am to work engine and brake van to Audley End. It then worked two round trips to Saffron Walden before departing for Bartlow at 12.15 pm. Returning at 2.00 pm, the locomotive then worked a further trip to Audley End before finishing. Most of the Cambridge-based locomotives, including Nos. D2001 to D2010, D2016, D2018 and D2028 worked the branch. The leading dimensions of the locomotives were:

Weight in working order	30 tons 4 cwt
Tractive effort	15,300 lb.
Wheelbase	9 ft 0 in.
Wheel diameter	3 ft 7 in.
Width overall	8 ft 6 in.
Length overall	26 ft 0 in.
Height overall	12 ft $2^7/_{16}$ in.
Minimum curve negotiable	2 chains
Maximum speed	28½ mph
Fuel tanks	300 gallons
Brakes	Compressed air, vacuum and hand
Sanding	Compressed air operated
Power equipment	8-cyl diesel engine – Gardner 8L3 type 204 hp at 1,200 rpm
Transmission	Fluid coupling – Vulcan Sinclair type '23', capacity 8½ gallons. Gearbox – Wilson Drewry CA5 R7 compressed air-operated. Reverse gear and final drive – type RF11

Demolition trains involved the use of Brush type '2' diesel-electric locomotives, class '31/0' and '31/1' as the wagons used for recovery of the permanent way and other assets required a locomotive to be in attendance at all times because of the steep gradients on the branch, especially between Saffron Walden and Bartlow. The leading dimensions of the Brush type '2' locomotives were:

Type	A1A-A1A
Weight in working order	104 tons*, 106 tons†
Tractive effort – maximum	42,000 lb.
Wheelbase	42 ft 10 in.
Wheel diameter	3 ft 7 in.
Bogie wheelbase	14 ft 0 in.
Bogie centres	28 ft 10 in.
Width overall	8 ft 9 in.
Length overall	56 ft 9 in.
Height overall	12 ft 7½ in.
Minimum curve negotiable	4½ chains
Maximum permitted speed	80 mph – D5520-D5534
	90 mph – D5535-D5699, D5800-on

Fuel tank capacity	550 gallons
Brakes	Compressed air and handbrakes on the locomotive. Vacuum brake equipment giving proportional air braking on the locomotive
Power equipment	*Mirlees 12-cyl* *English Electric diesel*
	diesel engine JVs engine 12SVT 1470hp
	12T 1,250hp at at 850 rpm
	900 rpm
Traction motors (4)	Brush DC type TM 73-68 4-pole force ventilated

* Mirlees engine. † English Electric engine.

The details quoted are those extant at the time the class were working the demolition trains. Many alterations were subsequently made.

Facilities and Staff

Saffron Walden shed was a sub-shed of Cambridge motive power depot, which always supplied locomotives to the line. In BR days the allocation code '31A' was given to Cambridge shed and the branch locomotives carried this shed plate on the smokebox door. The engine shed at Saffron Walden could accommodate one engine and the through road terminated on a turntable set in a cramped area between the shed and the high brick wall forming the abutment of the overbridge. The turntable was 40 ft in diameter, the smallest on the GER except for North Woolwich. This facility was removed in November 1953. The shed was brick built with wooden end gables. The roof ventilator extended the whole length of the structure and near one end was a wooden chimney, beneath which the locomotive chimney was positioned. The floor of the structure was paved with blue bricks and the inspection pit between the rails extended for most of the length of the shed. There were five arched bays on one side and four on the other, the buttresses between them being on the inside of the building. Three windows on each side had tall metal frames and as the shed in later years had no doors it was quite light inside, especially after the walls were whitewashed above shoulder height. The base of the water tower, which had two tall windows facing the track, formed an extension to the shed on one side. It contained a pumping engine and the tank supplied two cranes of distinctive pattern. These were located in the shed yard and the other at the Bartlow end of the station platform. A gas light was fixed to a bracket on the corner of the pump house and below it was a row of fire buckets. In the shed yard was a brick-built coaling stage adjacent to the shed road. On to this coal was offloaded and then re-shovelled into locomotive bunkers or tenders as required. Close to the stage was a receptacle for dry locomotive sand. A fireproof corrugated iron shed for oil and lamps stood in the angle between the shed and the base of the water tower.

When the line was opened only one set of footplate staff was stationed at Saffron Walden covering a full 12 hours shift. Following legislation on railway staff hours and the increase in traffic on the line, it was found necessary to allocate a second driver and fireman to the depot. By the 1880s the establishment was increased to four sets of footplatemen and two cleaners. The latter posts later alternated with one cleaner and one coalman. The cleaner or coalman was usually booked on at nights to coal and water the locomotives for the following day's duties.

In steam days the four sets of footplatemen shared two early and two later turns. Diagram 1 men signed on at 4.30 am to take up freight and passenger workings, whilst the second set signed on at approximately 5.45 am for passenger work only. The first set of men was relieved at about 12.30 pm by diagram 3 men, who took over passenger and freight workings for the afternoon. The final set of men relieved diagram 2 men at 2.45 pm, to work the remaining passenger services including the last train of the day. The two early turn sets of men were responsible for final preparation of their locomotives whilst the late turn men carried out disposal duties before handing over to the cleaner/coalman on nights.

During steam days when the 'C12' class 4-4-2Ts or other engines were used on the afternoon working, the locomotive was coupled and uncoupled from the coaching stock some 22 times during an eight hour shift by the locomotive fireman. Much time was thus saved with the introduction of push-and-pull working on the branch in 1951.

The locomotive foreman or, as he was later called, driver-in-charge, at Saffron Walden received a half day's extra pay per week for administrative duties which included the submission of drivers' tickets and coal and oil returns to the District Motive Power Office at Cambridge. The majority of drivers at Saffron Walden only signed the route knowledge sheets for the branch and occasionally to Cambridge via Whittlesford and or Linton. When the through service commenced to and from Liverpool Street, Saffron Walden drivers signed accordingly but when this was cut back to Bishop's Stortford the men followed suit and signed to the Hertfordshire town. Saffron Walden men later 'signed the road' to Haverhill and Cambridge, and Haverhill footplate staff signed for the Saffron Walden branch, over which they were responsible for working some of the freight services. Cambridge men also signed for the branch.

The drivers in GER days were strict with their fireman and cleaners, especially if Saffron Walden engines were not spotlessly clean. A common test was to wipe a clean rag along the footplate or the inside of the framing and wheels to make sure the cleaning had not been skimped. During the coal shortage in the 1920s, the cleaner and coalman were delegated to make briquettes from coal and cement to supplement the meagre coal supplies and cut up old sleepers for firelighters to light up the fire in the firebox.

In addition to other duties cleaners at one time emptied and refilled the footwarmers for the carriages, although when the coalman was appointed station staff carried out the work. The cleaner also offloaded the coal from wagons on to the coaling stage, a job later performed by the coalman.

Another aspect of this rural depot was boiler washing. As no facilities were on hand, a boiler washer and fitter travelled from Cambridge to carry out these tasks. After World War II, however, all boiler washing, tube cleaning and other remedial work was performed at Cambridge. Tube cleaning was for many years carried out by footplate staff at Saffron Walden and usually the senior fireman was paid four hours Sunday rate for the work.

View looking north from South Road overbridge facing towards Bartlow in 1910 showing from the left, the single main line protected by Saffron Walden up home signal. The branch train is stabled in long road and next to that is the carriage shed road with the carriage shed devoid of vehicles. The water crane and locomotive coaling stage are centre right beyond the water tank
GERS/Windwood Collection

A view of the single-road engine shed at Saffron Walden in 1910, with coaling stage to the left, water column and the water tank adjoining the shed building. The 40 feet diameter turntable is located in the space between the shed and South Road overbridge. *GERS/Windwood Collection*

As on most branch lines the motive power staff were 'characters' in their own right and a favourite tale often related is of one driver who was partial to pheasant for dinner. The Saffron Walden branch, passing as it did through various large estates, was rich with game birds as well as other wild animals venturing on to railway property. On many occasions the locomotive hit and killed a pheasant in full flight between Saffron Walden and Audley End. Noting roughly where the bird had fallen, our intrepid driver on arrival at Audley End removed his cap and stuffed it into his pocket or bag. The driver duly notified the signalman that he had lost his cap whilst leaning out of the side of the engine and requested the signalman to set the road out of the branch platform via the run-round loop so that he could set back towards Saffron Walden to rescue his headgear. The road duly set, the locomotive then ran light to the site of the incident where the pheasant was retrieved and the cap removed from pocket or bag and replaced on the driver's head. The locomotive then returned to Audley End to resume the booked working.

It appears the same ruse was attempted at Bartlow but the surprising regularity of the loss of the cap caused the signalmen to become suspicious and very often the 'trophy', if more than one bird, was shared. The coming of the push-and-pull working did not dampen the enthusiasm for game and our sympathies must lie with the fireman who had to uncouple the seven connections between engine and coaching stock and re-couple seven times on the return.

With the introduction of the railbuses on the branch the four firemen at Saffron Walden were transferred to Bishop's Stortford, Cambridge and other depots. The four drivers remained, three for the railbus and one for the diesel shunting locomotive. At first the railbus was stabled in the shed during the night but later stood on the main single line in the platform. The diesel shunting locomotive rarely visited the shed but was usually stabled in the siding opposite the platform. The withdrawal of the passenger services meant the transfer of a further three drivers leaving one man to handle the diesel shunting engine. Freight facilities were withdrawn on 28th December, 1964 and the shunting locomotive returned to Cambridge. Saffron Walden motive power depot was closed from the same date but the last driver remained for a further six months in a caretaker capacity before being transferred to Cambridge.

Drivers who served at Saffron Walden included William J. Baker who passed away in 1928 aged 80, David Faben who retired on 20th March, 1930 aged 65 years after nearly 50 years' service, 37 of them at Saffron Walden, and W.J.D. Green who died on 23rd November, 1938. Another character Alf Theobald, was said to handle his locomotive better after 'a few pints'. The final drivers at Saffron Walden included Reg Thake and Ken Brand who both transferred to Bishop's Stortford on the closure of the depot. Another Bishop's Stortford driver Albert Upton served at Saffron Walden as a fireman.

The Saffron Walden branch locomotive rarely travelled beyond the branch limits unless sent for changeover. It invariably travelled chimney first from Audley End to Bartlow and if it was received the wrong way round it was turned on the Saffron Walden turntable. If snow threatened Saffron Walden the signal box was kept open throughout the night and a light engine ran up and down the branch in an endeavour to keep the line clear.

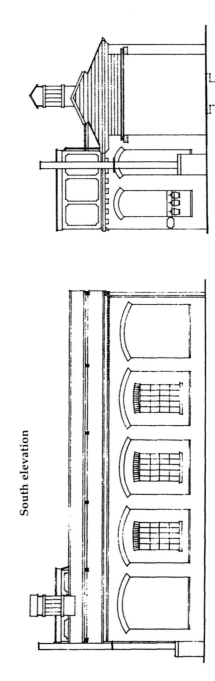

Saffron Walden engine shed

South elevation

West elevation

Courtesy GERS

Saffron Walden engine shed

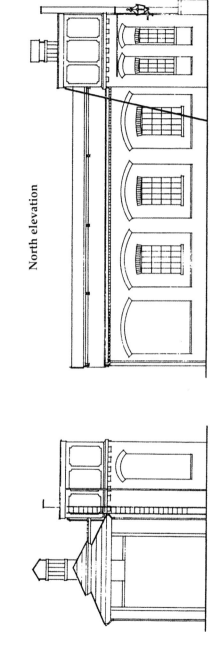

North elevation

East elevation

Courtesy GERS

Saffron Walden engine shed on 27th March, 1937 with 'G4' class 0-4-4T inside. Note the ornate gas lamps, which provided minimal illumination during periods of darkness.   *W.A. Camwell*

Saffron Walden engine shed from South Road overbridge on 4th August, 1952, showing the tank house with water tank raised aloft and the 40 ft diameter engine turntable which was removed in November 1953. Staff access to the shed was via the steps from the adjacent road but invariably footplate crews walked off the end of the station platform and under South Road bridge to the shed.   *D. Clayton*

Saffron Walden water was always regarded as hard for locomotive boilers and, except for engines based at the shed, few visiting footplatemen would use the supply to top up their locomotive tanks. The local men topped up the tank by the shed with water softening briquettes or molasses to stop the locomotive priming. One of the mixtures used was of a red base colour, which more often than not spread to other parts of the locomotive after a few days use on the branch. The supply was originally pumped from a well, but was later supplied by the local water company.

Initially the engine working the booked branch services carried no headlamp by day and one white light at the base of the chimney by night. Special trains only carried lights at night with the engine displaying a white light at the base of the chimney and another on the buffer beam, if fitted with a lamp bracket, or presumably attached to the coupling. By 1875 the headcode for ordinary trains was the same but special trains carried a white disc at the base of the chimney by day and two white lights at night. The branch headcode carried by locomotives hauling the branch trains in later GER days was a red light at the top of the smokebox by the chimney and a white light on the buffer beam. During daylight hours in place of the oil lamp a circular disc with red centre and white rim, was carried by the chimney. Special trains carried an additional white light by night or white disc by day on the buffer beam. By 1890 a red disc with white outer rim was carried at the base of the chimney by day and a red light under the chimney and a white light on the left-hand end of the buffer beam by night. Special trains then carried a red disc with white outer rim under the chimney and a white disc in the centre of the buffer beam by day, whilst at night a red lamp under the chimney and white lights on the left- and right-hand ends of the buffer beam were stipulated. In 1903 the headcode for the single line was again changed to a red disc with white rim under the chimney during daylight hours, and a red lamp under the chimney and green lamp on the left-hand end of the buffer beam by night. From 1910 ordinary and special trains carried the same code with red disc with white outer rim or red lamp under the chimney and a green disc with white outer rim or green lamp over the left-hand end of the buffer beam. After Grouping the LNER phased out the green lights and discs as a possible source of danger and replaced them with purple discs and lights. By 1926, however, the standard stopping passenger train code of one white light or white disc under the chimney was used on the Saffron Walden branch trains and remained in use until the elimination of steam traction on the line. Freight trains on the branch carried the appropriate class headcode.

The whistle code sounded by enginemen at Audley End was one distinct sound for the main line and three distinct sounds when taking a train main line to and from the Saffron Walden branch. At Bartlow Junction the whistle code was one distinct sound to and from the Sudbury line and three distinct sounds to and from the Saffron Walden branch.

In the event of a mishap or derailment the Cambridge breakdown crane was used to cover the Saffron Walden branch. Initially GER No. 1A, a 10 ton capacity crane dating from 1885 was utilized but this was later superseded by Ransomes & Rapier 35 tons crane, LNER No. 961601 built in 1932. Latterly Cowan & Sheldon 45 ton capacity steam crane LNER No. 961606 (Works No. 6873) dating from 1940, later renumbered by BR to 133 and then 330133, was used.

SAFFRON WALDEN DEPOT.

No. 1.

	arr. a.m.		dep. a.m.
On Duty			{ 4 45 M O { 5 0 M X
Loco			{ 5 30 L M O { 5 45 L M X
Sffr'n Wld'n			{ 5 45 G M O { 5 0 G M X
	M O 5 50 M X 6 5 }	Audley End	6 35 G
	6 42	Saffr'n Wald'n	7 12
	7 26	Bartlow	7 41
	8 4	Audley End	8 16
	8 20	Saffr'n Wald'n	8 42
	8 56	Bartlow	9 14
	9 34	Audley End	9 44
	9 48	Saffr'n Wald'n	9 53
	9 57	Audley End	10 7
	10 29	Bartlow	10 45
	11 12	Audley End	11 38
	11 42	Saffr'n W'ld'n	12 15
	p.m. 12 19	Audley End	1 4
	1 24	Bartlow	1 38
	1 52	S'ffr'n W'ld'n	{ 2 30 S X { 2 42 S O
	S X 2 34 S O 2 46 }	Audley End	3 2
	3 6	Saffr'n Wald'n	3 25
	3 29	Audley End	3 45
	3 49	Saffr'n Wald'n	4 20
	4 24	Audley End	4 38
	T X 4 58 T O 5 9 }	Bartlow	5 37
	5 59	Audley End	6 12
	6 16	Saffr'n Wald'n	6 46
	6 50	Audley End	7 14
	7 34	Bartlow	7 55
	8 9	Saffr'n Wald'n	L Loco'

Men change at Saffron Walden 1.8 pm

No. 2.

	arr. a.m.		dep. a.m.
On Duty			6 5
Loco'			6 50 L
Saffron Wal.			7 5
	7 9	Audley End	7 40
	7 44	Saffron Wal.	8 52
	8 56	Audley End	9 20
			p.m.
	9 24	Saff'n Wal.GP	{ 1 10 G S X { 1 34 S O
	p.m.		
S X	1 17 }	Audley End	{ 1 55 G S X { 1 54 S O
S O	1 38		
S X	2 2 }	Saffron Wal.	2 15 G S O
S O	1 58		
	2 22	Audley End	2 50 G S O
	2 57	Saffron Wal.	3 35
	4 5	Bp's Stortf'd	5 13
	5 43	Saff'n W.GP	{ 7 20 G S X { 7 20 L S O
	7 28	Audley End	8 22
	8 28	Saffron Wal.	9 0
	9 4	Audley End	9 38
	9 42	Saffron Wal. Loco'	L

Men change at Saffron Walden 2.5 p.m.

Right: Locomotive and enginemen's diagrams for Saffron Walden depot, July 1925.

Below: 'N7/3' class No. 69692 standing outside Saffron Walden engine shed in August 1957. In the background is the water column and coal stage, at this period not used as the engines were hand-coaled from wagons.

D. Campbell

Coaching stock

The GER placed no weight or loading gauge restrictions for coaching stock on the Saffron Walden branch and conventional branch line rolling stock was used. The company supplied some of their most modern stock for the opening of the Saffron Walden line obviously to impress local travellers but within a week or so, older vehicles were placed into service on the branch. No new stock appeared for the opening of the Bartlow section, the usual branch formation of four 4-wheel vehicles forming the train. Thus for 30 years or more regular Saffron Walden branch passengers were subjected to rides in old Gooch- or Sinclair-designed iron or wooden-framed 24 ft-long, 4-wheel coaches, with oil lighting and minimal springing. Complaints made by Saffron Walden Directors were later supplemented by the travelling public but ignored at GER headquarters.

Initially the coaching stock was very primitive, with first, second and third class accommodation as well as catering for Parliamentary fare paying passengers who travelled in third class on selective trains. The first class vehicles had fully upholstered seating in compartments, whilst at the other end of the scale third class passengers were subjected to sitting on bare wooden boards. Until 1900 the coaching stock was exclusively four-wheel, provided with oil lighting and latterly equipped with the Westinghouse brake. During the 1860s and 1870s the stock provided was Sinclair's design for the Eastern Counties Railway with four-compartment first/second composites to diagram 33, five-compartment thirds to diagram 34, both with 24 ft body length, and a full brake van to diagram 39 with 21 ft body. The branch train usually comprised four vehicles with one composite, two full thirds and one brake van as the formation. On Tuesday, Saffron Walden market day, an additional full third and composite were attached. The leading dimensions of these vehicles were:

GER diagram No.	33	34	39
	4 wheel	4 wheel	4 wheel
	Composite	Third	Full Brake
Length over body	24 ft 0 in.	24 ft 0 in.	21 ft 0 in.
Body height	6 ft 1 ¾ in.	6 ft 5 ¾ in.	6 ft 2½ in.
Wheelbase	13 ft 6 in.	13 ft 6 in.	12 ft 0 in.
Seating 1st class	16	–	–
3rd class	20*	50	–
Weight empty	8 tons 2 cwt	7 tons 5 cwt	7 tons 17 cwt

* Second or third class

By the late 1880s and during the 1890s, six-wheel coaches were introduced on main line services and subsequently the older stock was superseded by GER four-wheel vehicles of 26 to 27 ft body length which cascaded down to work on branch line and cross-country services. A set of three or four coaches formed of four-compartment first/third composite to diagram 216, one or two five-compartment thirds to diagram 401 and a brake third to diagram 502, usually sufficed for most periods of the year, although if the train required strengthening an additional five-compartment third was added. Prior to the

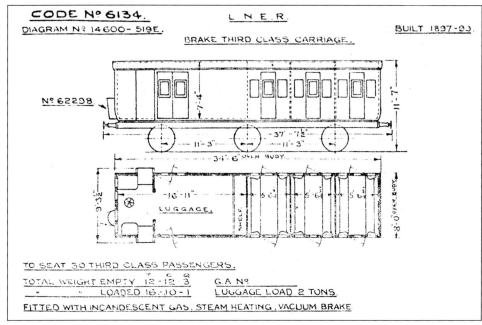

GER diagram 519 six-wheel brake/third.

GER diagram 533 six-wheel brake/third.

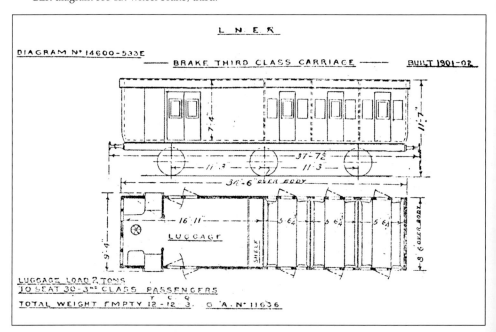

abolition of second class accommodation outside the London suburban area, the composite would have provided first/second class accommodation. The leading dimensions of these vehicles were:

GER diagram No.	216 4 wheel Composite	401 4 wheel Third	502 4 wheel Brake/Third
Length over body	26 ft 0 in.	26 ft 0¾ in.	27 ft 0 in.
Height overall	10 ft 11 in.	10 ft 10 in.	10 ft 11 in.
Body height	6 ft 8 in.	6 ft 8 in.	6 ft 8 in.
Width over body	8 ft 0 in.	8 ft 0 in.	8 ft 0 in.
Width over guard's lookout	–	–	9 ft 0 in.
Wheelbase	15 ft 3 in.	15 ft 3 in.	15 ft 3 in.
Seating 1st class	16	–	–
3rd class	20*	50	30
Luggage	–	–	15 cwt
Weight empty	8 tons 1 cwt	8 tons 9 cwt	9 tons 5 cwt

* Second or third class

By 1895 the four-wheel stock used on the branch was replaced by six-wheel vehicles displaced from main line duties. Dating from the 1880s the vehicles were a considerable improvement over the older carriages and were equipped with gas lighting. A three- or four-coach train formed of first/third composite with luggage accommodation to diagram 200, one or two six-compartment thirds to diagram 403 and a brake/third to diagram 511 or 514 usually sufficed for normal workings. On occasions a four-wheel brake van to diagram 505 may have been used in preference to the six-wheel brake/third, especially on Saffron Walden or Bishop's Stortford market days, when additional produce was conveyed. The leading dimensions of these vehicles were:

GER diagram No.	200 6 wheel Composite	403 6 wheel Third	511 6 wheel Brake/Third	505 4 wheel Brake
Length over buffers	35 ft 1½ in.	37 ft 7½ in.	35 ft 1½ in.	
Length over body	31 ft 6 in.	34 ft 0 in.	31 ft 6 in.	26 ft 0 in.
Height overall	10 ft 11½ in. 11 ft 2½ in.	11 ft 3 in.	11 ft 2 in.	10 ft 11 in.
Width over body	8 ft 0 in.	8 ft 0 in.	8 ft 0 in.	8 ft 0 in.
Width over guard's lookout	–	–	9 ft 0 in.	9 ft 3½ in.
Wheelbase	20 ft 0 in.	21 ft 0 in.	20 ft 0 in.	15 ft 3 in.
Seating 1st class	12	–	–	–
3rd class	20	60	30	–
Luggage	15 cwt	–	2 tons	3 tons
Weight empty	12 tons 15 cwt	13 tons 3 cwt	12 tons 18 cwt	8 tons 18 cwt

Six-wheel coaching stock remained in use on the line until the late 1930s.

During the early 1930s two-coach sets were used on the branch comprising a bogie composite and six-wheel brake third. One set was formed of bogie

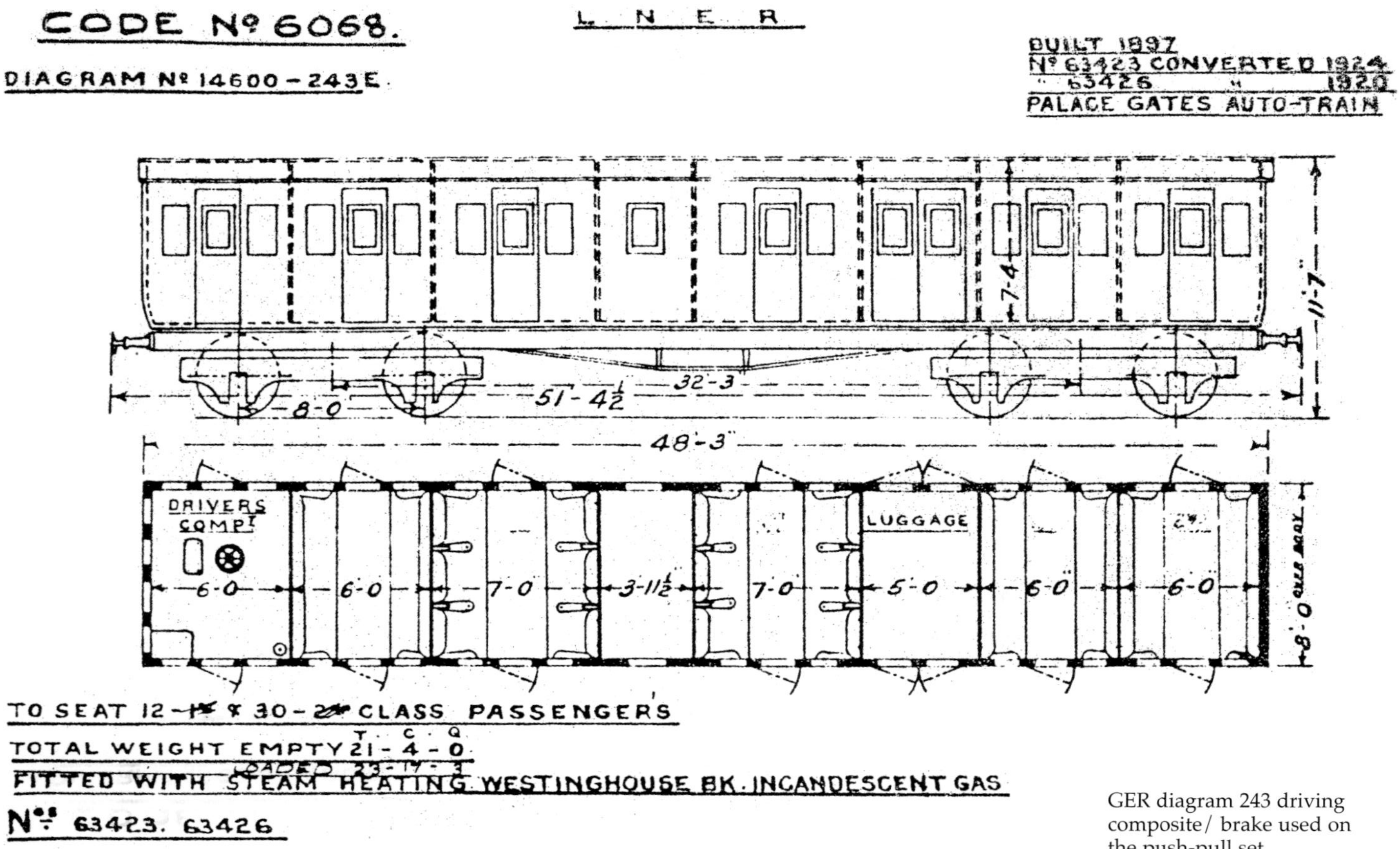

CODE Nº 6068.

L N E R

DIAGRAM Nº 14600 - 243 E.

BUILT 1897
Nº 63423 CONVERTED 1924
63426 " 1920
PALACE GATES AUTO-TRAIN

7 - 11

7 - 4

8 - 0

32 - 3

51 - 4½

48 - 3"

8 - 0 over max.

6 - 0   6 - 0   5 - 0   C.W.

LUGGAGE   7 - 0

3 - 11½   7 - 0

6 - 0   6 - 0

DRIVERS COMPT   6 - 0

TO SEAT 12 1ST & 30 2ND CLASS PASSENGERS

TOTAL WEIGHT EMPTY 21 - 4 - 0   T. C. Q.

FITTED WITH STEAM HEATING WESTINGHOUSE BK. INCANDESCENT GAS

Nºs 63423. 63426.

GER diagram 243 driving composite / brake used on the push-pull set.

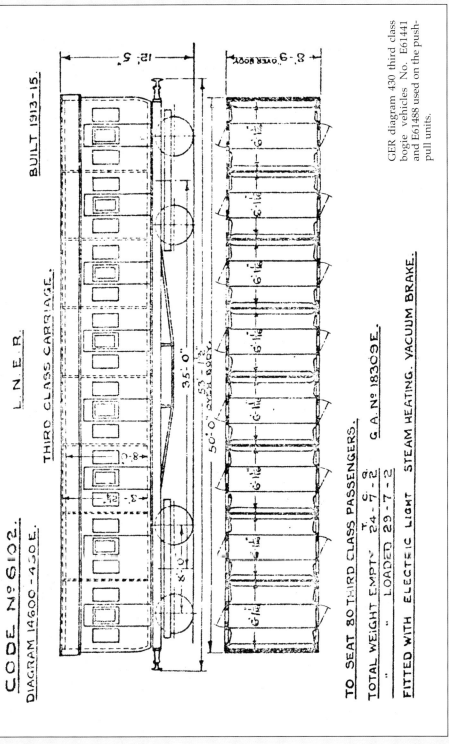

CODE No. 6102.

L. N. E. R.

DIAGRAM 14600-450 E.

BUILT 1913-15.

THIRD CLASS CARRIAGE.

12' 5".

8' 9" OVER BODY.

35'-0"

53'-1½"

50'-0" OVER BODY.

8'-0"

8'-0"

3'-2½"

6'-1½"

6'-1½"

6'-1½"

6'-1½"

6'-1½"

6'-1½"

6'-1½"

TO SEAT 80 THIRD CLASS PASSENGERS.

	T.	C.	Q.
TOTAL WEIGHT EMPTY	24	7	2
" " LOADED	29	7	2

G. A. No. 18309E.

FITTED WITH ELECTRIC LIGHT STEAM HEATING. VACUUM BRAKE.

GER diagram 430 third class bogie vehicles No. E61441 and E61488 used on the push-pull units.

GER diagram 212 bogie composite.

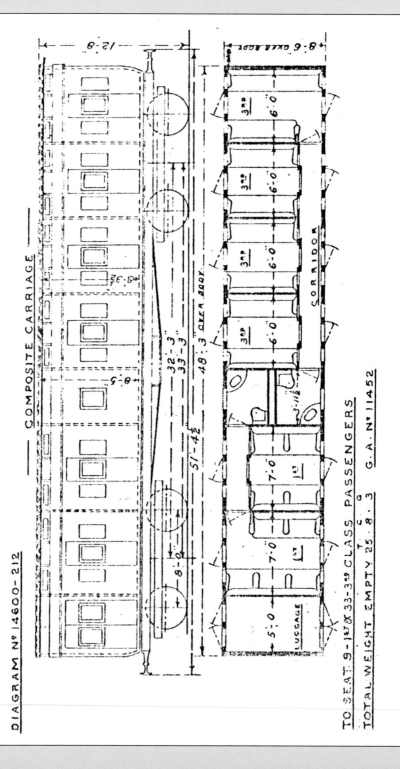

DIAGRAM Nº 14600-212

— COMPOSITE CARRIAGE —

TO SEAT 9-1ST & 33-3RD CLASS PASSENGERS

TOTAL WEIGHT EMPTY 25.8.3   G.A. Nº 11452

composite LNER No. 63472 formerly GER No. 584 built in 1901 to diagram 212, and withdrawn in June 1940 following damage sustained during enemy action. The six-wheel brake third, LNER No. 62305, formerly GER No. 781, was built in November 1897 to diagram 519 and withdrawn in August 1937, and sold to the North Sunderland Railway. In addition to the brake thirds to diagram 519, similar vehicles to diagram 533 were also used on services, but both types were replaced in the late 1930s, although the brake thirds to diagram 533 did not become extinct in East Anglia until 1952. The principal dimensions were:

GER diagram No.	212	519	533
	Bogie	6 wheel	6 wheel
	Composite	Brake/Third	Brake/Third
Length over buffers	51 ft 4½ in.	37 ft 7½ in.	37 ft 7½ in.
Length over body	48 ft 3 in.	34 ft 6 in.	34 ft 6 in.
Height overall	12 ft 8 in.	11 ft 7 in.	11 ft 7 in.
Width over body	8 ft 6 in.	8 ft 0 in.	8 ft 6 in.
Width over			
guard's lookout	–	9 ft 3½ in.	9 ft 4 in.
Wheelbase	40 ft 3 in.	22 ft 6 in.	22 ft 6 in.
	41 ft 3 ins		
Wheelbase to bogie centre	8 ft 0 in.	–	–
Seating 1st class	9	–	–
3rd class	33	30	30
Luggage	–	2 tons	2 tons
Weight empty	25 tons 9 cwt	12 tons 13 cwt	12 tons 13 cwt

The departure of the 'G4' class 0-4-4Ts and the arrival of the vacuum-braked 'C12' class 4-4-2Ts in 1938 led the LNER to introduce a motley collection of coaching vehicles to the Saffron Walden service, although these replacements were more modern than the ageing ex-GER vehicles. The branch train throughout the late 1930s and the war years was usually formed of two bogie vehicles, one an ex-GER corridor coach and the other an ex-North Eastern Railway clerestory or Great Central Railway compartment suburban coach.

By 1946 LNER Gresley compartment suburban stock had infiltrated into the two-coach formation, but former North Eastern, Great Eastern and Great Central Railway vehicles, usually formed of brake third and first/third composite, could be found on the line until push-and-pull trains displaced the ordinary hauled stock in 1951.

The carriage workings for the branch from September 1950 showed two sets to cover the service each formed of a 'BT' (non-gangway brake third) with four 3rd class compartments and a 'CL' (non-gangway composite lavatory) with two 1st class and four 3rd class compartments, having a combined weight of 52 tons, and with accommodation for 11 first and 73 third class passengers. The diagrams Nos. 118 and 119 worked turn and turn about on weekdays.

In 1951 a couple of two-coach ex-GER push-and-pull sets were transferred from the Palace Gates to Seven Sisters line along with the 'G5' class 0-4-4Ts to Cambridge for use on the Saffron Walden branch. The push-pull units were fitted with air-operated gear instead of the more usual vacuum-controlled motor equipment and were formed of a composite brake and a full third. The

Composite/brake No. E63423 at Bartlow on 25th August, 1956. Built by the GER as No. 520 in May 1897 for the Liverpool Street to Cromer service. Converted to push-pull operation in March 1924 for the Palace Gates branch it was transferred to the Audley End to Saffron Walden branch in 1951.   *R.C. Riley*

Close up of driving brake composite No. E63423 showing the 1897 maker's plate.   *H.C. Casserley*

composite brake vehicles were numbered E63423 and E63426 and built as GER Nos. 520 and 523 in May 1897 to diagram 209, for the Liverpool Street to Cromer services, and were converted in March 1924 and June 1920 respectively to diagram 243 for the Palace Gates auto-trains.

These were the first general service type of main line bogie coach built by the GER and had low arc roofs. The centre compartment was formerly two lavatories, whilst the driver's compartment was formed out of the end third class compartment. Two of the third class carriages used in the sets were Nos. E61328 and E61330, originally built in 1906 as GER Nos. 522 and 524, and converted for auto-train working in 1917. These vehicles were distinguishable by their clerestory roofs. In July 1955 they were displaced and withdrawn. The other third class carriages had elliptical roofs and were numbered E61441 and E61488, originally built in February 1913 and June 1915 as eight-compartment non-corridor stock to diagram 430 numbered GER 242 and 273.

Following the introduction of the LNER Gresley-designed push-and-pull vacuum-fitted units the two sets were withdrawn from traffic in February 1957. Whilst on the branch the two motor driving trailers were labelled at each end with a small plate bearing the legend 'Audley End-Saffron Walden-Bartlow'.

The principal dimensions of the vehicles were:

GER Diagram No.	243	430
	Driving Brake/Composite	Third
Length over buffers	51 ft 4½ in.	53 ft 1½ in.
Length over body	48 ft 3 in.	50 ft 0 in.
Height overall	11 ft 7 in.	12 ft 5 in.
Width over body	8 ft 0 in.	8 ft 9 in.
Wheelbase	40 ft 3 in.	43 ft 0 in.
Wheelbase to bogie centre	8 ft 0 in.	8 ft 0 in.
Seating 1st class	12	–
3rd class	30	80
Luggage	2 tons	–
Weight empty	21 tons 4 cwt	24 tons 7 cwt

With the transfer of the 'N7' class 0-6-2Ts to the line, two sets of Gresley-designed vacuum-controlled push-and-pull sets were introduced. Motor driving trailers coded OBDTC (Ordinary Brake Third Driving Carriage), Nos. E86147 and E86149 and trailer composites remained in use until the introduction of diesel railbuses in June 1958.

	OBTDC	C
Length over buffers	54 ft 3 in.	54 ft 3 in.
Length over body	51 ft 1½ in.	51 ft 1½ in.
Height overall	12 ft 10 in.	12 ft 10 in.
Width over body	9 ft 3 in.	9 ft 3 in.
Wheelbase	43 ft 0 in.	43 ft 0 in.
Wheelbase to bogie centre	8 ft 0 in.	8 ft 0 in.
Seating 1st class	–	32
3rd class	40	30

Most GE coaching vehicles could travel on the Saffron Walden branch but there were restrictions. GE carriage vans Nos. 1600 to 1649 and 1888 to 1922 measuring 35 ft in length could not be turned on ordinary wagon turntables. In order that they could be used for general parcels, milk, fruit and fish traffic or as covered carriage trucks they were constructed with both side and end doors for loading and unloading. The vans were not to be used for loading private carriages, motor cars, long theatrical scenery or any other traffic which could not be unloaded through the side doors at Audley End and Saffron Walden, as the loading docks at both stations could not be reached without the use of the small wagon turntables.

Three static items of rolling stock located on the branch were also of considerable age and interest. The passenger waiting accommodation at Ashdon Halt was formerly a five-compartment, second class coach built in October 1883 as GER No 342. It was transferred from main line to suburban work in the 1890s following the withdrawal of second class travel on the main line. The vehicle was widened from 8 ft to 9 ft sometime between 1902 and 1904 after which it re-entered traffic, and was subsequently withdrawn from traffic on 31st December, 1915. Soon afterwards the body was removed from the underframe and sent to Ashdon as passenger accommodation where the compartment partitions were removed and replaced by wooden seats around the wall of the vehicle.

The 32 ft 2 in. carriage body at Audley End close to the up main line near the junction points, was taken from a six-wheel vehicle built by the Great Northern Railway in 1897. It was transferred to the Midland & Great Northern Railway prior to 1919 becoming that company's No. 149 and was renumbered in 1936 as LNER 81994 before being withdrawn in October 1941, when the body was placed at Audley End as a signal fitters' store.

Behind the goods shed at Saffron Walden was the third static item of rolling stock, a van body from a vehicle built for the GER by the Metropolitan Railway Carriage & Wagon Co. to an order between 1881 and 1882. The van was probably withdrawn prior to 1920 and the body utilized at Saffron Walden as a store.

A view of the body of former Midland & Great Northern Joint Railway coach No. 149, renumbered 81994 in 1936 and withdrawn from traffic in October 1941, used by the signal and telegraph department as a store at Audley End, seen on 2nd May, 1964. The vehicle was built originally built by the GNR as a third/lavatory in 1897.   *J. Watling*

Wagon stock

The wagons used by the GER in the early years were wooden open vehicles with side doors and fitted with dumb buffers. Where grain, straw or merchandise was susceptible to wet weather, a tarpaulin sheet was used to cover the contents of the wagon. The brake van at the tail end of the train would have been a 10 ton vehicle. In the years prior to the turn of the century the GER utilized four-plank-bodied, open wagons with wooden frames, dating from 1882 for the conveyance of general merchandise and minerals. From 1887, these wagons were gradually superseded by five-plank 9 ton capacity, later 10 ton opens, to diagram 16 with 9 ft 6 in. wheelbase and measuring 15 ft 0 in. over headstocks. Later 10 ton, five-plank open wagons to diagram 17, with a length of 15 ft 0 in. over headstocks and 9 ft 0 in. wheelbase, were also used. Another variation was the use of 10 ton, seven-plank opens to diagram 55, measuring 17 ft 0 in. over headstocks and 9 ft 6 in. wheelbase for vegetable and root traffic. For fruit and perishable traffic, 10 ton ventilated vans to diagram 15 were provided, measuring 16 ft 1 in. over headstocks, with 9 ft 0 in. wheelbase and overall height of 11 ft 0 ¾ in. Later covered goods vans to diagram 47 were also used. They measured 17 ft 3 in. over headstocks, had a wheelbase of 10 ft 6 in. and were 11 ft 2 in. in height. A third variation was the 10 tons capacity covered goods wagon to diagram 72, which measured 19 ft 0 in. over headstocks whilst maintaining a 10 ft 6 in. wheelbase.

The extensive cattle traffic conveyed to and from Saffron Walden would have entailed the use of three types of cattle wagons of the branch. The first of 8 ton capacity was to diagram 5 and was 18 ft 7 in. over headstocks, had a 10 ft 6 in. wheelbase and was 10 ft 10¾ in. in height. The second to diagram 6 was of 9 tons capacity and measured 19 ft 0 in. over headstocks, with a 10 ft 6 in. wheelbase and overall height of 10 ft 10½ in. The third GE variant of cattle wagon to diagram 7 was of 10 tons capacity, 19 ft 3 in. over headstocks with 10 ft 6 in. wheelbase and overall height of 11 ft 2 in. At the tail of the train was usually a 20 ton four-wheel brake van to GE diagram 56, measuring 17 ft 6 in. over headstocks, a 10 ft 3 in. wheelbase and 3 ft 1 in. diameter wheels. In addition many wagons owned by other railway companies were used to deliver and collect agricultural and livestock traffic, whilst coal and coke supplies came in private owner coal wagons. These fell into two categories, those belonging to the collieries consigning the coal, and merchants and coal factors wagons, which were loaded at the collieries.

After Grouping the GER wagons continued to be utilized but gradually LNER-designed wagons made an appearance. The most numerous were probably the 12 ton, five-plank opens with an 8 ft 0 in. wheelbase to code 2, and 12 ton capacity six-plank opens with 10 ft 0 in. wheelbase to code 91 built after 1932. Later variations included a 13 ton, seven-plank open wagon to code 162 measuring 16 ft 6 in. over headstocks and with a 9 ft 0 in. wheelbase. All were used on vegetable and sugar beet traffic. Fitted and unfitted 12 ton, 9 ft 0 in. wheelbase covered vans to code 16 conveyed perishable goods, fruit and malt and later some were designated for fruit traffic only. From 1934 12 ton capacity vans to code 171, with steel underframe and pressed corrugated steel ends, were introduced whilst at the same time the wheelbase was extended to a length of 10 ft 0 in. Specific fruit vans with both 9 ft 0 in. and 10 ft 0 in. wheelbase also saw service on the Saffron Walden line. Agricultural machinery destined for local farms was delivered on 12 ton 'Lowfit' wagons with 10 ft wheelbase and overall length over headstocks of 17 ft 6 in. Larger machinery would have arrived or departed on one of the ex-GER 14 ton, 25 ft 6 in. 'Mac K2' machinery wagons to diagram 75 and later LNER builds. LNER brake vans provided for the branch traffic included 20 ton 'Toad B' to code 34 and 'Toad E' to code 64 vehicles, with 10 ft 6 in. wheelbase and measuring 22 ft 5 in. over buffers. Later 'Toad D' brake vans to code 61 with 16 ft 0 in. wheelbase and measuring 27 ft 5 in. over buffers were employed. After nationalization many of the older wooden wagons were scrapped and much of the traffic conveyed in open wagons in the standard 16 ton all-steel mineral wagons. Malt traffic was conveyed in 20 ton bulk grain wagons.

In GER days the body, solebars and headstocks of the open wagons were painted slate grey, whilst the ironwork below solebar level, buffer guides, buffers, drawbars, drawbar plates and couplings were black. The LNER wagon livery was grey for non-fitted wagons, covered vans and brake vans, whilst all vehicles fitted with automatic brakes, including brake vans were painted red oxide, which changed to bauxite around 1940. Similar liveries were carried in BR days.

The maintenance of wagon stock used on the branch was carried out at the wagon repair shop at Cambridge. In the event of the failure or defect of a wagon on the branch, a travelling wagon repairer carried out the repairs locally.

Former GER van body used as a store in Saffron Walden goods yard on 20th July, 1963. The vehicle was built by the Metropolitan Railway Carriage & Wagon Co. and dated from 1881/2.   *J. Watling*

Appendix One

Length of Platforms, Sidings, etc.

Location	Ex-Liverpool Street m. c.		Platforms Up ft	Down ft	Loop ft	Sidings
Audley End	41	57		205	255	Long storage (1,017 ft) Shunting spur (80 ft)
Saffron Walden	43	41		202	270	Gas House/Long (912 ft) Bell/Railway Foundry (395 ft) Dix's Road (637 ft) New Road (210 ft) Straight Road (200 ft) Coal Road (160 ft) No. 1 Shed Road (110 ft) Shed Road (372 ft) Dock Road (152 ft) Engine shed (190 ft)
Acrow Halt	44	47		230		
Ashdon Halt	46	64	210			
Bartlow	48	78	210		260	Trolley Siding (170 ft) Trap siding (35 ft)

The timber-faced 210 ft- long platform at Ashdon Halt facing Saffron Walden.

Author's Collection

225

Appendix Two

Bridges

No.	Location	Mileage (m. ch.)	Name	Under or over	Type	Spans (No.)	Square span between abutments or supports (ft in.)	Skew span between abutments or supports (ft in.)	Width to parapet abutments (ft in.)	Depth of construction (ft in.)	Distance from road or surface of water to rail (ft in.)	Construction
	Junction points	41 44	From Liverpool Street									
2107	Audley End and Saffron Walden	41 68	Fighting Cocks	Under	Public	1	35 0	36 8	13 0	2 6	18 9	Brick abutments, No. 2 side girder, cross girders, longitudinal timbers, plank floor, corrugated iron, parapet TR. Removed Sunday 10th August, 1968.
2108	Audley End and Saffron Walden	42 00	Culvert	Under	Water	2	6 0	– –	150 0	32 0	38 0	Twin culverts, brick abutments, brick arches and inverts 6 ft 10 in. deep, 9 in. of strengthening walls in centre of each arch.
2109	Audley End and Saffron Walden	42 08	River Cam	Under	River	2	9 0	– –	150 0	32 0	38 0	Brick arches, brick abutments.
2110	Audley End and Saffron Walden	42 11		Under	Occupation	1	11 10	– –	24 0	3 6	27 6	Brick abutments, brick arches and parapets.
2111	Audley End and Saffron Walden	42 32		Over	Occupation	3			12 8	4 0	43 9	Brick arches and piers. Brick arch and parapet piers encased with reinforced concrete 1938.
2112	Audley End and Saffron Walden	42 56	Fulfen Slade a.k.a. Beechy Ride	Under	Public path and stream	1	21 0	– –	62 0	18 0	43 0	Brick abutments, brick invert for stream 9 ft 0 in., roadway 12 ft 0 in. wide, brick arch and parapets.
2113	Audley End and Saffron Walden	42 72		Over	Occupation	3			12 2	2 6	28 0	Brick arches and piers, brick arches and parapets. Removed and cutting filled in 1968.

No.	Parish	Mile	Road	Over/Under	Status	No. of spans						Remarks
2114	Audley End and Saffron Walden	43 14	London Road	Over	Public	1	24 0	38 5	20 7	3 9	18 9	Brick abutments, brick arch and parapets. Maintenance by Saffron Walden Council from 1st December, 1914. Removed and cutting filled in 1969.
2115	Audley End and Saffron Walden	43 20	Borough Lane	Over	Public	1	24 0	– –	25 1	3 6	18 0	Brick abutments, cast-iron girders, part brick jack arches, part concrete slabs, brick parapets. Maintenance by Saffron Walden Council from 1914. Filled in 1969.
2116	Audley End and Saffron Walden	43 32	Debden Road	Over	Public	1	24 0	24 5	25 0	3 6	18 0	Brick abutments, cast-iron girders with brick jack arches. Maintenance by Saffron Walden Council from 1914.
2117	Saffron Walden and Bartlow	43 45	South Road	Over	Public	2	24 0 / 25 0	West side / East side	26 2	2 6	17 6	Brick abutments, cast-iron girder, brick jack arch west side, wrought-iron girder, corrugated steel troughing east side, brick parapets. East side superstructure renewed with 24 ft x 7½ in. RSJ set in concrete 1957 Sold 23rd January, 1970.
2118	Saffron Walden and Bartlow	43 65	Thaxted Road	Under	Public	1	35 1	36 5	24 0	4 9	20 9	Brick abutments, brick arch and parapets. Maintenance by Saffron Walden Council by 1914. Removed in 1975.
2119	Saffron Walden and Bartlow	44 20	Sewards End Road a.k.a. Radwinter Road	Under	Public	1	25 0	28 10	25 0	5 6	21 6	Brick abutments, brick arch and parapets. Demolished 1970, one abutment left.
2120	Saffron Walden and Bartlow	44 44	Ashdon Road	Under	Public	1	25 0	26 0	14 6	2 0	16 0	Brick abutments No. 2 side girder corrugated cross troughing. Plate parapet ballast LR, reconstructed 1894, demolished 1970.

No.	Location	Mileage	Name	Under or over	Type	Spans	Square span between abutments or supports	Skew span between abutments or supports	Width to parapet abutments	Depth of construction	Distance from road or surface of water to rail	Construction
		m. ch.				No.	ft in.	ft in.	ft in.	ft in.	ft in.	
2121	Saffron Walden and Bartlow	45 00	Keeper's Bridge	Under	Occupation	1	12 0	– –	24 0	2 6	14 9	Brick abutments, brick arch and parapets. Included in sale of land to Audley End Estates 22nd July, 1967.
2122	Saffron Walden and Bartlow	45 40	Painter's Bridge	Over	Public	3			19 8	2 9	17 9	Brick abutments and piers, brick arches and parapets.
2123	Saffron Walden and Bartlow	46 25	Nutts Bridge	Under	Public	1	15 0	– –	24 0	3 6	18 6	Brick abutments, brick arch and parapets.
2124	Saffron Walden and Bartlow	47 20	Rickett's Bridge	Under	Occupation	1	14 9	– –	25 0	4 0	23 6	Brick abutments, brick arch and parapets.
2125	Saffron Walden and Bartlow	47 42	Puddlewort Bridge	Over	Occupation							Removed.
2126	Saffron Walden and Bartlow	48 03	Ashdon Road	Over	Public	1	24 0	26 1	15 9	2 9	18 0	Brick abutments, brick arch and parapets.
2127	Saffron Walden and Bartlow	48 28	River Bourne	Under	River	1	9 0	9 6	14 0	2 0	6 6	Brick abutments, longitudinal corrugated steel troughing, ballast LR. Sold to Bartlow Estates.

Cross section of Fulfen Slade underbridge No. 2112.

BRIDGE AT 42 56

Between AUDLEY END and SAFFRON WALDEN

Appendix Three

Level Crossings

No.	Location	Mileage m. ch.		Local name	Status	Protection
1	Audley End & Saffron Walden	41	63	Private Road	Accommodation	Gates
2	Audley End & Saffron Walden	42	18	Dennis No. 1	Accommodation	Gates
3	Audley End & Saffron Walden	42	51	Dennis No. 2	Accommodation	Gates
4	Saffron Walden & Bartlow	44	08	Engleman	Accommodation	Gates
5	Saffron Walden & Bartlow	44	63	Metcalfe No. 1	Accommodation	Gates
6	Saffron Walden & Bartlow	45	24	Metcalfe No. 2	Accommodation	Gates
7	Saffron Walden & Bartlow	45	62	Metcalfe No. 3	Accommodation	Gates
8	Saffron Walden & Bartlow	45	70	Metcalfe No. 4	Accommodation	Gates
9	Saffron Walden & Bartlow	46	18	Metcalfe No. 5	Accommodation	Gates
10	Saffron Walden & Bartlow	46	44	Bell No. 1	Accommodation	Gates
11	Saffron Walden & Bartlow	46	51	Bell No. 2	Accommodation	Gates
12	Saffron Walden & Bartlow	46	58		Footpath	
13	Saffron Walden & Bartlow	46	66	Ashdon Halt	Public	Gates
14	Saffron Walden & Bartlow	46	70	Wiseman	Accommodation	Gates
15	Saffron Walden & Bartlow	47	01		Footpath	
16	Saffron Walden & Bartlow	47	12	Bridle Path	Accommodation	Gates
17	Saffron Walden & Bartlow	47	32	Smith's No. 1	Accommodation	Gates
18	Saffron Walden & Bartlow	47	37		Footpath	
19	Saffron Walden & Bartlow	47	61		Footpath	
20	Saffron Walden & Bartlow	47	67	Smith's No. 2	Accommodation	Gates
21	Saffron Walden & Bartlow	47	79	Smith's No. 3	Accommodation	Gates
22	Saffron Walden & Bartlow	48	15	Brocklebank's No. 1	Accommodation	Gates
23	Saffron Walden & Bartlow	48	41	Brocklebank's No. 2	Accommodation	Gates
24	Saffron Walden & Bartlow	48	66	Brocklebank's No. 3	Accommodation	Gates

Ashdon Halt and public crossing No. 13 facing Audley End on 5th September, 1964.

Author

Acknowledgements

This publication would not have been possible without the help of many people who have been kind enough to assist. In particular I should like to thank:

The late A.R. Cox, A, Keeler, J. Mott, R. Thake, J. White, A Theobald, the late R. Debenham, A. Upton, K. Brand, the late H.C. Casserley, the late R.C. Riley, the late B.D. J. Walsh, J. Watling, G. Parslew, the late Mrs K. Connor, the late G. Woodcock, W. Pledger, the late P. Proud, the late G. Pember, M. Barnes, M. Brooks, P. Webber, C. Cock and R. Powell who kindly checked the manuscript.

Also many other active and retired railway staff who worked on the line, and members of the Great Eastern Railway Society.
And to:

The Public Record Office (now National Archives)
British Rail Eastern Region
The Editor and Staff, *Herts and Essex Observer*, Bishop's Stortford
L.W. Pole and Staff, Saffron Walden Museum
The House of Lords Record Office
Essex County Record Office
Cambridge County Record Office
County of Cambridge Library

Between 1949 and 1951 ten of the Gresley-designed 'N7' class 0-6-2Ts were fitted with vacuum-controlled push-pull gear but did not work on the GE section services until 1954 when members of the class replaced 'F5' class 2-4-2Ts on the Lowestoft to Beccles and Lowestoft to Yarmouth services. After trials in 1956, three locomotives and two sets of coaching stock were transferred to Cambridge to work the Saffron Walden branch in place of the ailing 'G5' class 0-4-4Ts. With their introduction through services were resumed from the Saffron Walden branch to Haverhill and here 'N7/5' class No. 69651 stands at Haverhill after working a through service from Audley End via Bartlow in 1957.
Dr I.C. Allen

Bibliography

General works

The Great Eastern Railway, C.J. Allen, Ian Allan
Regional History of the Railways of Great Britain, Vol. 5 Eastern Counties,
    D.I. Gordon, David & Charles
Our Home Railways, Vol. 1, W.J. Gordon
Forgotten Railways of East Anglia, R.S. Joby, David & Charles
Story of British Railways, B. Tatford
Locomotives of the LNER (various volumes), RCTS
GER Locomotives, C.L. Aldrich

Periodicals
Bradshaw's Railway Guides
Bradshaw's Railway Manuals
British Railways (Eastern Region) Magazine
Buses
Essex Countryside
Essex Review
Great Eastern Railway Magazine
Herapath's Journal
Locomotive Carriage and Wagon Review
Locomotive Magazine
LNER Magazine
Railway Magazine
Railway Times
Railway World
Railway Year Book
Trains Illustrated

Newspapers
Herts and Essex Journal
Herts and Essex Observer
Royston Crow
Cambridge Chronicle
Cambridge Independent Press
Saffron Walden Weekly News

Miscellaneous
Minute Books of the Eastern Counties Railway
Minute Books of the Great Eastern Railway
Minute Books of the London and North Eastern Railway
Working and Public Timetables from the GER, LNER and BR (ER)
Appendices to the Working Timetables from the GER, LNER and BR (ER)

Index